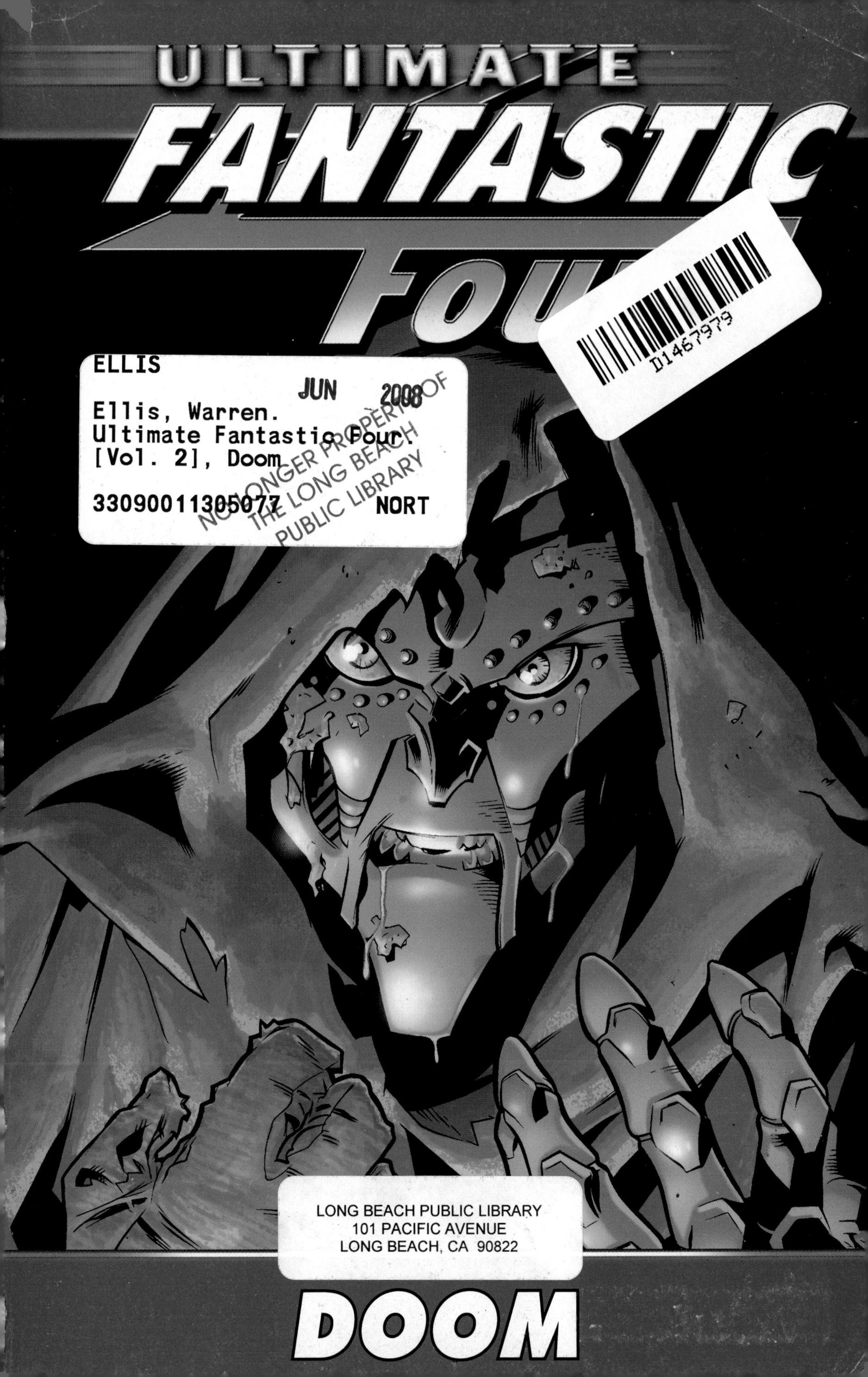
ULTIMATE
FANTASTIC
FOUR
DOOM

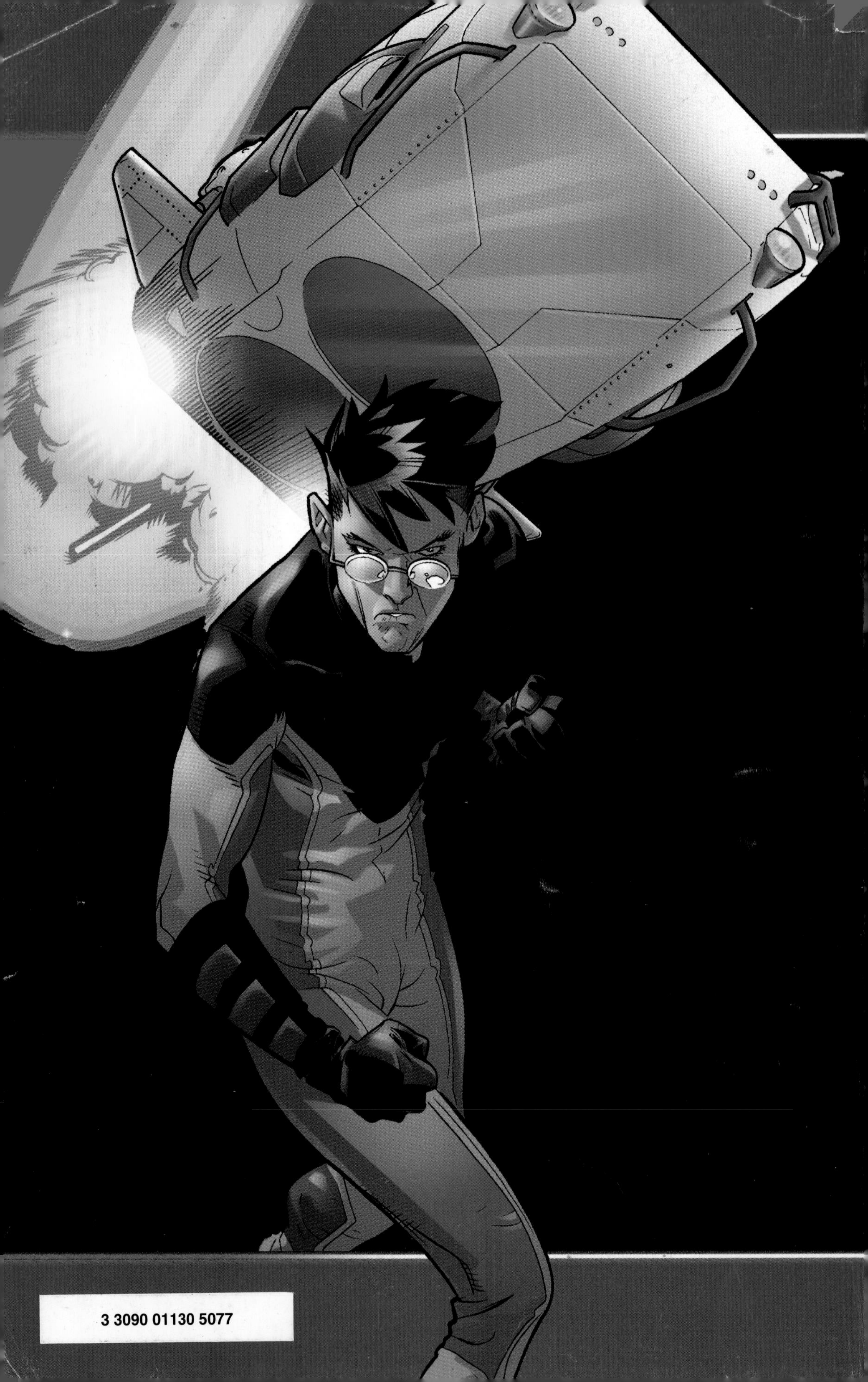

ULTIMATE FANTASTIC FOUR

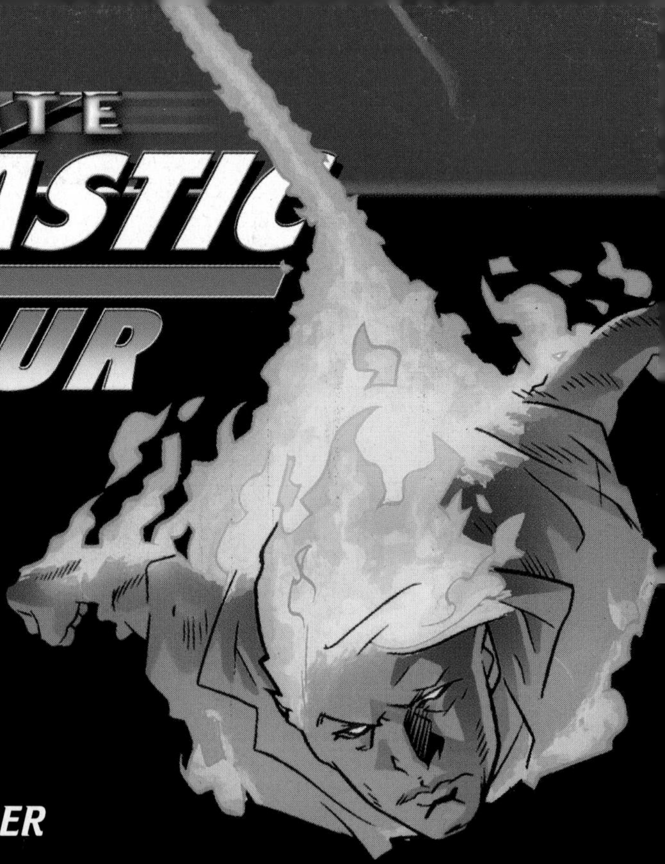

writer
WARREN ELLIS
pencils
STUART IMMONEN
inks
WADE VON GRAWBADGER
colors
DAVE STEWART
letters
CHRIS ELIOPOULOS

assistant editor
NICK LOWE
editor
RALPH MACCHIO

collections editor
JEFF YOUNGQUIST
assistant editor
JENNIFER GRÜNWALD
book designer
MEGHAN KERNS
creative director
TOM MARVELLI
editor in chief
JOE QUESADA
publisher
DAN BUCKLEY

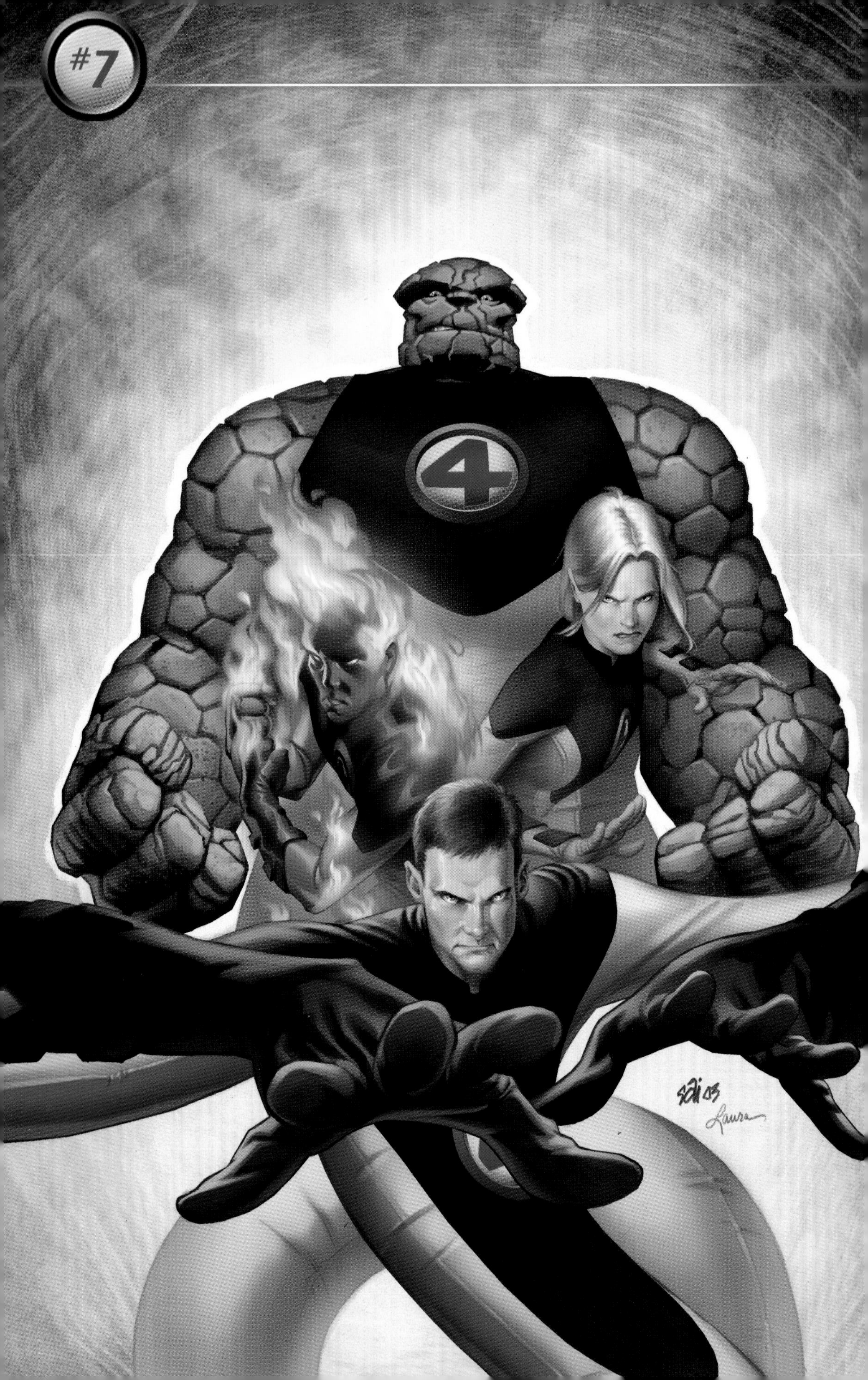
#7
4

PREVIOUSLY IN ULTIMATE FANTASTIC FOUR:

Reed Richards, hand-picked to join the Baxter Building think-tank of young geniuses, spent his entire youth and young adulthood developing a teleport system that would transport solid matter through a parallel universe.

Its first full-scale test was witnessed by Reed, fellow think-tank members Sue Storm and Victor Van Damme, Sue's younger brother Johnny, and Reed's childhood friend Ben Grimm.

There was an accident.

Their genetic structures were scrambled and recombined in a fantastically strange way. Reed's body stretches and flows like water. Ben looks like a thing carved from desert rock. Sue can become invisible. Johnny generates flame.

The four remain in the Baxter Building under the guidance of think-tank head Doctor Storm, father of Sue and Johnny.

Victor Van Damme has not been seen since the accident.

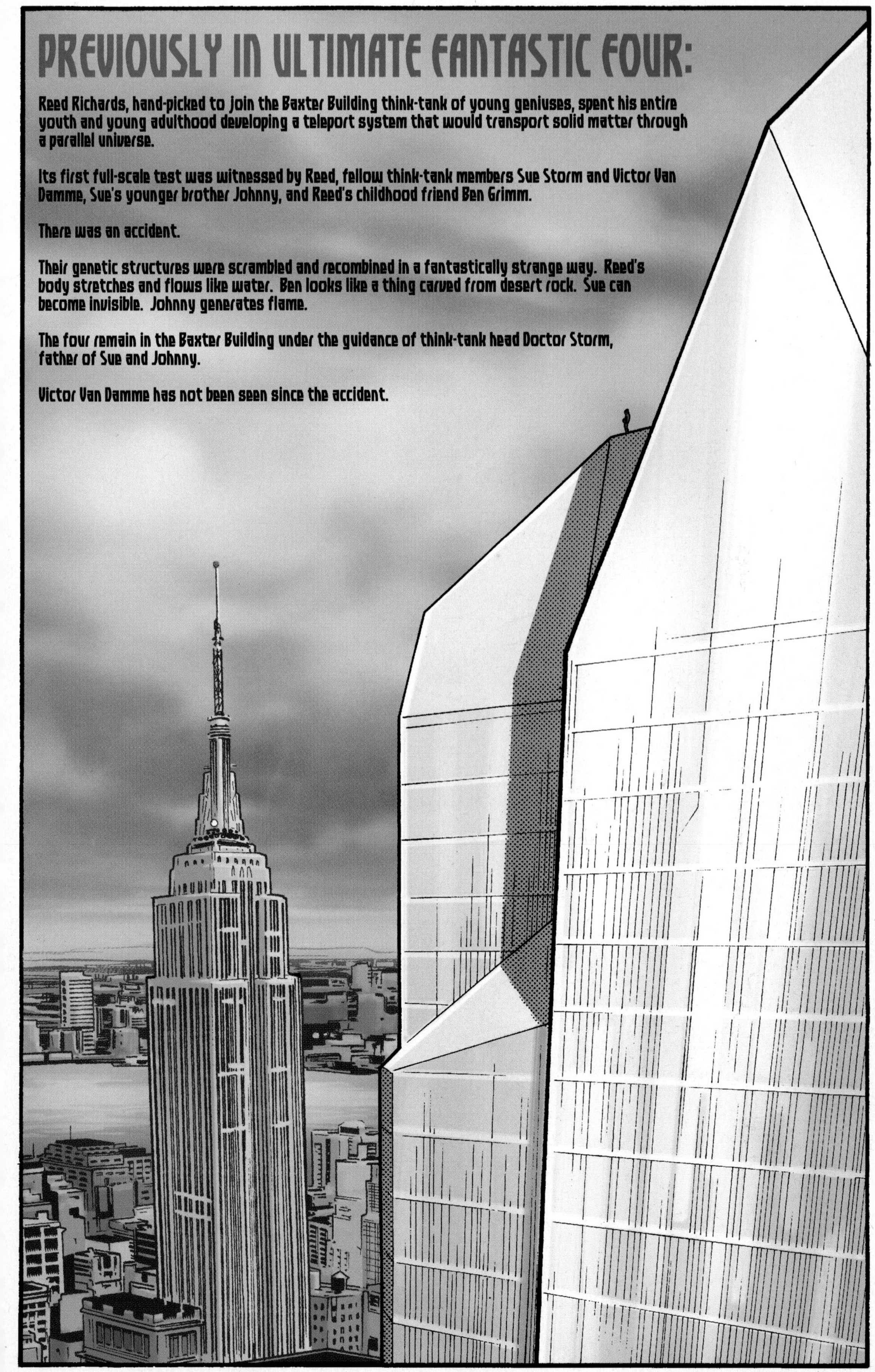

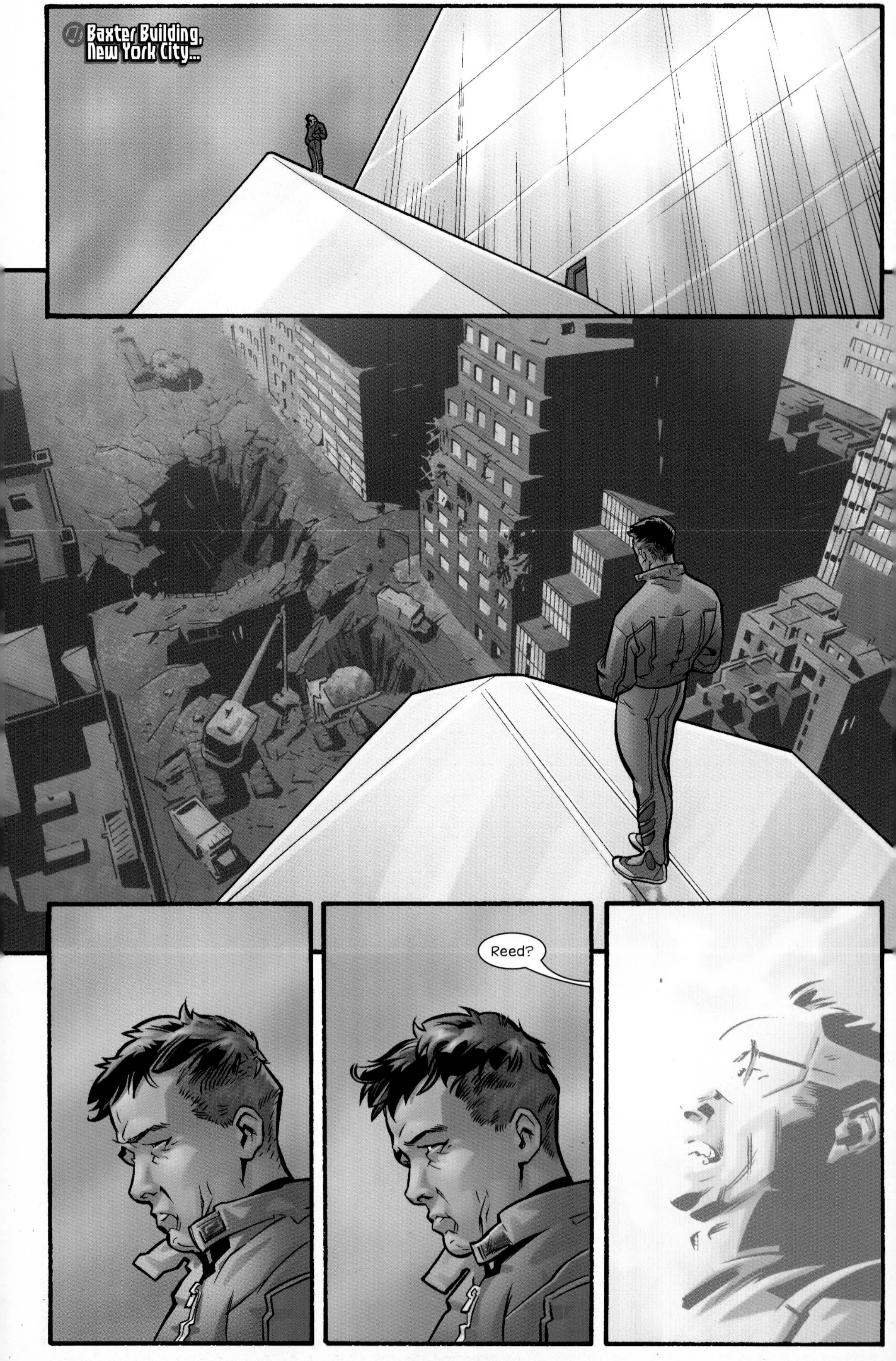
Baxter Building, New York City...
Reed?

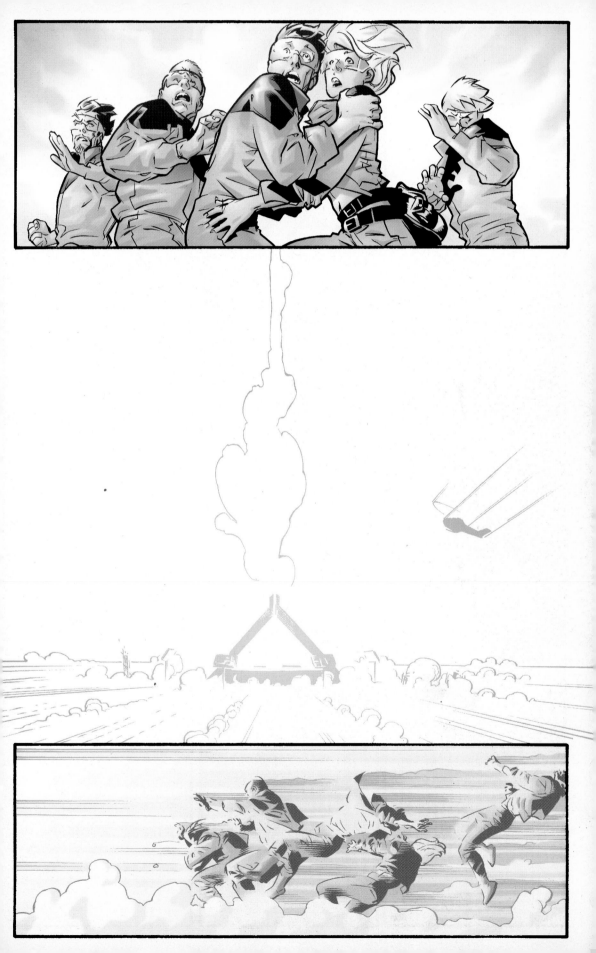

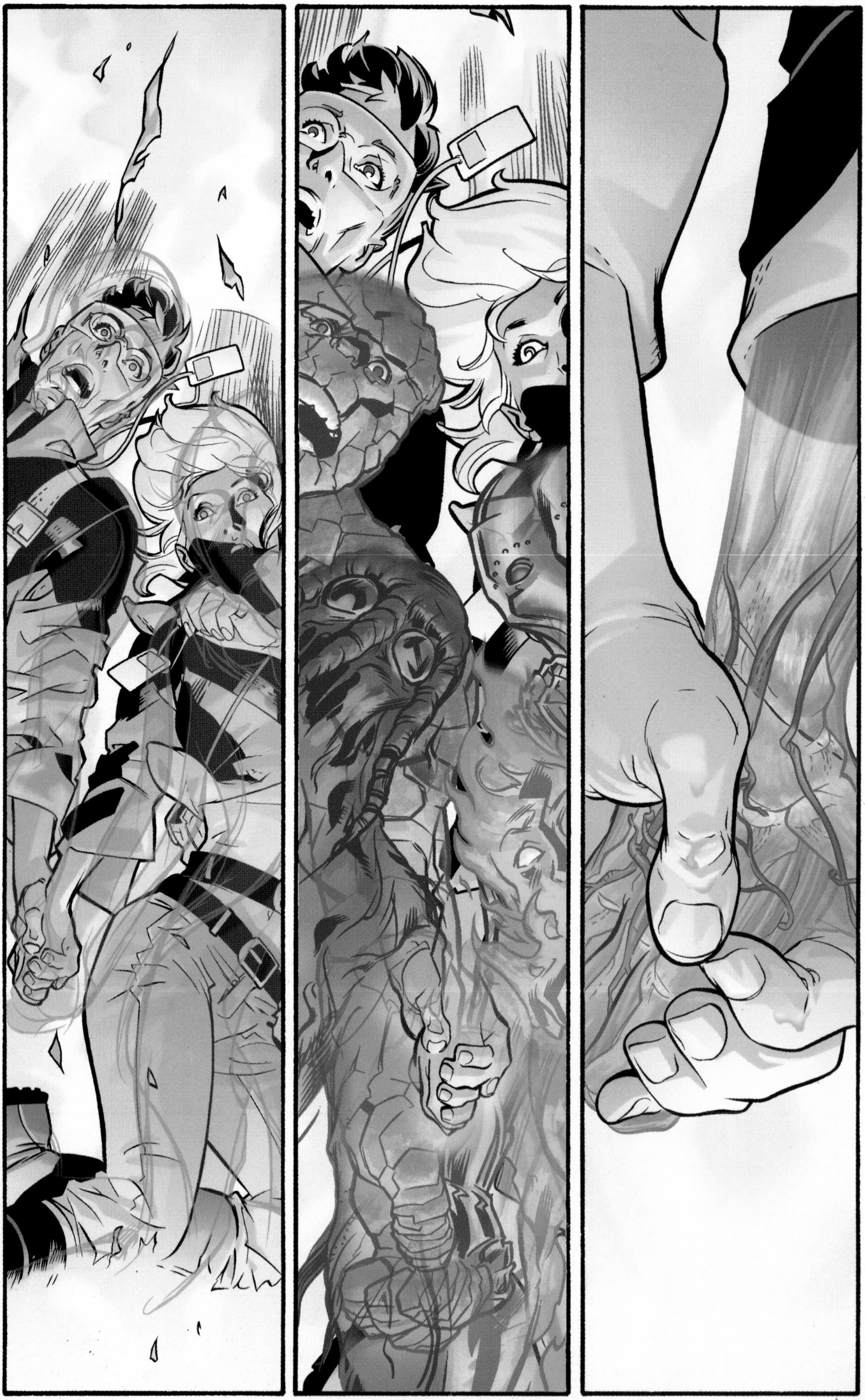

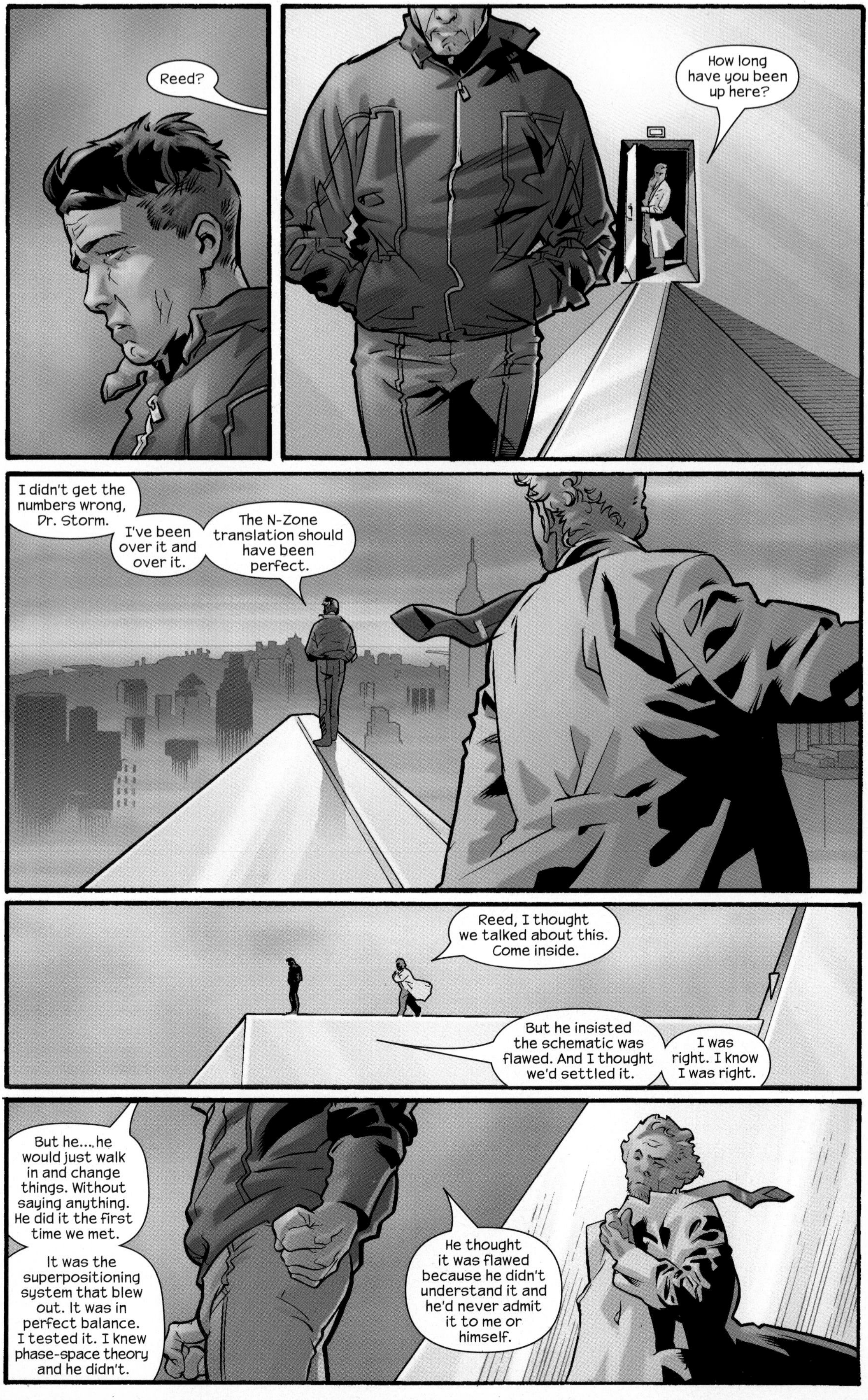
Reed?
How long have you been up here?
I didn't get the numbers wrong, Dr. Storm.
I've been over it and over it.
The N-Zone translation should have been perfect.
Reed, I thought we talked about this. Come inside.
But he insisted the schematic was flawed. And I thought we'd settled it.
I was right. I know I was right.
But he... he would just walk in and change things. Without saying anything. He did it the first time we met.
It was the superpositioning system that blew out. It was in perfect balance. I tested it. I knew phase-space theory and he didn't.
He thought it was flawed because he didn't understand it and he'd never admit it to me or himself.

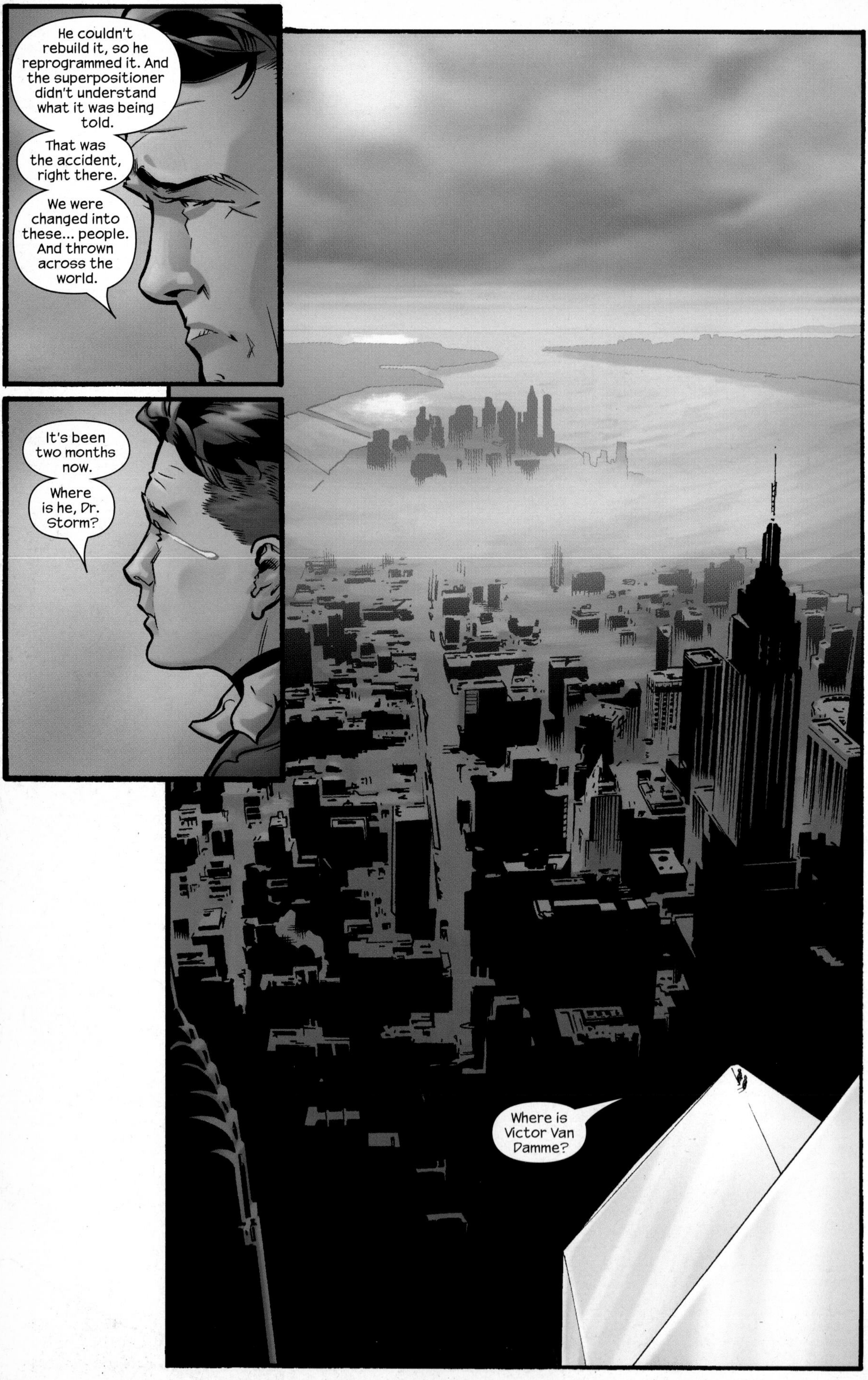
He couldn't rebuild it, so he reprogrammed it. And the superpositioner didn't understand what it was being told.
That was the accident, right there.
We were changed into these... people. And thrown across the world.
It's been two months now.
Where is he, Dr. Storm?
Where is Victor Van Damme?

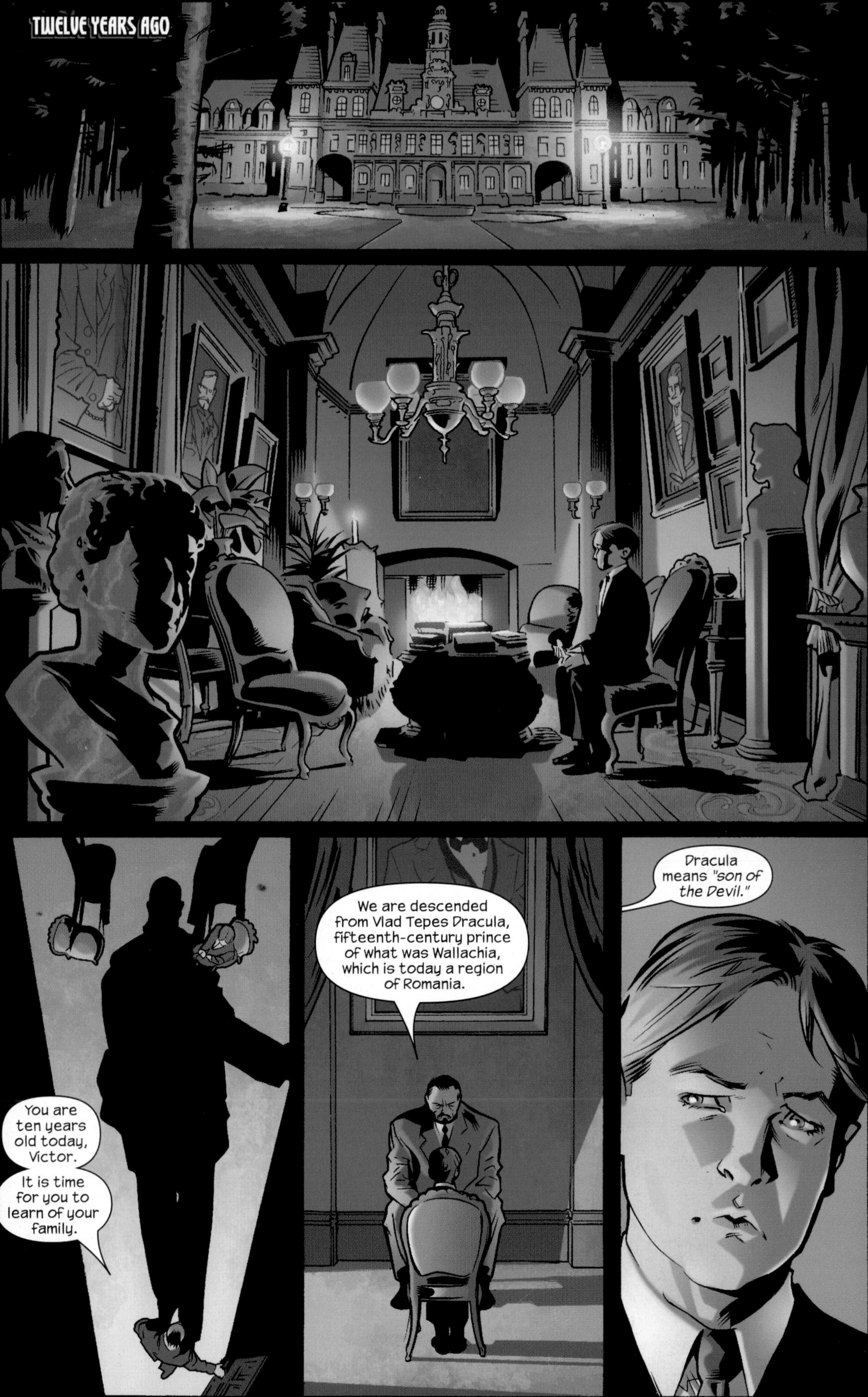
TWELVE YEARS AGO
You are ten years old today, Victor.
It is time for you to learn of your family.
We are descended from Vlad Tepes Dracula, fifteenth-century prince of what was Wallachia, which is today a region of Romania.
Dracula means "*son of the Devil.*"

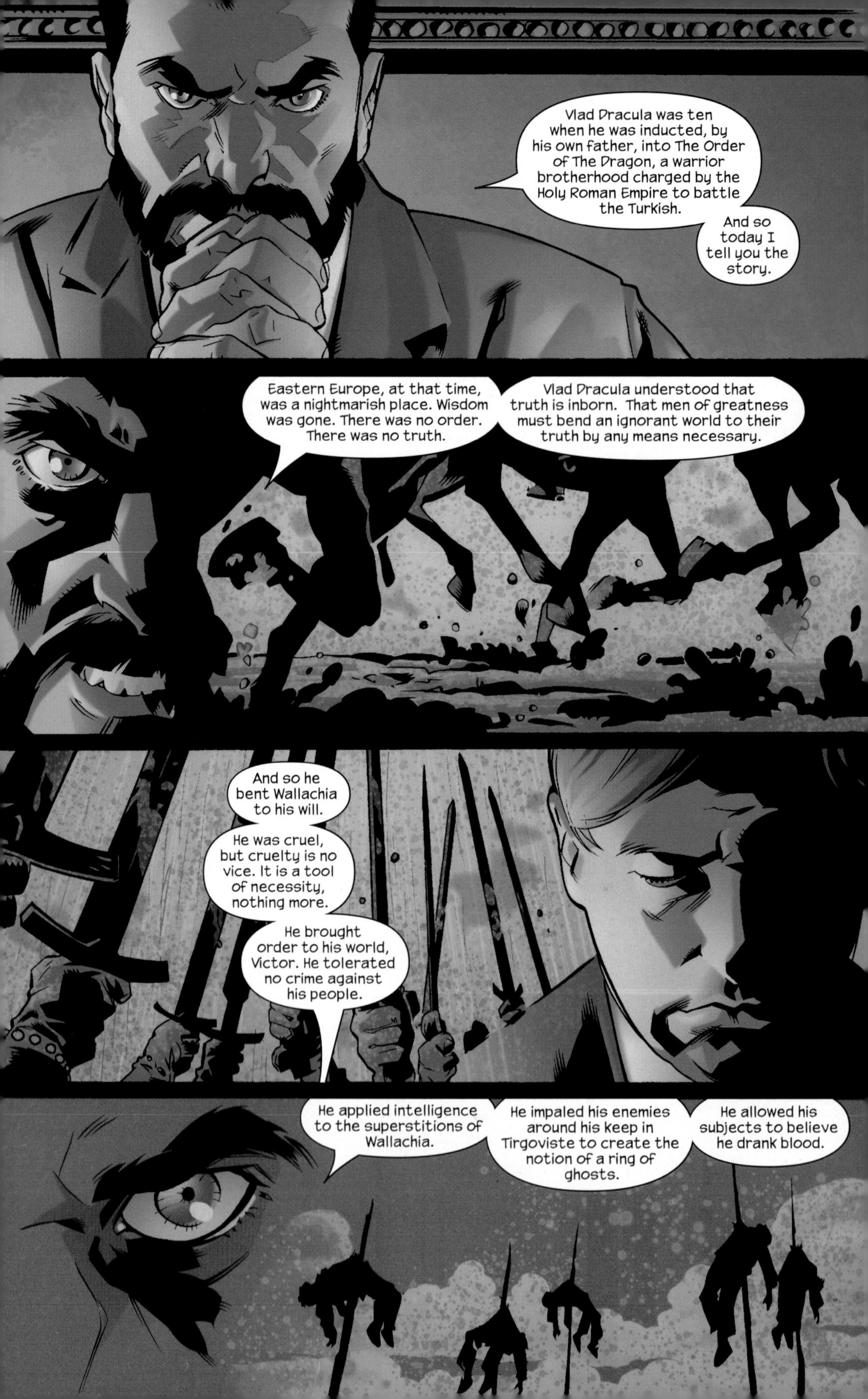

Vlad Dracula was ten when he was inducted, by his own father, into The Order of The Dragon, a warrior brotherhood charged by the Holy Roman Empire to battle the Turkish.
And so today I tell you the story.
Eastern Europe, at that time, was a nightmarish place. Wisdom was gone. There was no order. There was no truth.
Vlad Dracula understood that truth is inborn. That men of greatness must bend an ignorant world to their truth by any means necessary.
And so he bent Wallachia to his will.
He was cruel, but cruelty is no vice. It is a tool of necessity, nothing more.
He brought order to his world, Victor. He tolerated no crime against his people.
He applied intelligence to the superstitions of Wallachia.
He impaled his enemies around his keep in Tirgoviste to create the notion of a ring of ghosts.
He allowed his subjects to believe he drank blood.

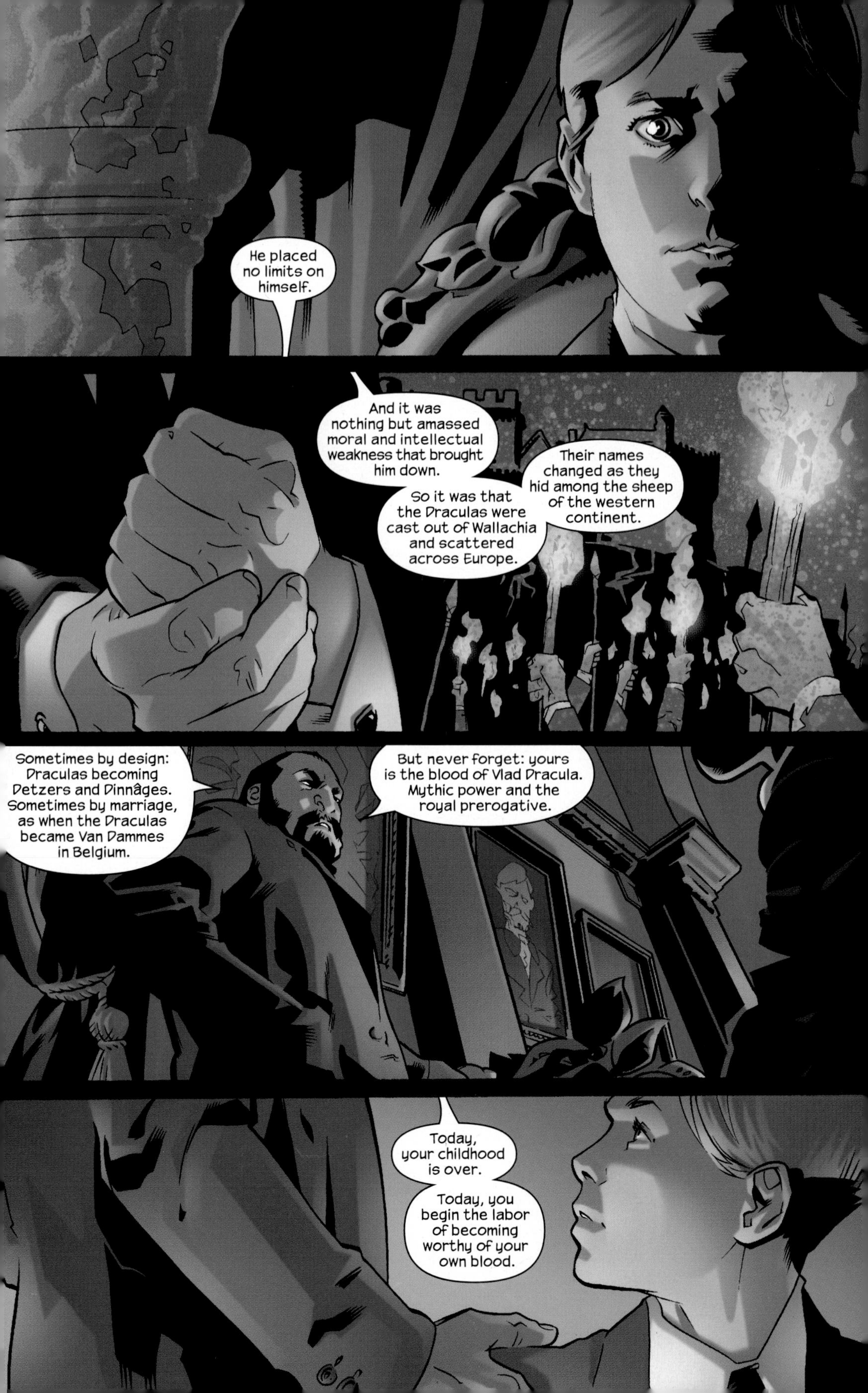
He placed no limits on himself.
And it was nothing but amassed moral and intellectual weakness that brought him down.
So it was that the Draculas were cast out of Wallachia and scattered across Europe.
Their names changed as they hid among the sheep of the western continent.
Sometimes by design: Draculas becoming Detzers and Dinnâges. Sometimes by marriage, as when the Draculas became Van Dammes in Belgium.
But never forget: yours is the blood of Vlad Dracula. Mythic power and the royal prerogative.
Today, your childhood is over.
Today, you begin the labor of becoming worthy of your own blood.

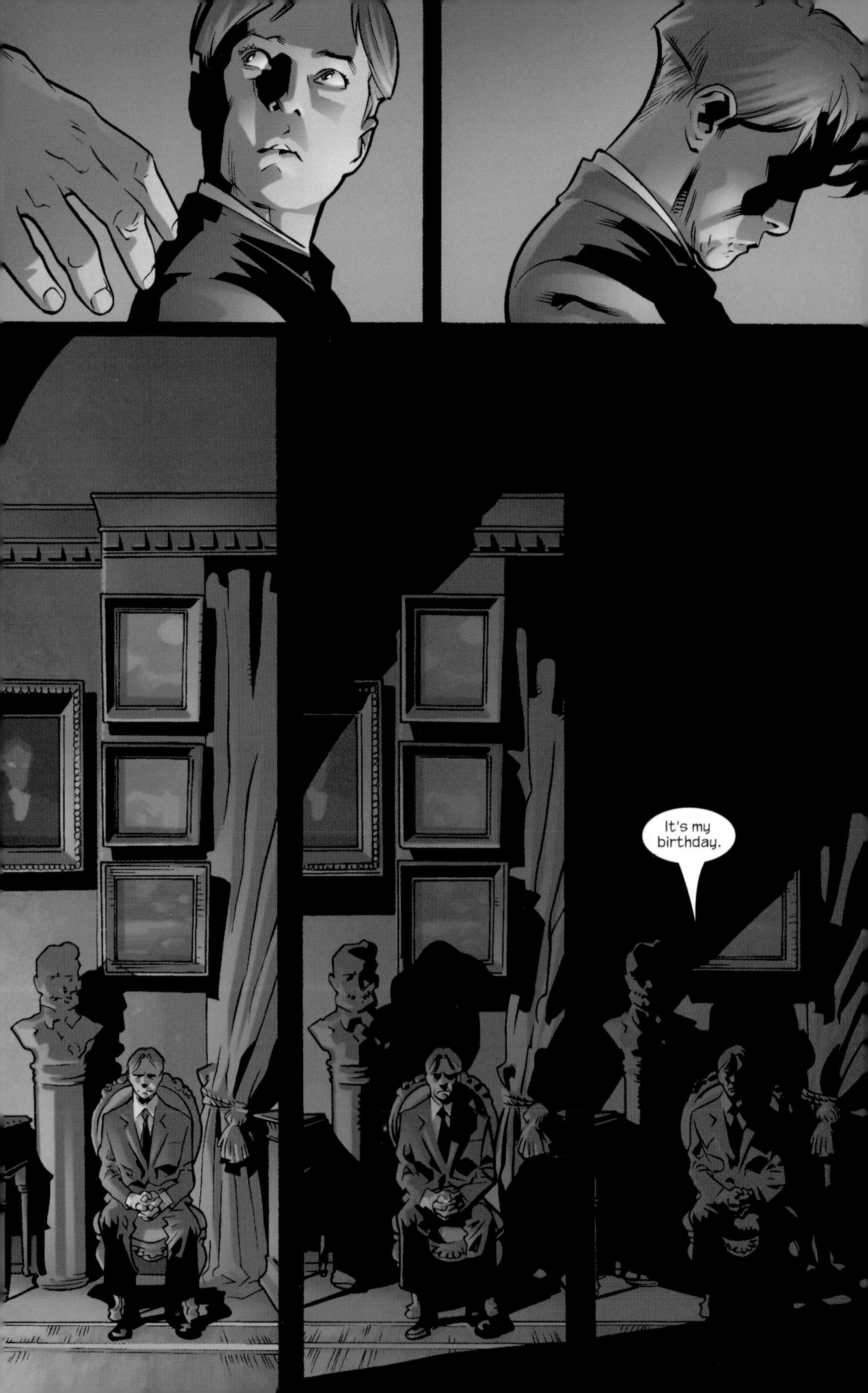
It's my birthday.

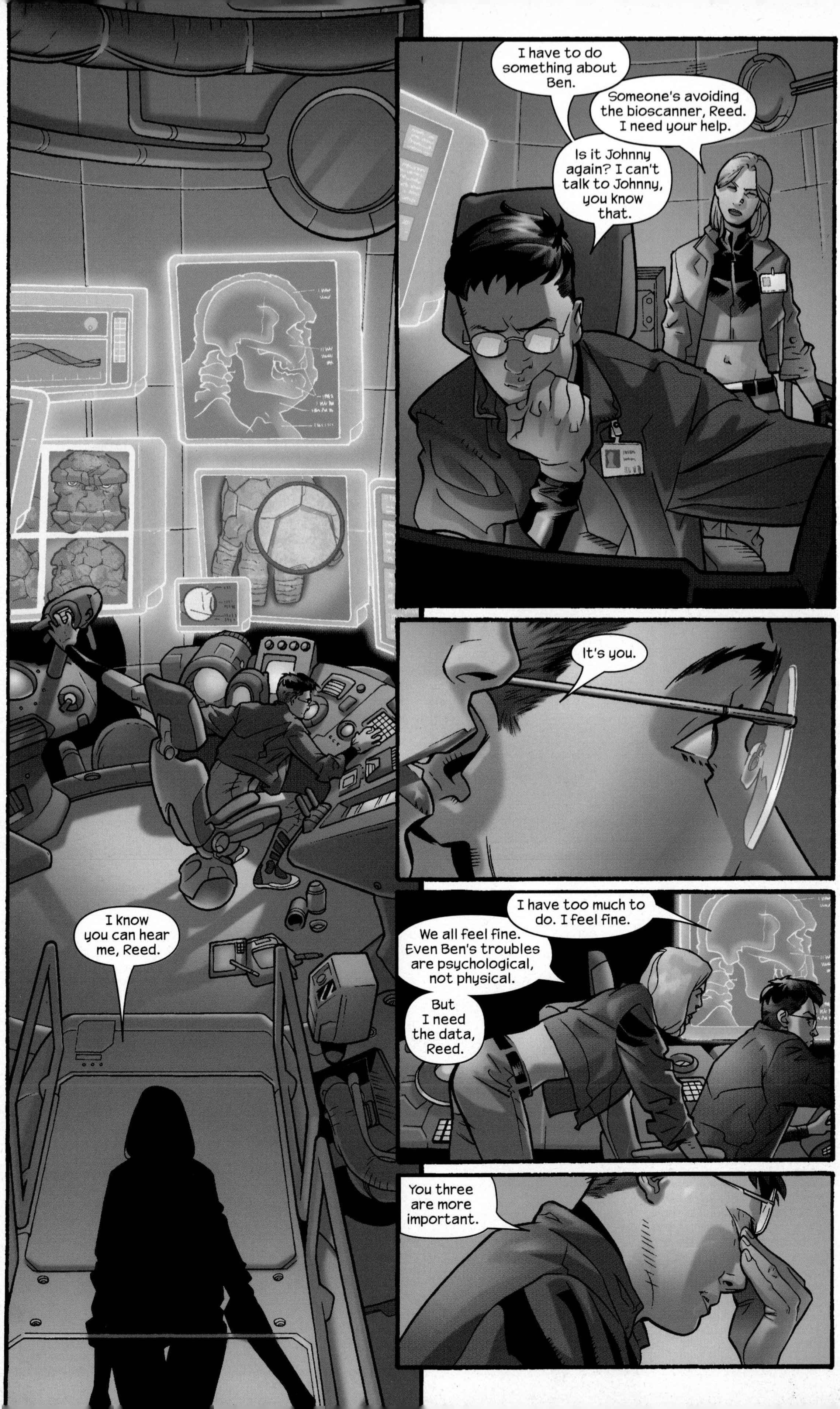
I have to do something about Ben.
Someone's avoiding the bioscanner, Reed. I need your help.
Is it Johnny again? I can't talk to Johnny, you know that.
It's you.
I know you can hear me, Reed.
I have too much to do. I feel fine.
We all feel fine. Even Ben's troubles are psychological, not physical.
But I need the data, Reed.
You three are more important.

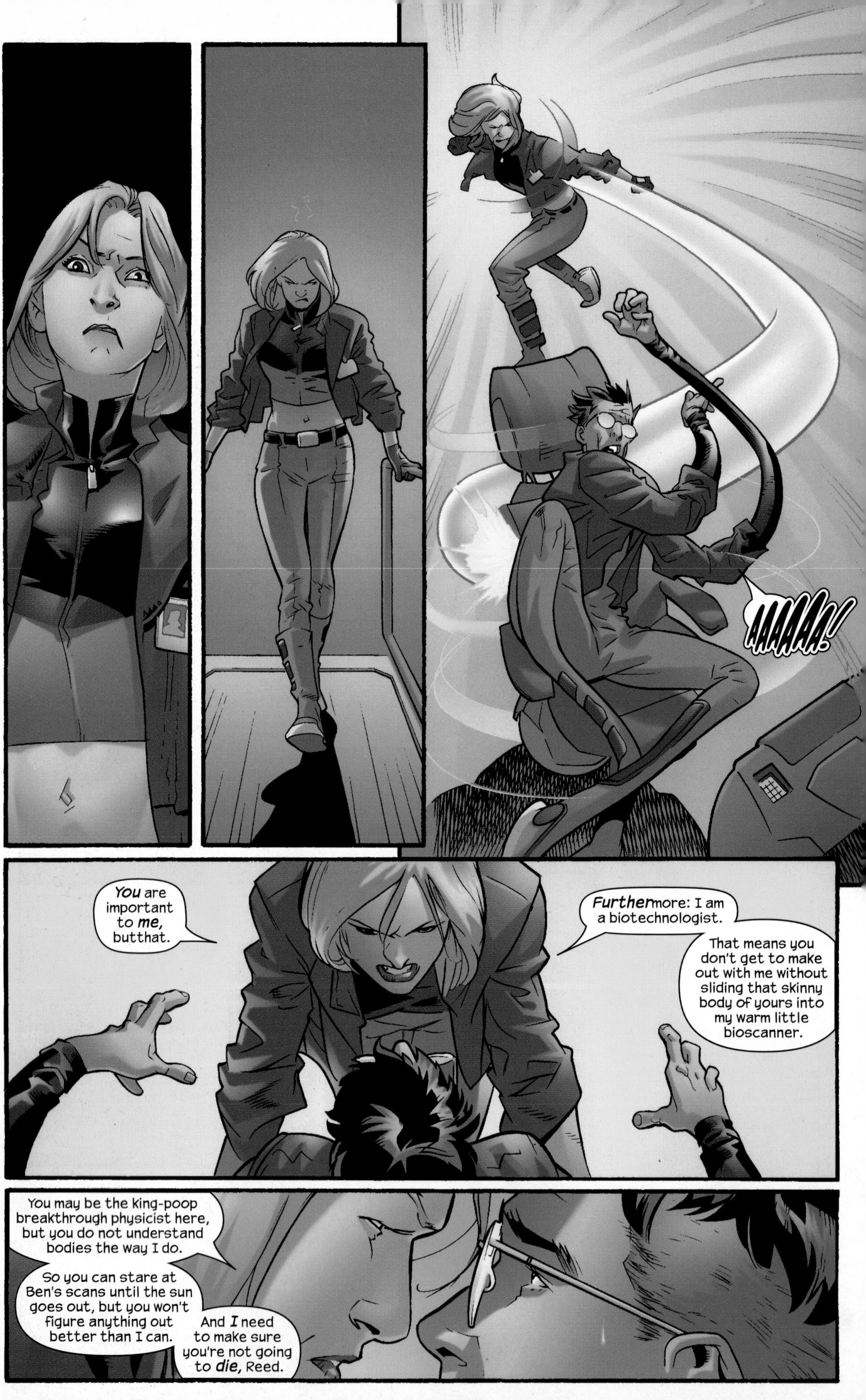
AAAAAA!
You are important to me, butthat.
Furthermore: I am a biotechnologist.
That means you don't get to make out with me without sliding that skinny body of yours into my warm little bioscanner.
You may be the king-poop breakthrough physicist here, but you do not understand bodies the way I do.
So you can stare at Ben's scans until the sun goes out, but you won't figure anything out better than I can.
And I need to make sure you're not going to die, Reed.

Can we make out afterwards?

It's just that I think I'm getting good at it.

You started out good at it. You're getting fantastic.

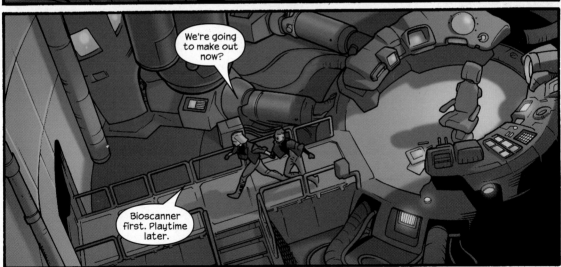

We're going to make out now?

Bioscanner first. Playtime later.

Have you looked at Ben's scans? They're kind of spare.

I need to reconfigure the bioscanner. I can't get it to tunnel through his hide properly.

I'm not even sure how he's breathing.

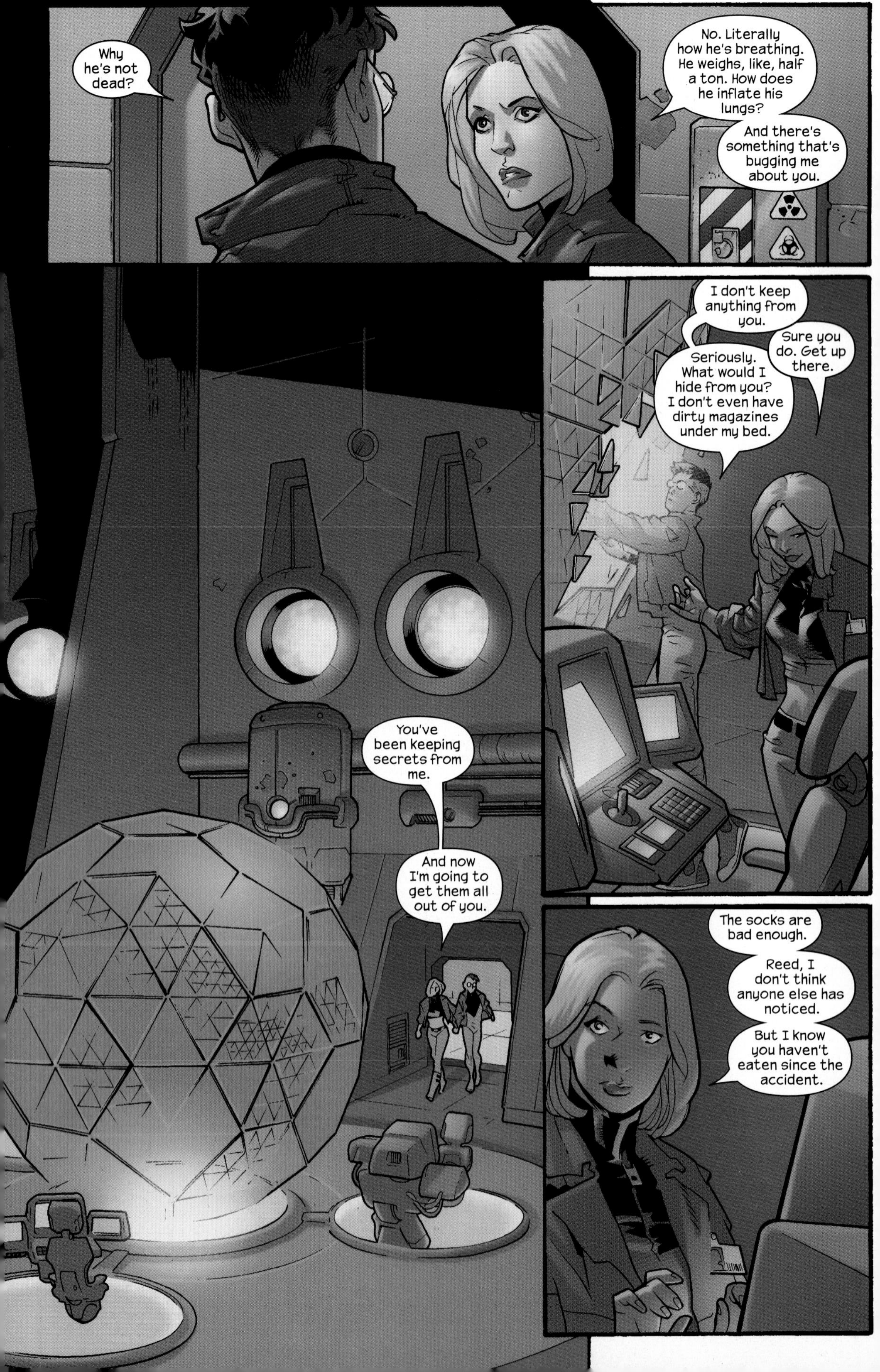
Why he's not dead?
No. Literally how he's breathing. He weighs, like, half a ton. How does he inflate his lungs?
And there's something that's bugging me about you.
You've been keeping secrets from me.
And now I'm going to get them all out of you.
I don't keep anything from you.
Sure you do. Get up there.
Seriously. What would I hide from you? I don't even have dirty magazines under my bed.
The socks are bad enough.
Reed, I don't think anyone else has noticed.
But I know you haven't eaten since the accident.

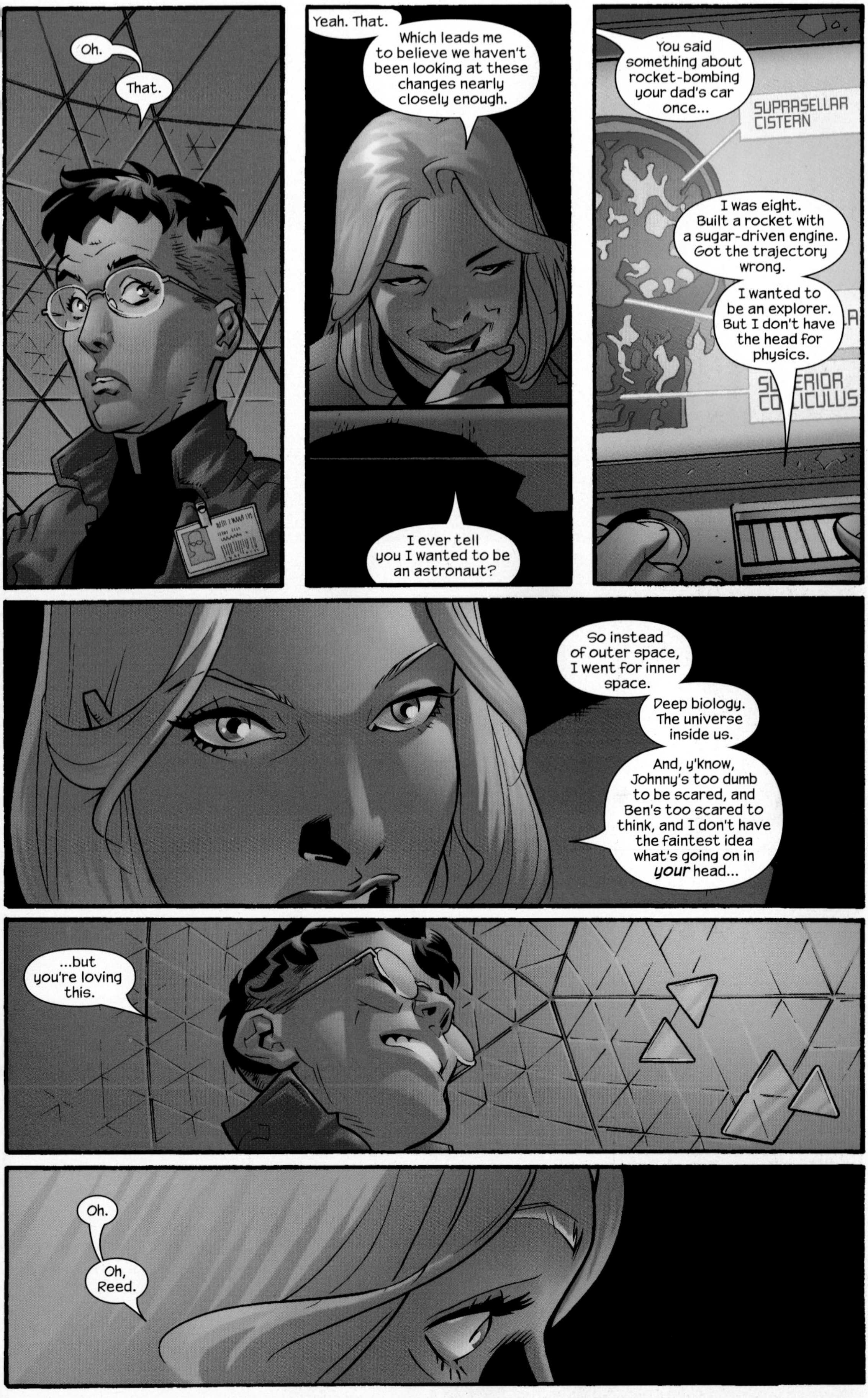
Oh.
That.
Yeah. That.
Which leads me to believe we haven't been looking at these changes nearly closely enough.
I ever tell you I wanted to be an astronaut?
You said something about rocket-bombing your dad's car once...
SUPRASELLAR CISTERN
I was eight. Built a rocket with a sugar-driven engine. Got the trajectory wrong.
I wanted to be an explorer. But I don't have the head for physics.
So instead of outer space, I went for inner space.
Deep biology. The universe inside us.
And, y'know, Johnny's too dumb to be scared, and Ben's too scared to think, and I don't have the faintest idea what's going on in *your* head...
...but you're loving this.
Oh.
Oh, Reed.

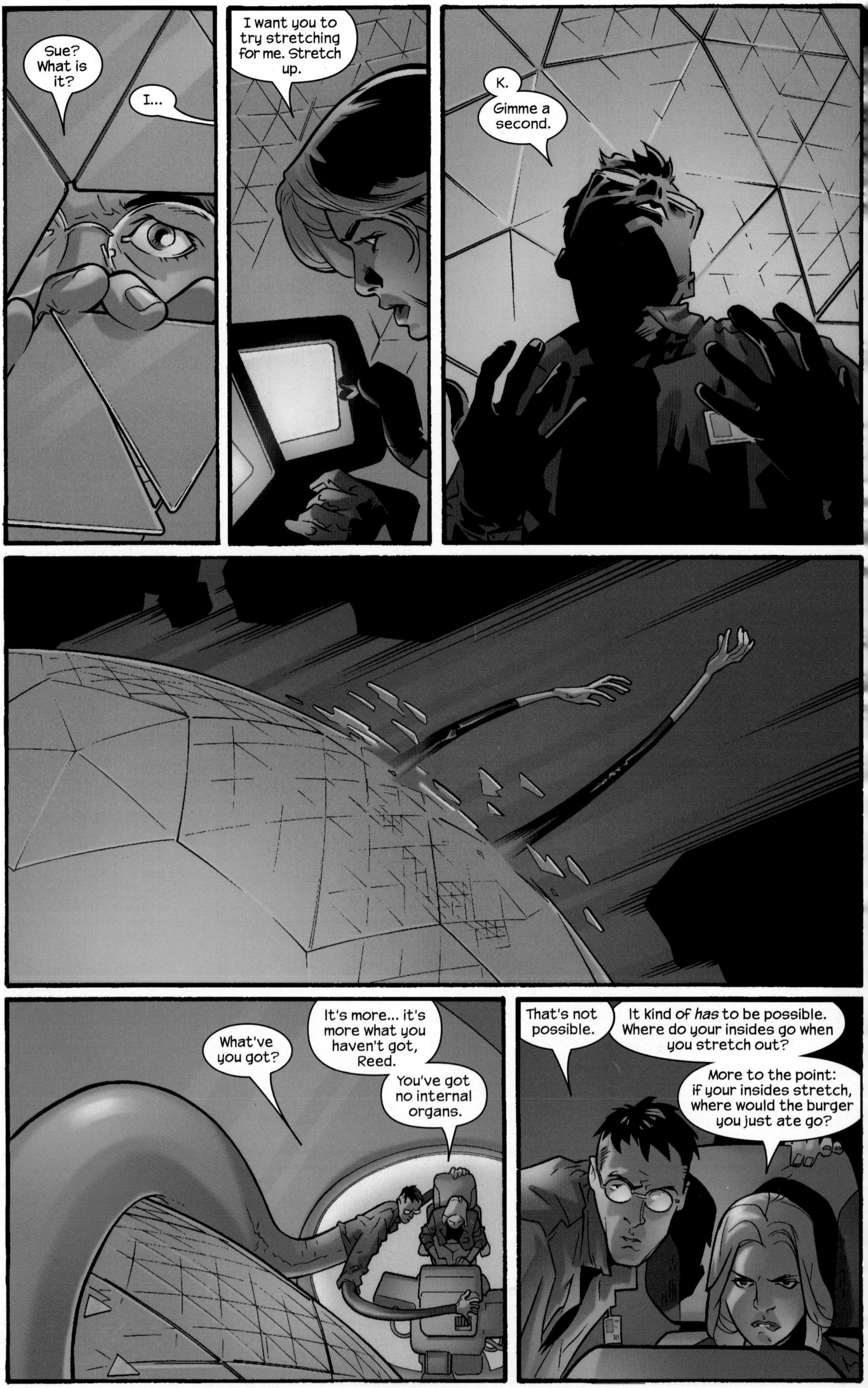

Sue? What is it?
I...
I want you to try stretching for me. Stretch up.
K.
Gimme a second.
What've you got?
It's more... it's more what you haven't got, Reed.
You've got no internal organs.
That's not possible.
It kind of *has* to be possible. Where do your insides go when you stretch out?
More to the point: if your insides stretch, where would the burger you just ate go?

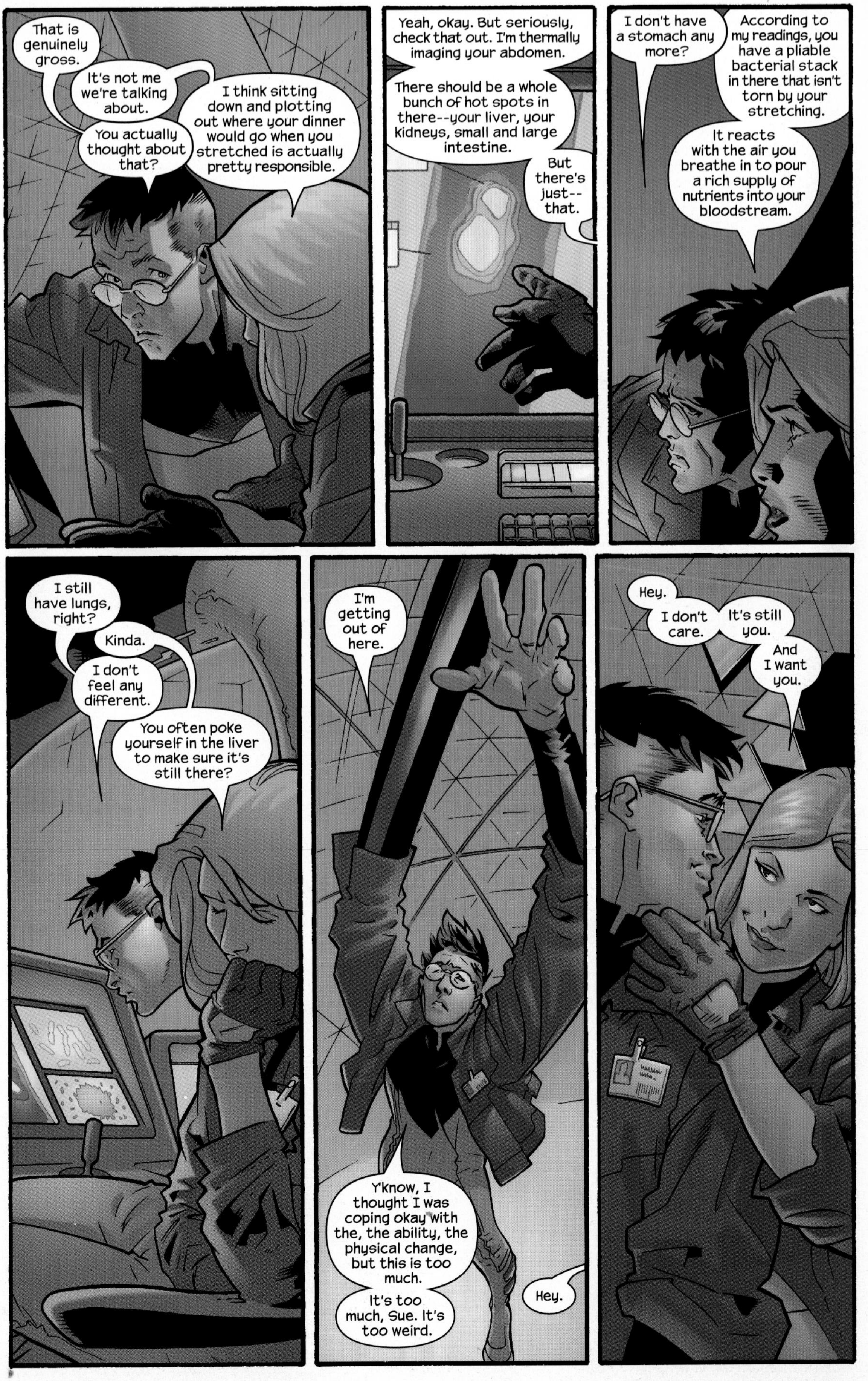
That is genuinely gross.
It's not me we're talking about.
You actually thought about that?
I think sitting down and plotting out where your dinner would go when you stretched is actually pretty responsible.
Yeah, okay. But seriously, check that out. I'm thermally imaging your abdomen.
There should be a whole bunch of hot spots in there--your liver, your kidneys, small and large intestine.
But there's just--that.
I don't have a stomach any more?
According to my readings, you have a pliable bacterial stack in there that isn't torn by your stretching.
It reacts with the air you breathe in to pour a rich supply of nutrients into your bloodstream.
I still have lungs, right?
Kinda.
I don't feel any different.
You often poke yourself in the liver to make sure it's still there?
I'm getting out of here.
Y'know, I thought I was coping okay with the, the ability, the physical change, but this is too much.
It's too much, Sue. It's too weird.
Hey.
Hey.
I don't care.
It's still you.
And I want you.

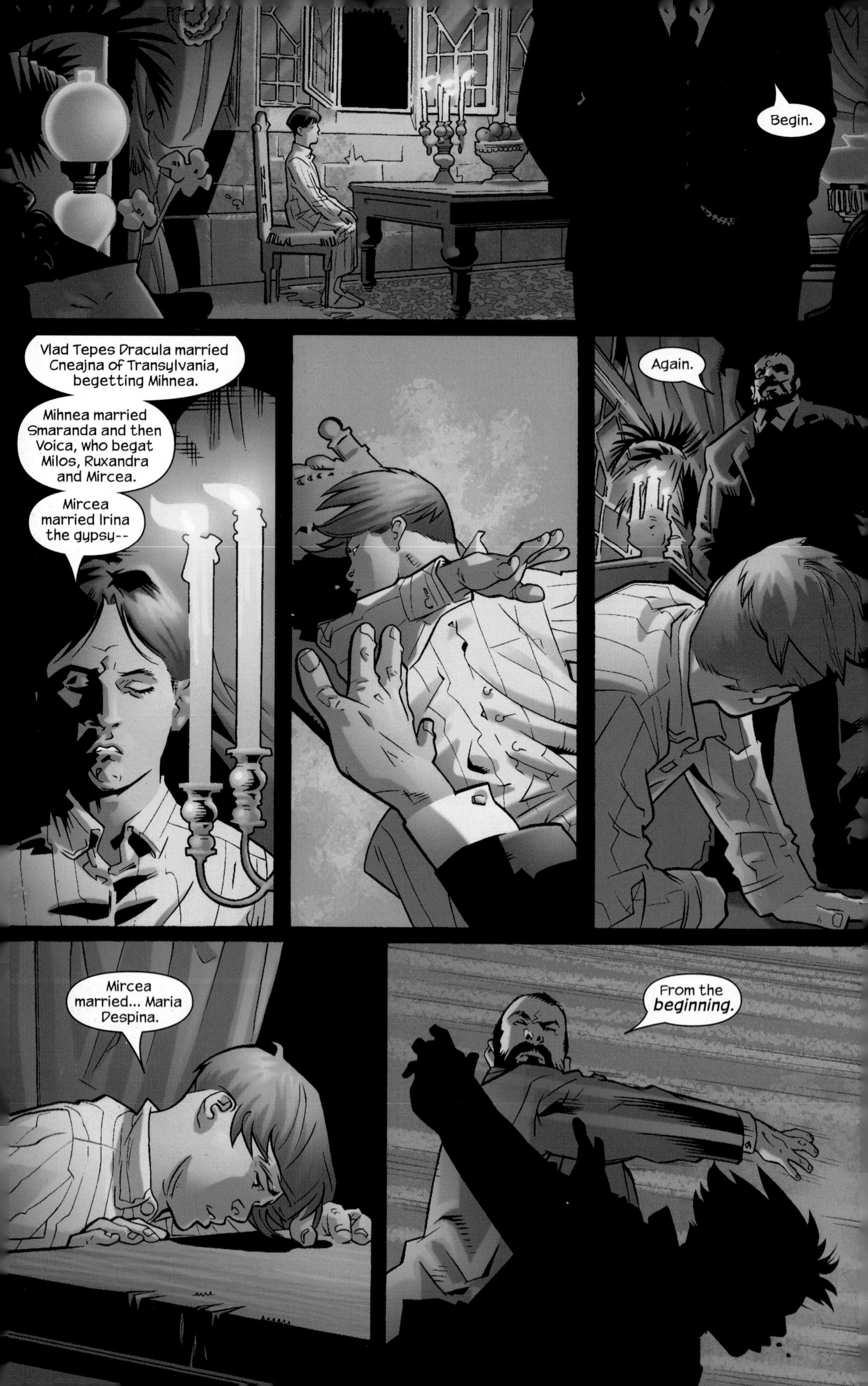
Begin.
Vlad Tepes Dracula married Cneajna of Transylvania, begetting Mihnea.
Mihnea married Smaranda and then Voica, who begat Milos, Ruxandra and Mircea.
Mircea married Irina the gypsy--
Again.
Mircea married... Maria Despina.
From the *beginning.*

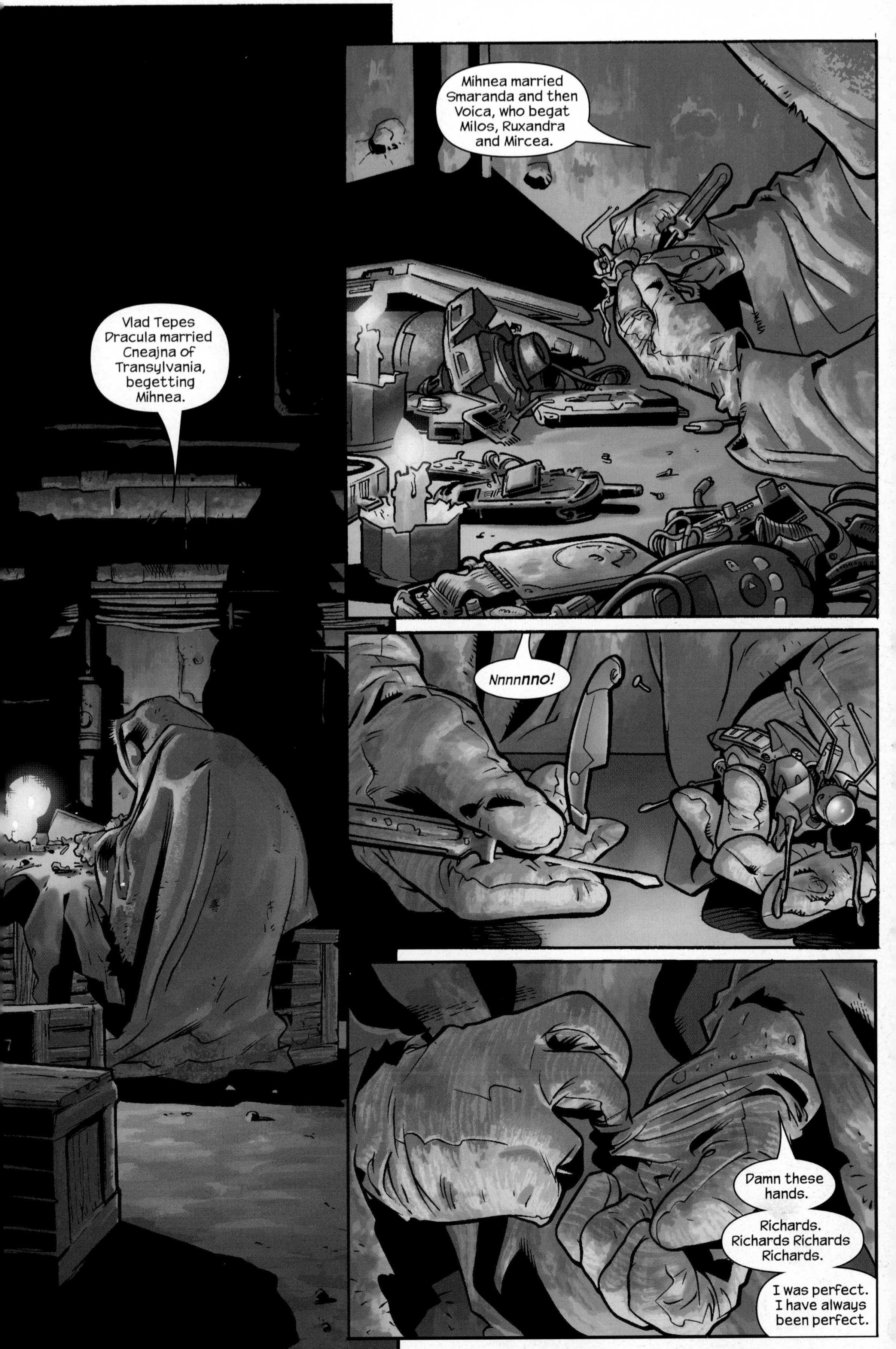
Mihnea married Smaranda and then Voica, who begat Milos, Ruxandra and Mircea.
Vlad Tepes Dracula married Cneajna of Transylvania, begetting Mihnea.
Nnnnnno!
Damn these hands.
Richards. Richards Richards Richards.
I was perfect. I have always been perfect.

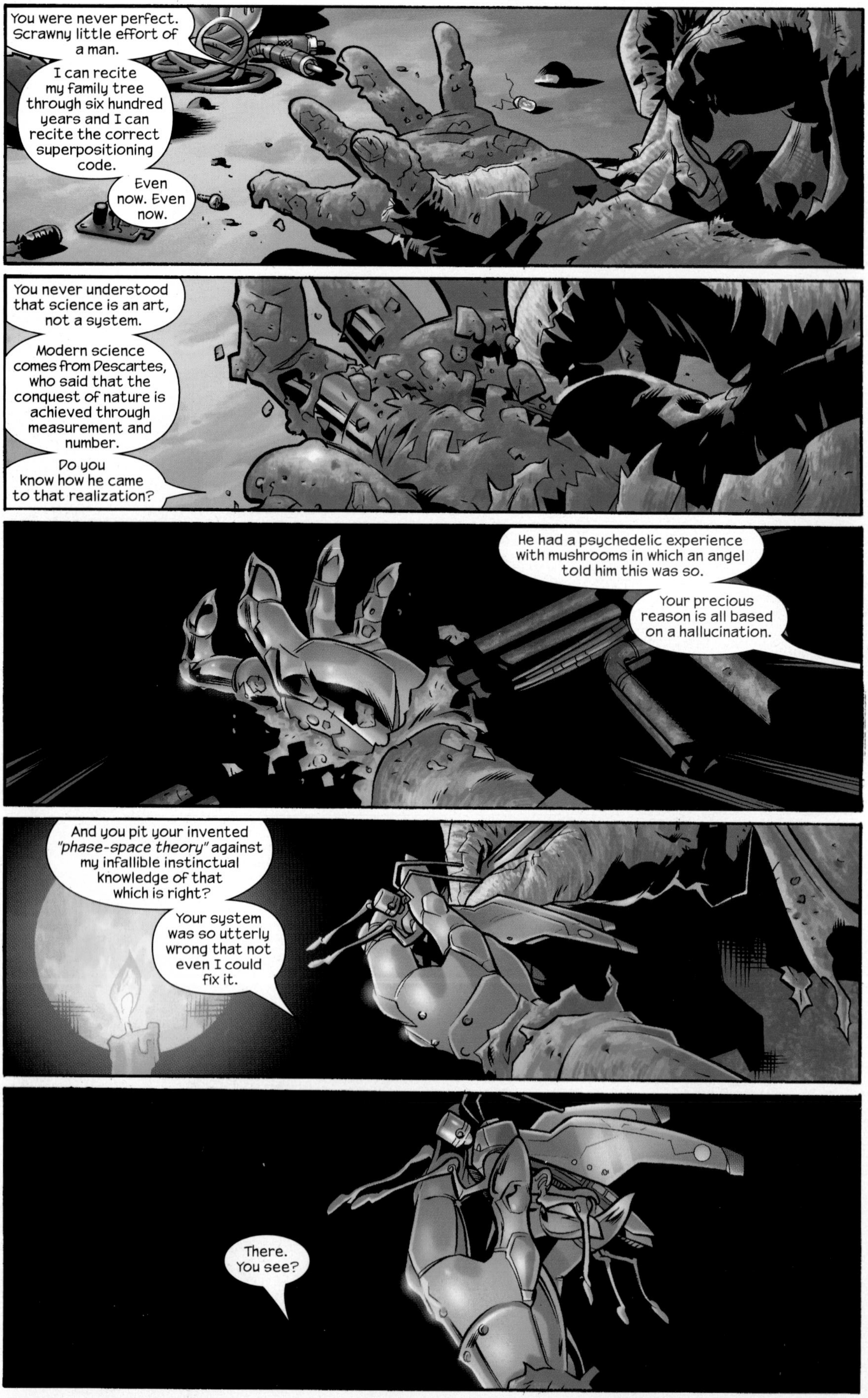
You were never perfect. Scrawny little effort of a man.
I can recite my family tree through six hundred years and I can recite the correct superpositioning code.
Even now. Even now.
You never understood that science is an art, not a system.
Modern science comes from Descartes, who said that the conquest of nature is achieved through measurement and number.
Do you know how he came to that realization?
He had a psychedelic experience with mushrooms in which an angel told him this was so.
Your precious reason is all based on a hallucination.
And you pit your invented "phase-space theory" against my infallible instinctual knowledge of that which is right?
Your system was so utterly wrong that not even I could fix it.
There. You see?

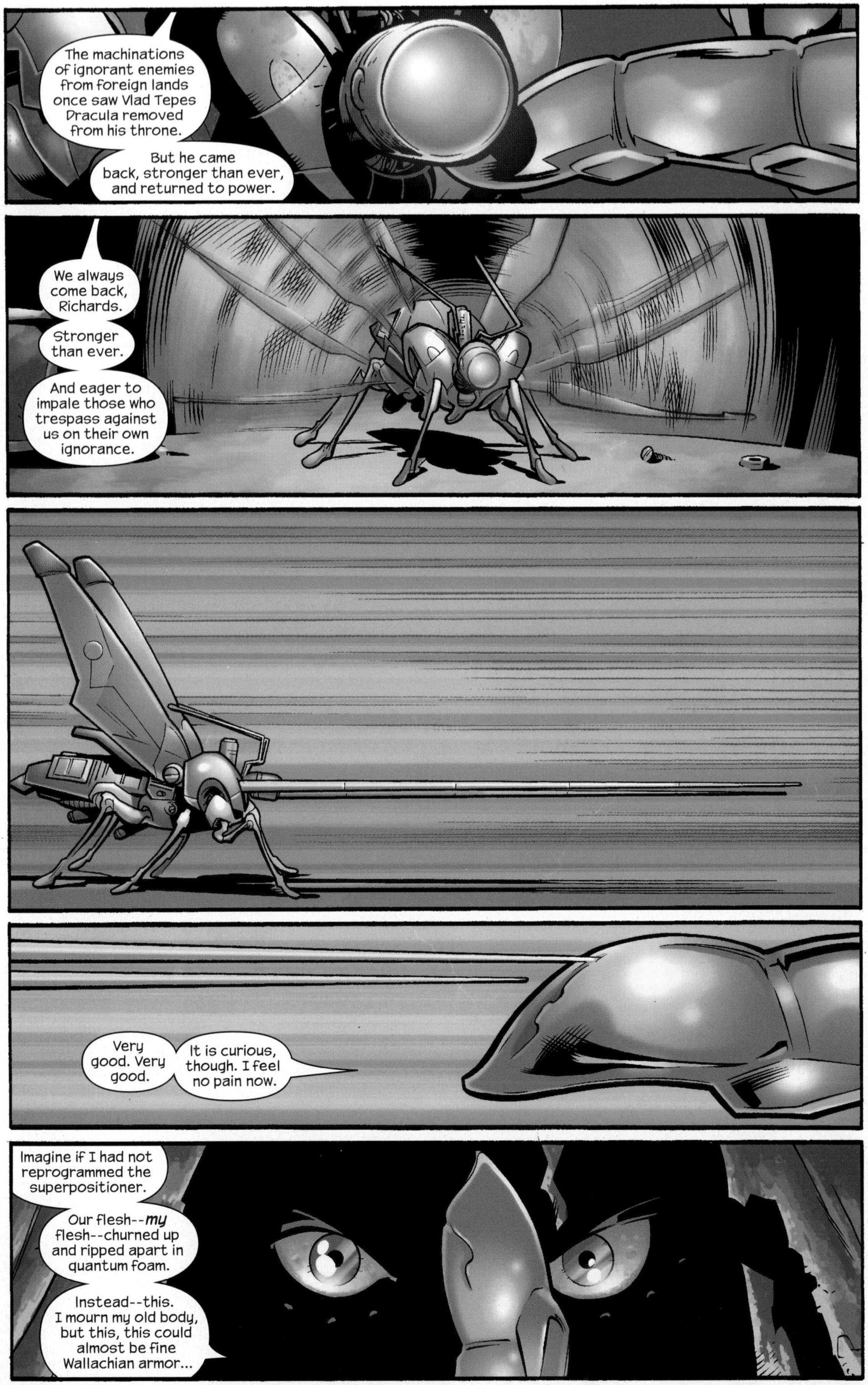

The machinations of ignorant enemies from foreign lands once saw Vlad Tepes Dracula removed from his throne.
But he came back, stronger than ever, and returned to power.
We always come back, Richards.
Stronger than ever.
And eager to impale those who trespass against us on their own ignorance.
Very good. Very good.
It is curious, though. I feel no pain now.
Imagine if I had not reprogrammed the superpositioner.
Our flesh--*my* flesh--churned up and ripped apart in quantum foam.
Instead--this. I mourn my old body, but this, this could almost be fine Wallachian armor...

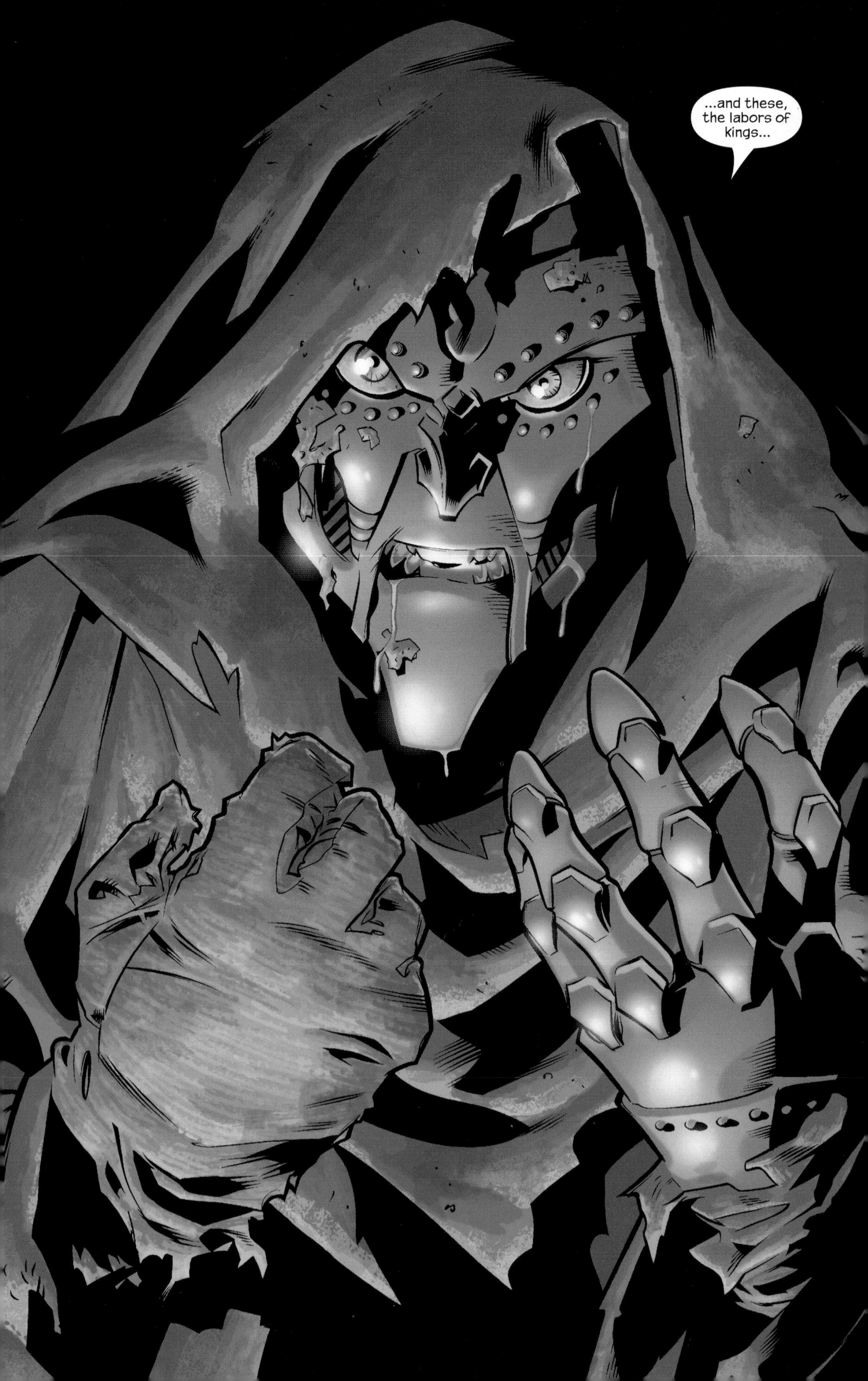
...and these, the labors of kings...

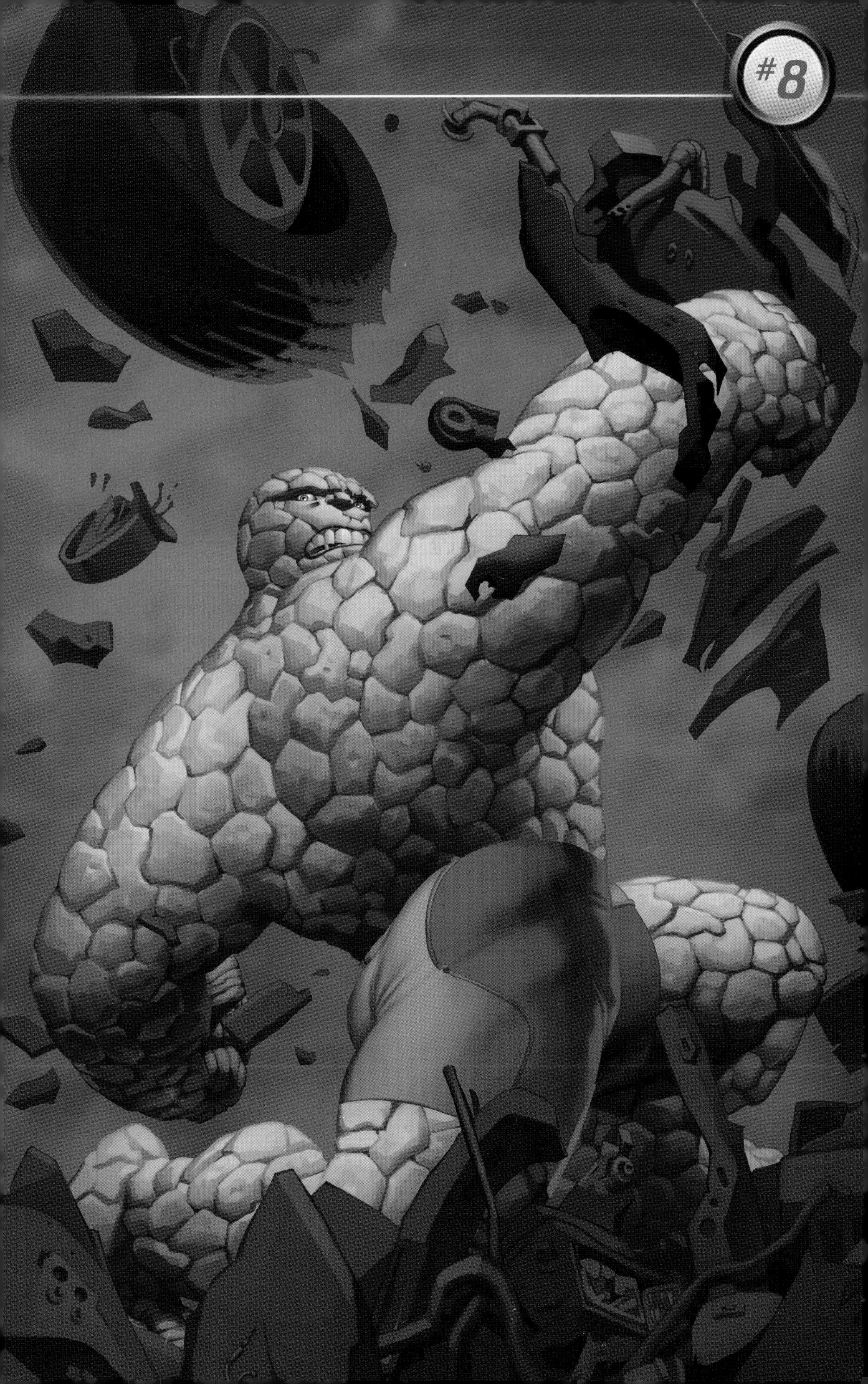
#8

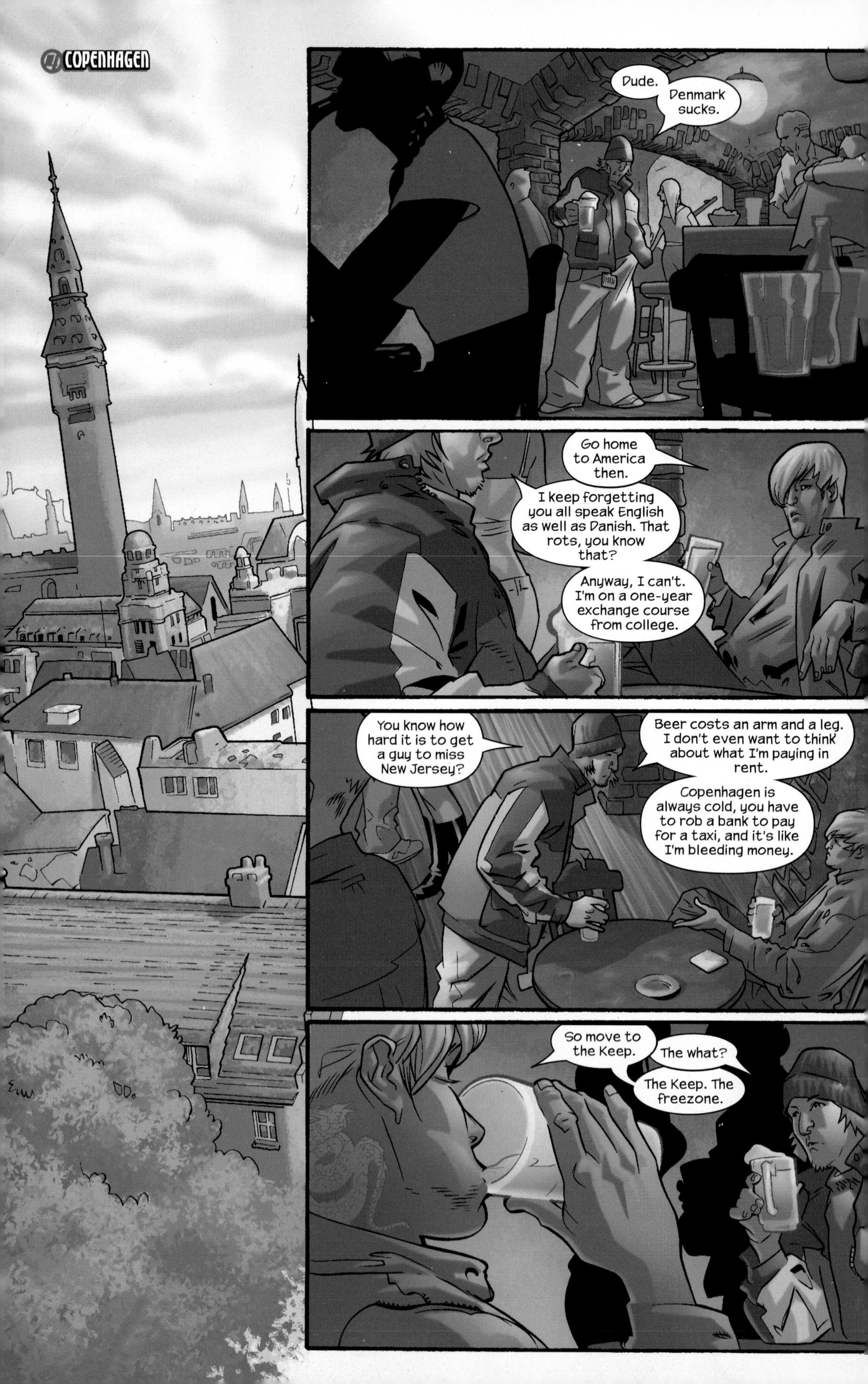
COPENHAGEN
Dude.
Denmark sucks.
Go home to America then.
I keep forgetting you all speak English as well as Danish. That rots, you know that?
Anyway, I can't. I'm on a one-year exchange course from college.
You know how hard it is to get a guy to miss New Jersey?
Beer costs an arm and a leg. I don't even want to think about what I'm paying in rent.
Copenhagen is always cold, you have to rob a bank to pay for a taxi, and it's like I'm bleeding money.
So move to the Keep.
The what?
The Keep. The freezone.

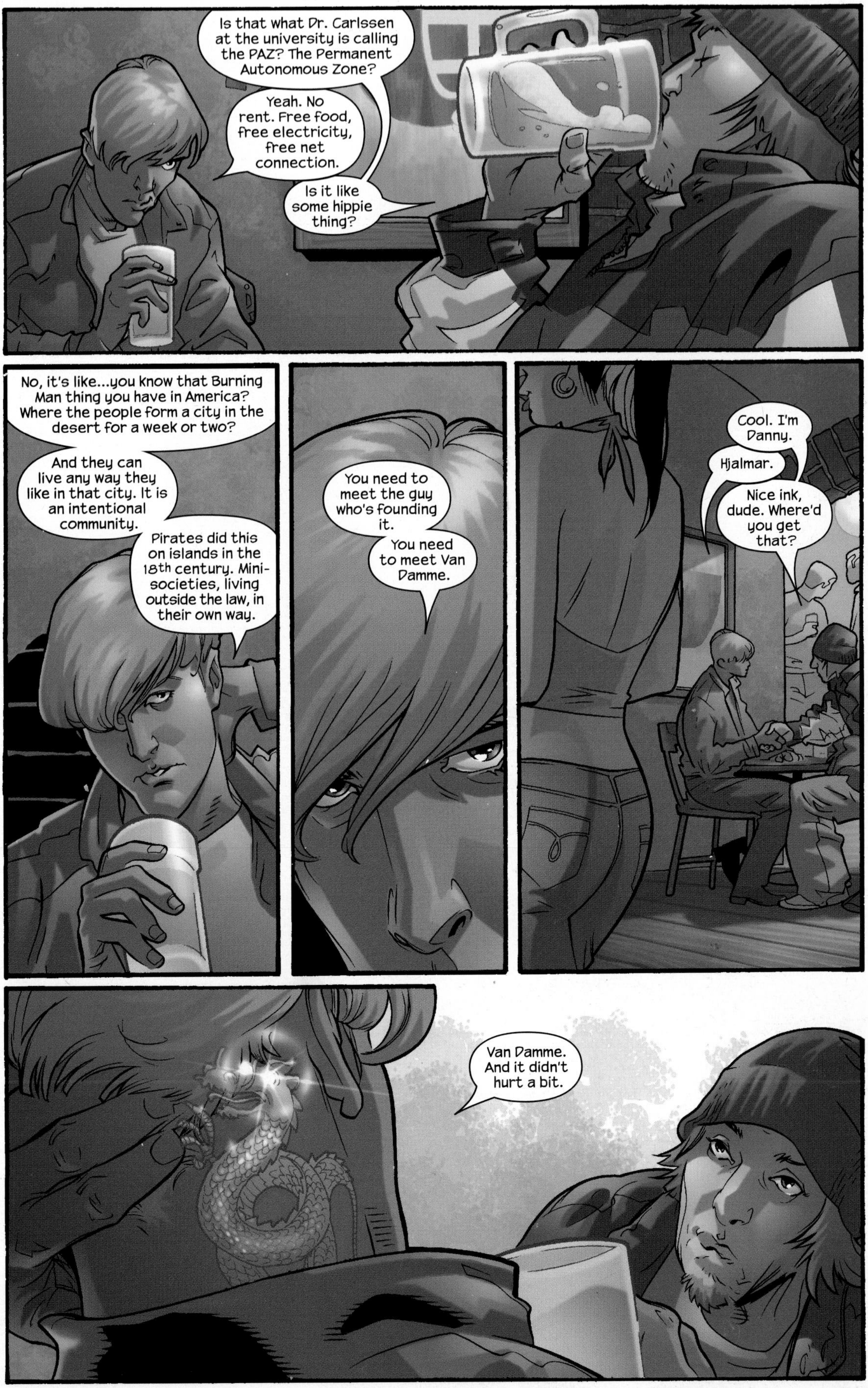
Is that what Dr. Carlssen at the university is calling the PAZ? The Permanent Autonomous Zone?
Yeah. No rent. Free food, free electricity, free net connection.
Is it like some hippie thing?
No, it's like...you know that Burning Man thing you have in America? Where the people form a city in the desert for a week or two?
And they can live any way they like in that city. It is an intentional community.
Pirates did this on islands in the 18th century. Mini-societies, living outside the law, in their own way.
You need to meet the guy who's founding it.
You need to meet Van Damme.
Cool. I'm Danny.
Hjalmar.
Nice ink, dude. Where'd you get that?
Van Damme. And it didn't hurt a bit.

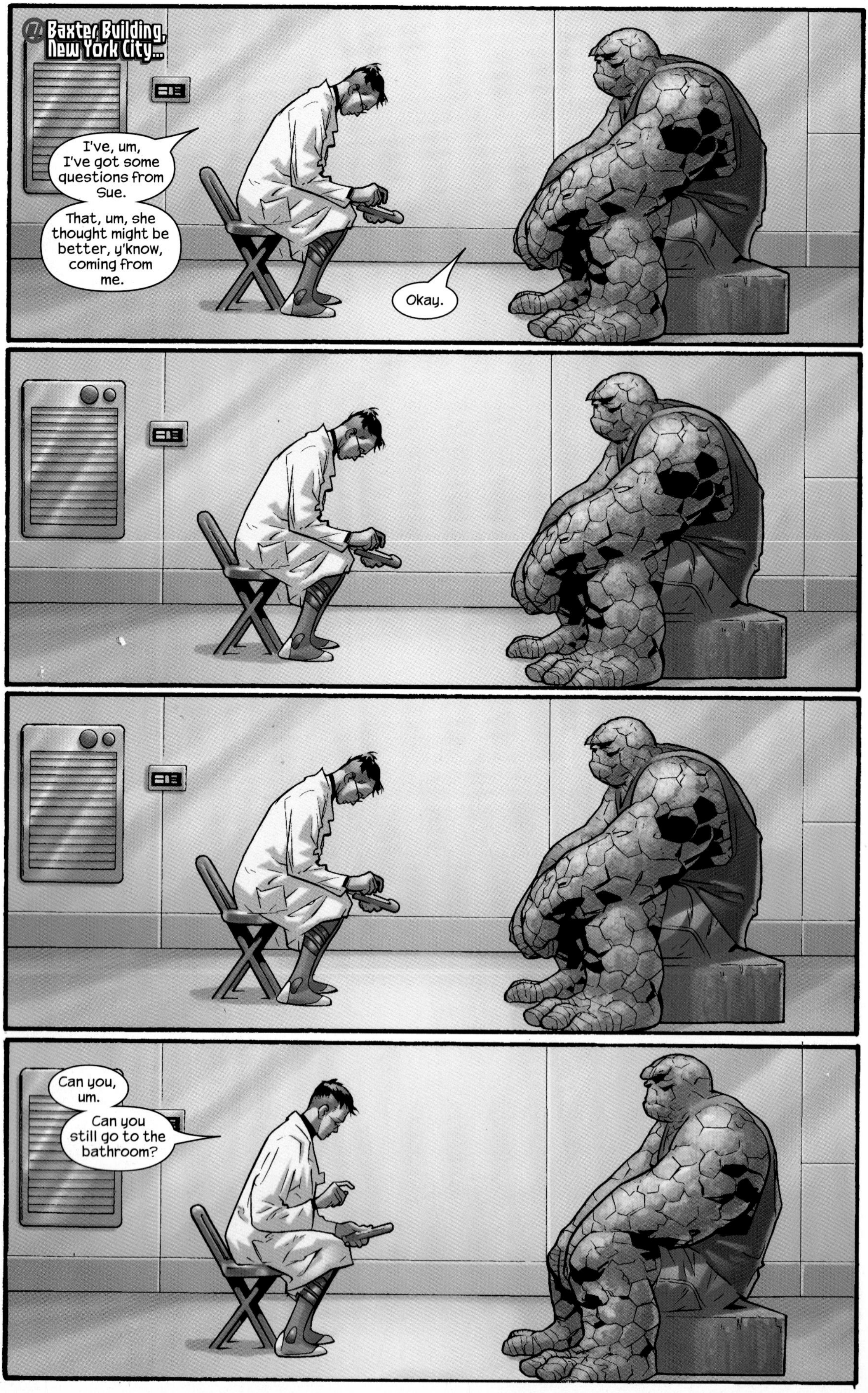
Baxter Building, New York City...
I've, um, I've got some questions from Sue.
That, um, she thought might be better, y'know, coming from me.
Okay.
Can you, um.
Can you still go to the bathroom?

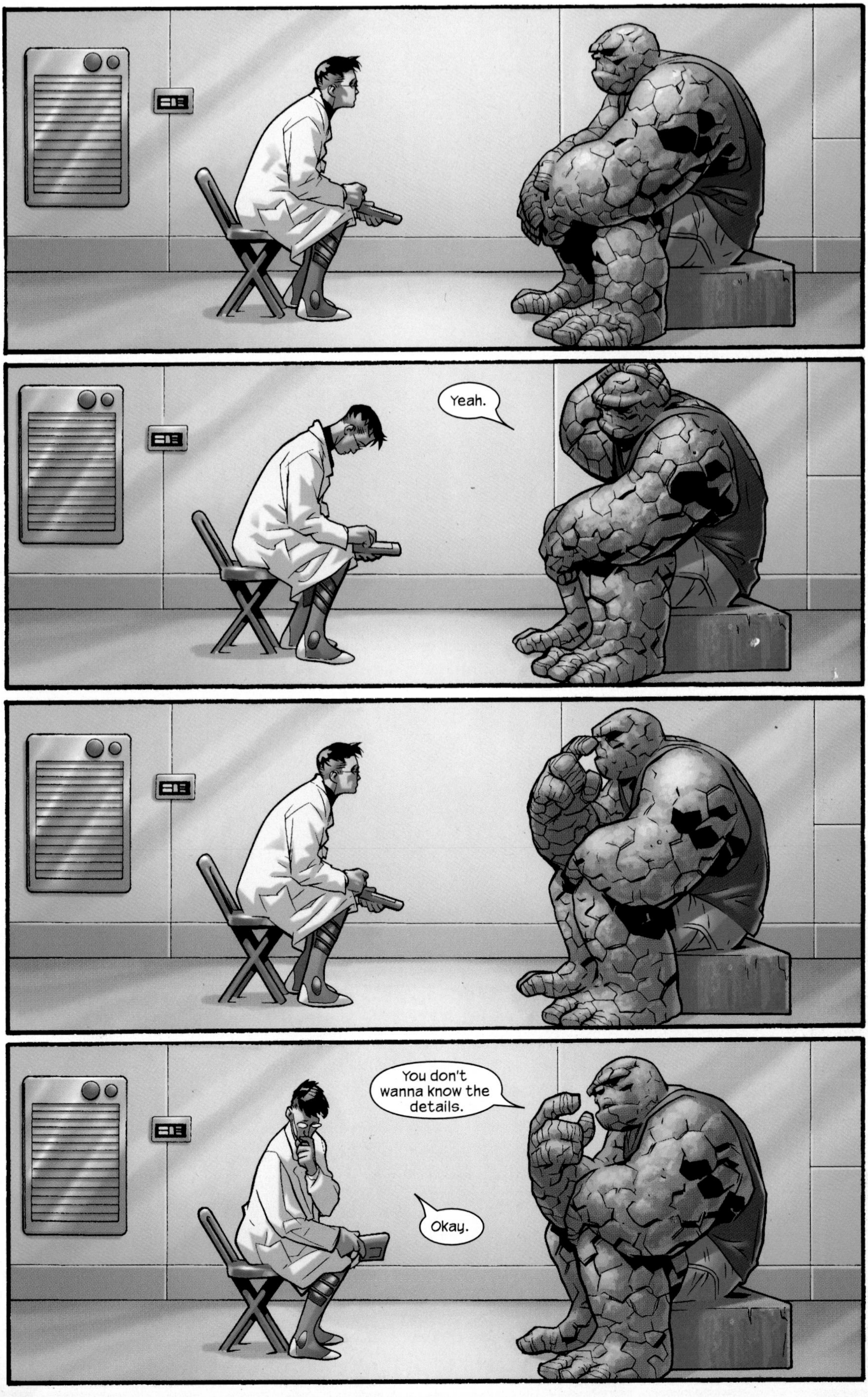
Yeah.
You don't wanna know the details.
Okay.

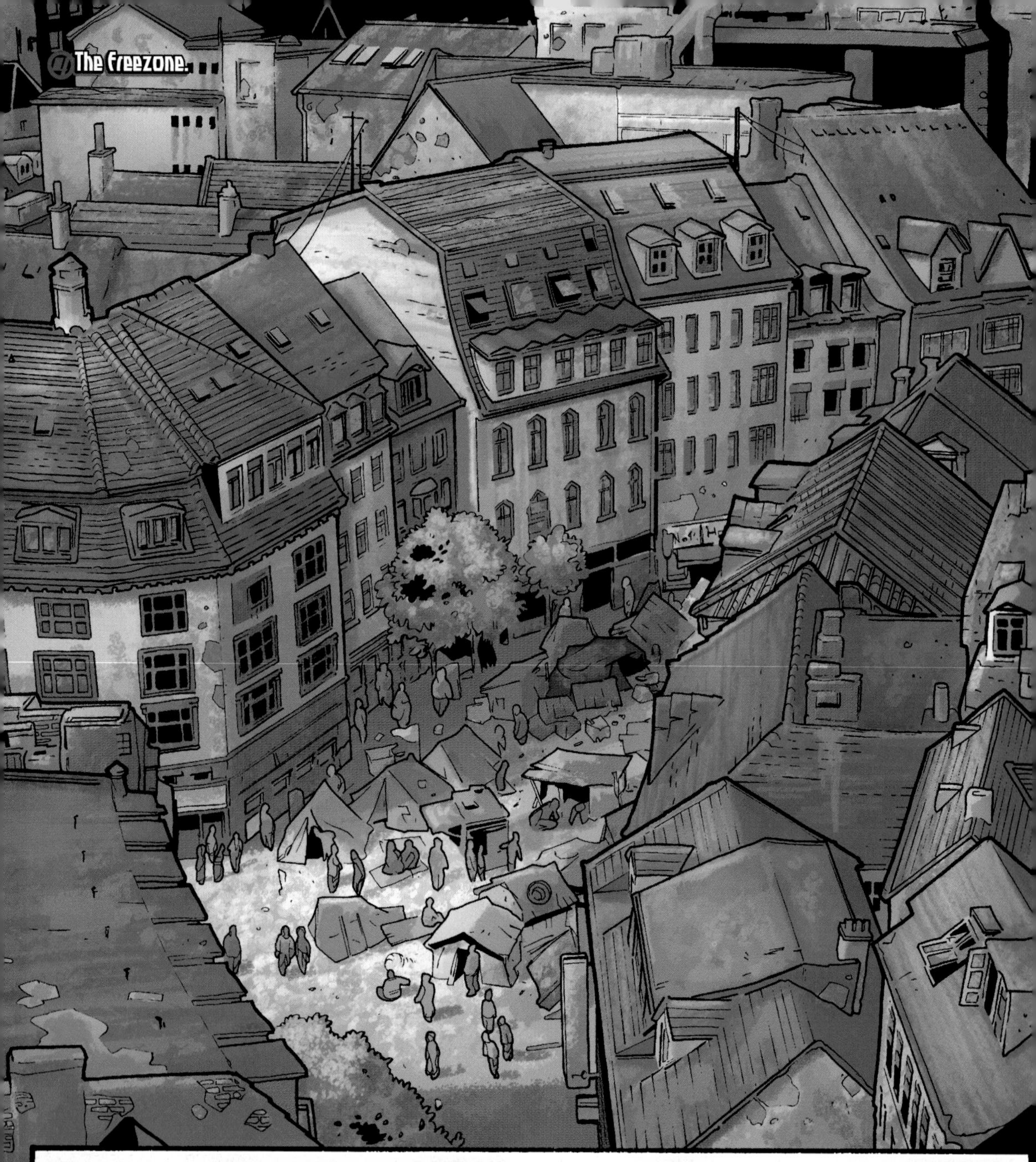
The Freezone.

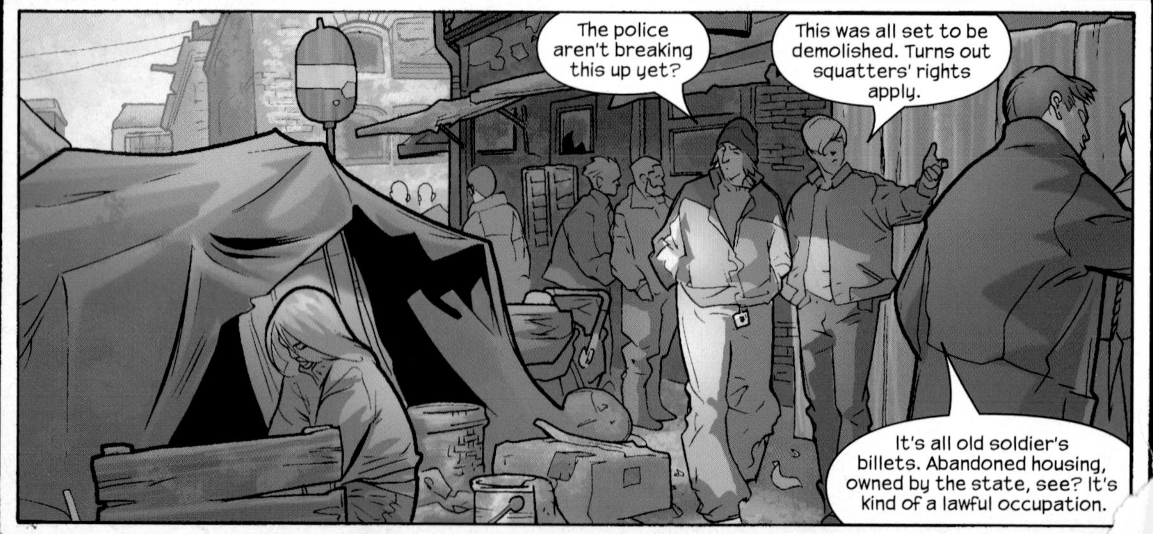
The police aren't breaking this up yet?
This was all set to be demolished. Turns out squatters' rights apply.
It's all old soldier's billets. Abandoned housing, owned by the state, see? It's kind of a lawful occupation.

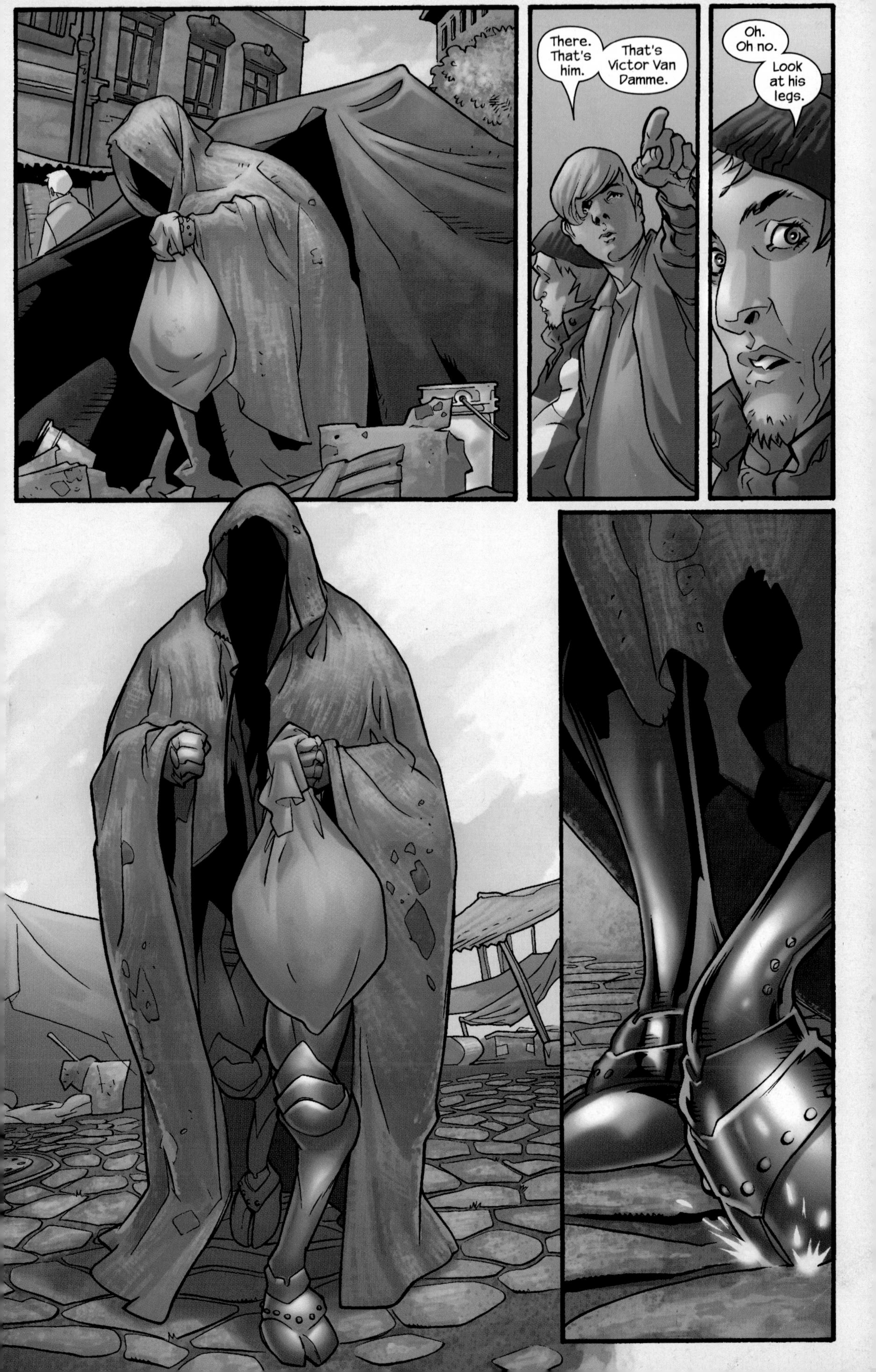
There. That's him.
That's Victor Van Damme.
Oh. Oh no.
Look at his legs.

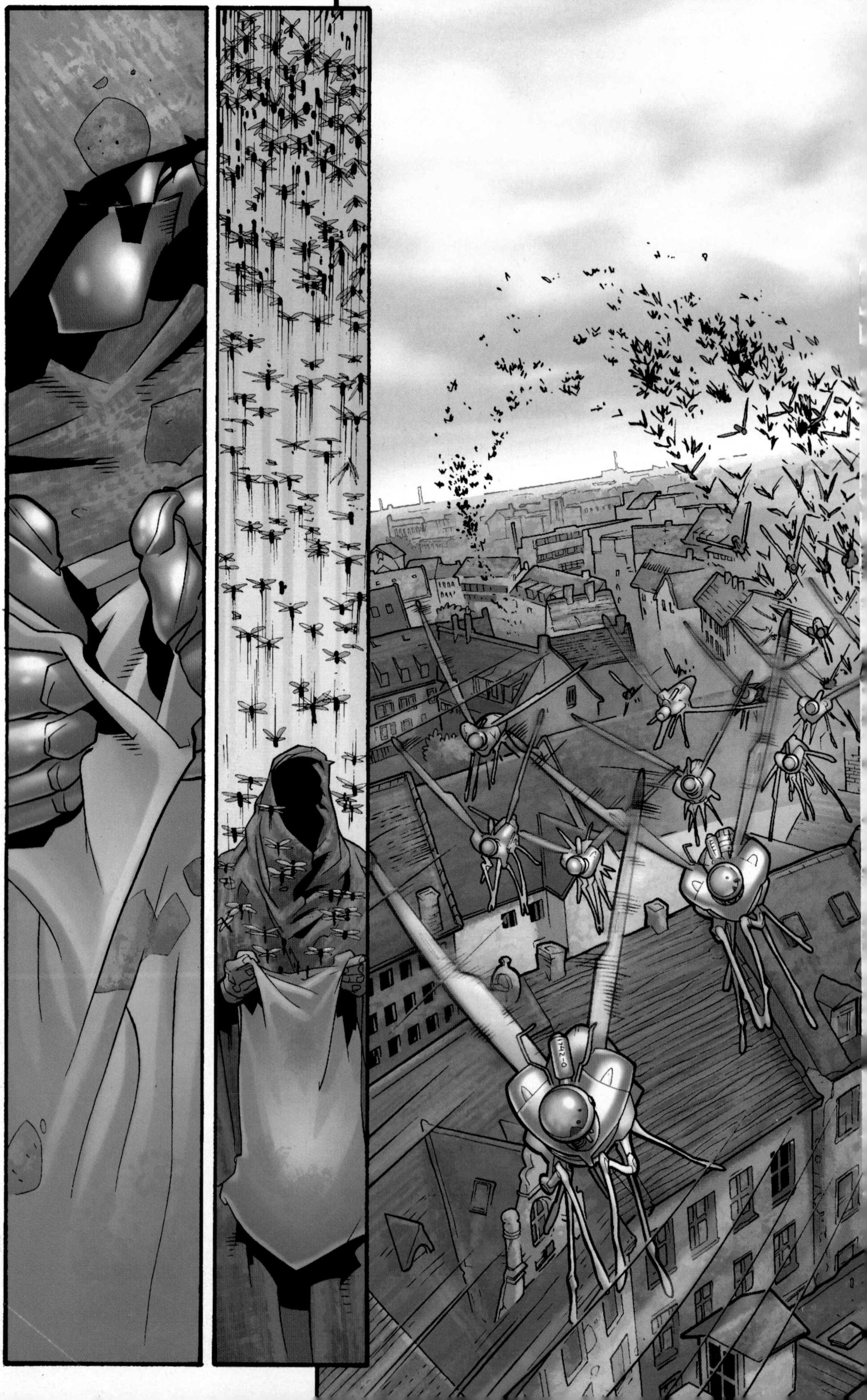

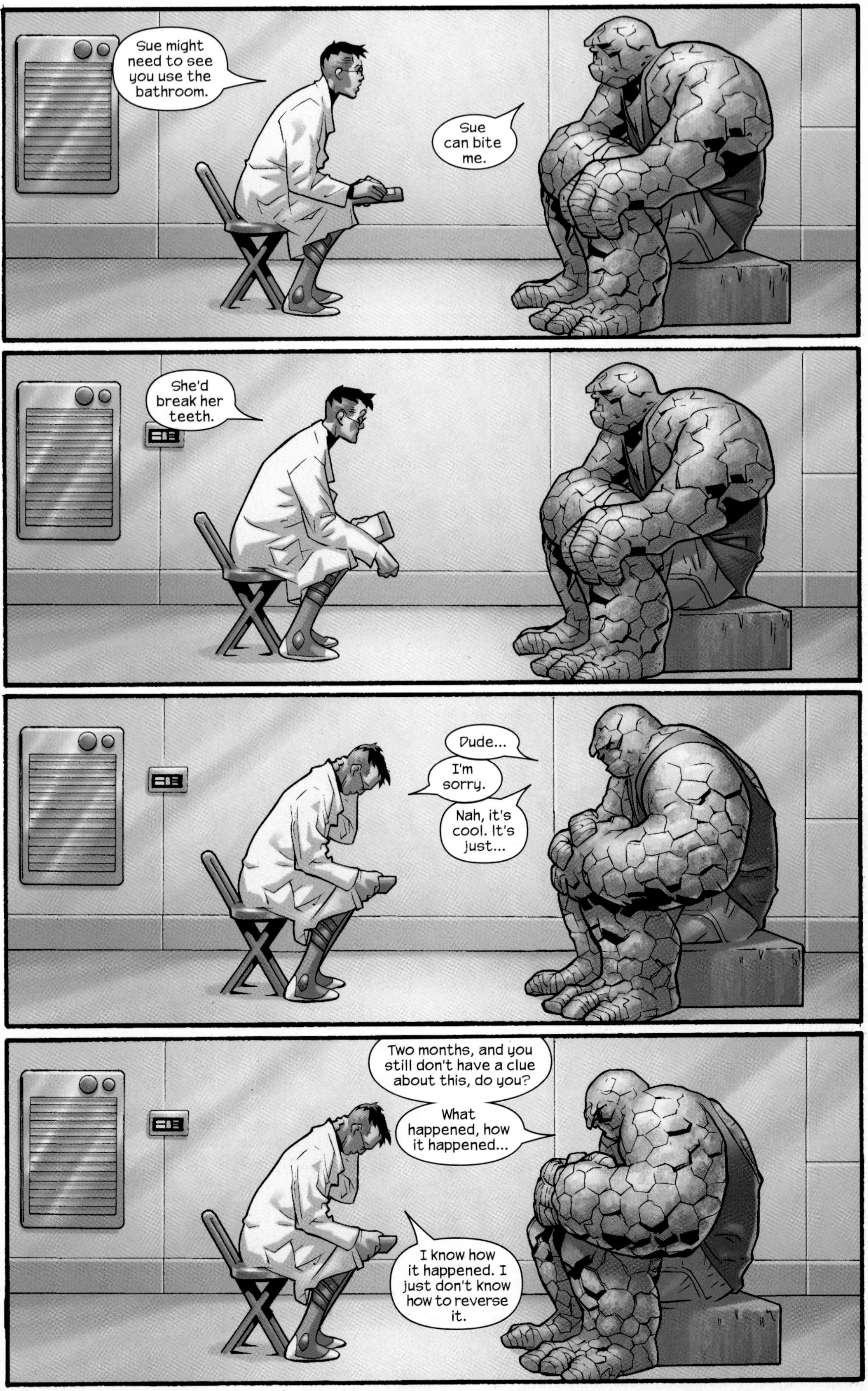
Sue might need to see you use the bathroom.
Sue can bite me.
She'd break her teeth.
Dude...
I'm sorry.
Nah, it's cool. It's just...
Two months, and you still don't have a clue about this, do you?
What happened, how it happened...
I know how it happened. I just don't know how to reverse it.

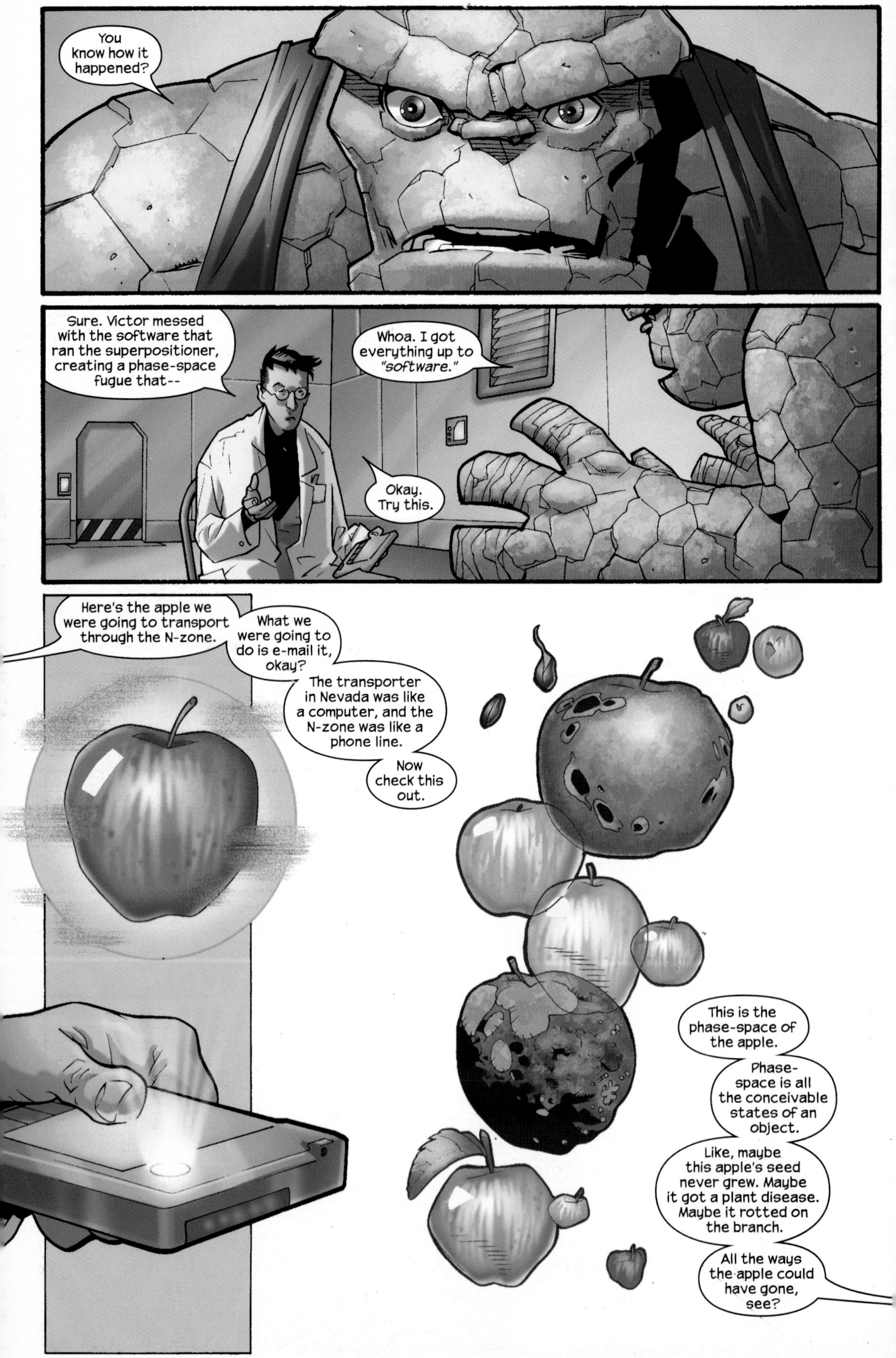
You know how it happened?
Sure. Victor messed with the software that ran the superpositioner, creating a phase-space fugue that--
Whoa. I got everything up to "software."
Okay. Try this.
Here's the apple we were going to transport through the N-zone.
What we were going to do is e-mail it, okay?
The transporter in Nevada was like a computer, and the N-zone was like a phone line.
Now check this out.
This is the phase-space of the apple.
Phase-space is all the conceivable states of an object.
Like, maybe this apple's seed never grew. Maybe it got a plant disease. Maybe it rotted on the branch.
All the ways the apple could have gone, see?

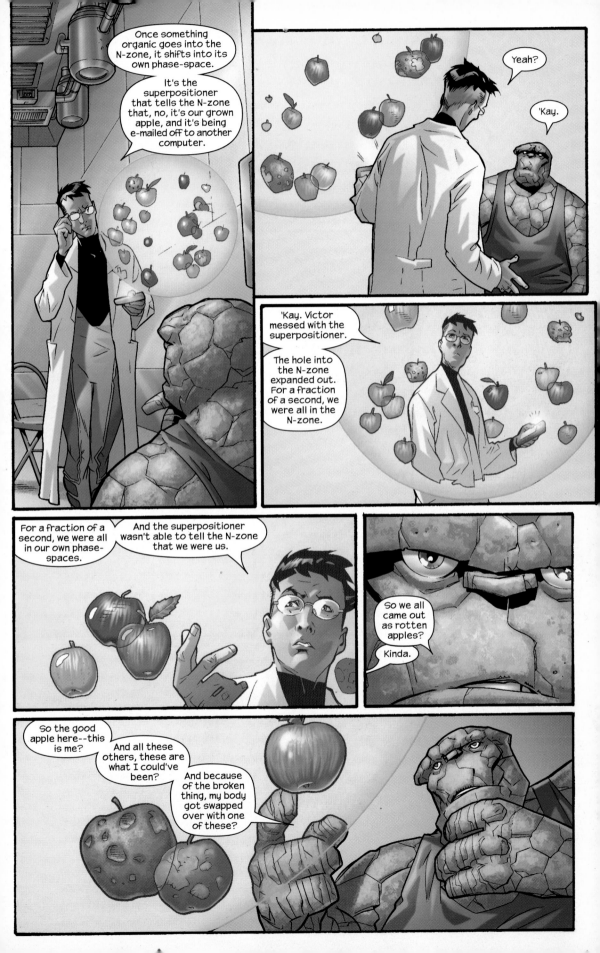

Once something organic goes into the N-zone, it shifts into its own phase-space.

It's the superpositioner that tells the N-zone that, no, it's our grown apple, and it's being e-mailed off to another computer.

Yeah?

'Kay.

'Kay. Victor messed with the superpositioner.

The hole into the N-zone expanded out. For a fraction of a second, we were all in the N-zone.

For a fraction of a second, we were all in our own phase-spaces.

And the superpositioner wasn't able to tell the N-zone that we were us.

So we all came out as rotten apples?

Kinda.

So the good apple here--this is me?

And all these others, these are what I could've been?

And because of the broken thing, my body got swapped over with one of these?

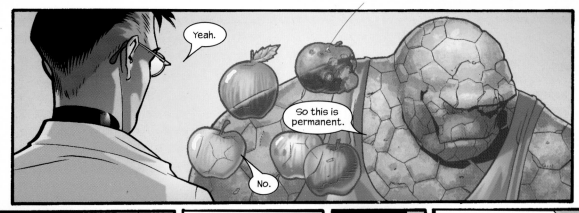

Yeah.

So this is permanent.

No.

See, if I knew how Victor changed the code, I could eventually rerun the whole thing.

Put us back in the phase-space condition, select out a modality and--

Put me back in the apple.

Right. We're going to need a better understanding of the N-zone, I need to work on the theory--

And you need Van Damme.

...yeah.

But I'm telling you, Ben--in theory, I can fix this.

So what do I do in the meantime?

I'm still quarantined in here, dude. I only get to phone my folks once a week. My mom's going crazy.

Yeah. Dr. Storm says New York City isn't ready for Big Fat Rock Guy yet.

They let Ozzy Osbourne out on the street but I have to stay indoors?

Johnny Storm catches fire but they let him out?

Johnny's not doing the fire thing when he's outside. And they put guards on him anyway.

C'mon. Sue's got something she wants you to try.

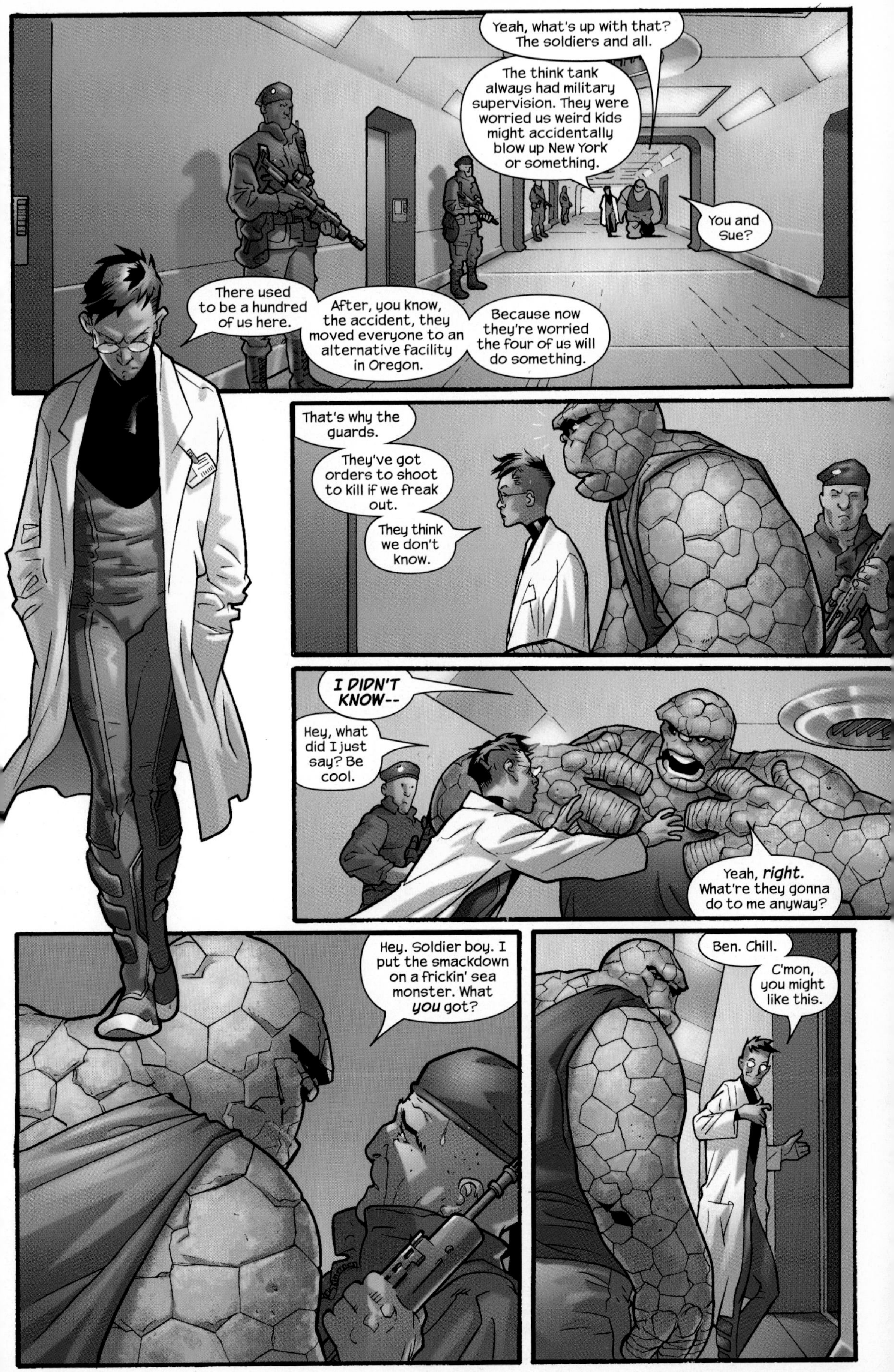
Yeah, what's up with that? The soldiers and all.
The think tank always had military supervision. They were worried us weird kids might accidentally blow up New York or something.
You and Sue?
There used to be a hundred of us here.
After, you know, the accident, they moved everyone to an alternative facility in Oregon.
Because now they're worried the four of us will do something.
That's why the guards.
They've got orders to shoot to kill if we freak out.
They think we don't know.
I DIDN'T KNOW--
Hey, what did I just say? Be cool.
Yeah, right. What're they gonna do to me anyway?
Hey. Soldier boy. I put the smackdown on a frickin' sea monster. What you got?
Ben. Chill.
C'mon, you might like this.

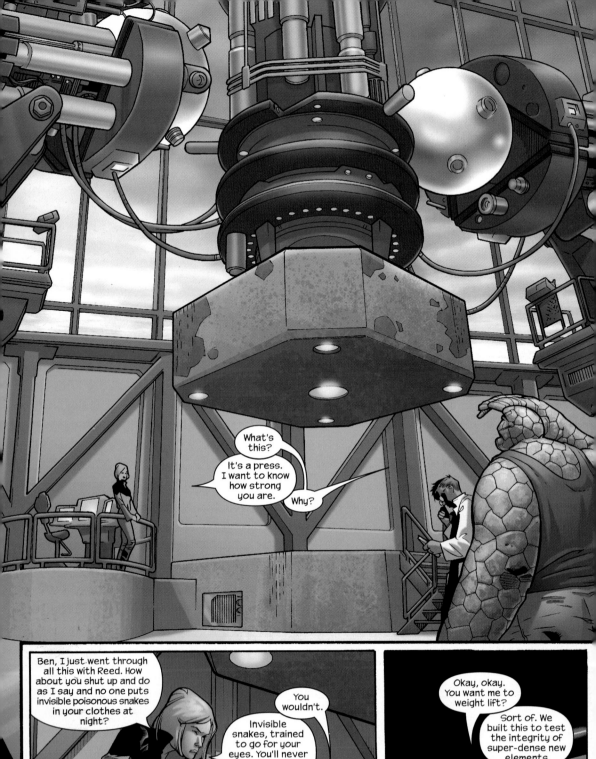

What's this?

It's a press. I want to know how strong you are.

Why?

Ben, I just went through all this with Reed. How about you shut up and do as I say and no one puts invisible poisonous snakes in your clothes at night?

You wouldn't.

Invisible snakes, trained to go for your eyes. You'll never know how many or where they are.

Okay, okay. You want me to weight lift?

Sort of. We built this to test the integrity of super-dense new elements.

This was Mad Billy's thing?

Yeah.

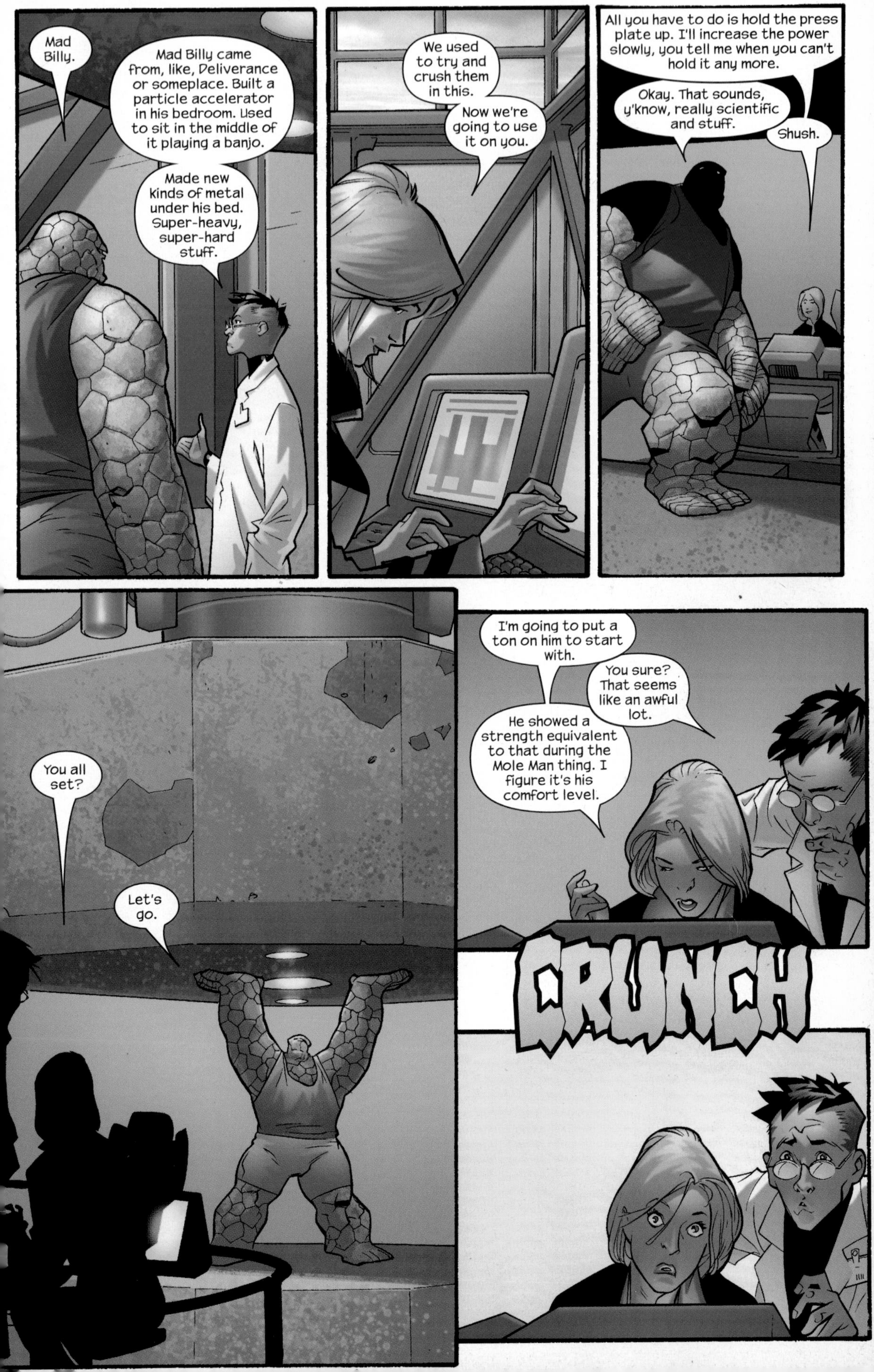
Mad Billy.
Mad Billy came from, like, Deliverance or someplace. Built a particle accelerator in his bedroom. Used to sit in the middle of it playing a banjo.
Made new kinds of metal under his bed. Super-heavy, super-hard stuff.
We used to try and crush them in this.
Now we're going to use it on you.
All you have to do is hold the press plate up. I'll increase the power slowly, you tell me when you can't hold it any more.
Okay. That sounds, y'know, really scientific and stuff.
Shush.
You all set?
Let's go.
I'm going to put a ton on him to start with.
You sure? That seems like an awful lot.
He showed a strength equivalent to that during the Mole Man thing. I figure it's his comfort level.
CRUNCH

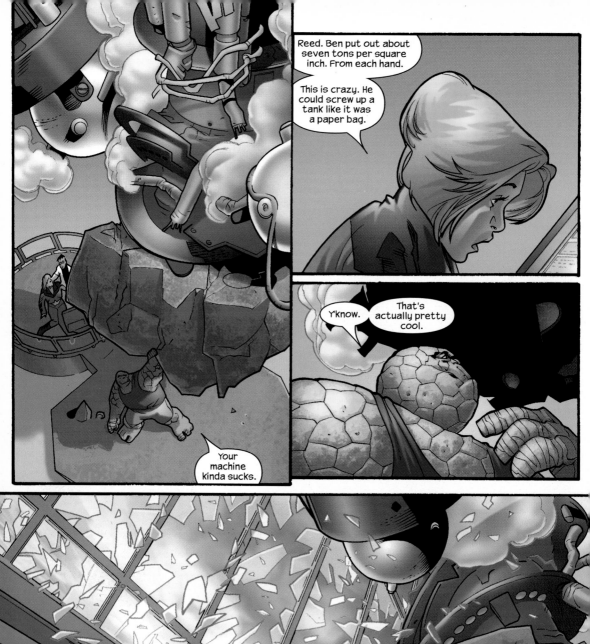

Reed. Ben put out about seven tons per square inch. From each hand.

This is crazy. He could screw up a tank like it was a paper bag.

Your machine kinda sucks.

Y'know.

That's actually pretty cool.

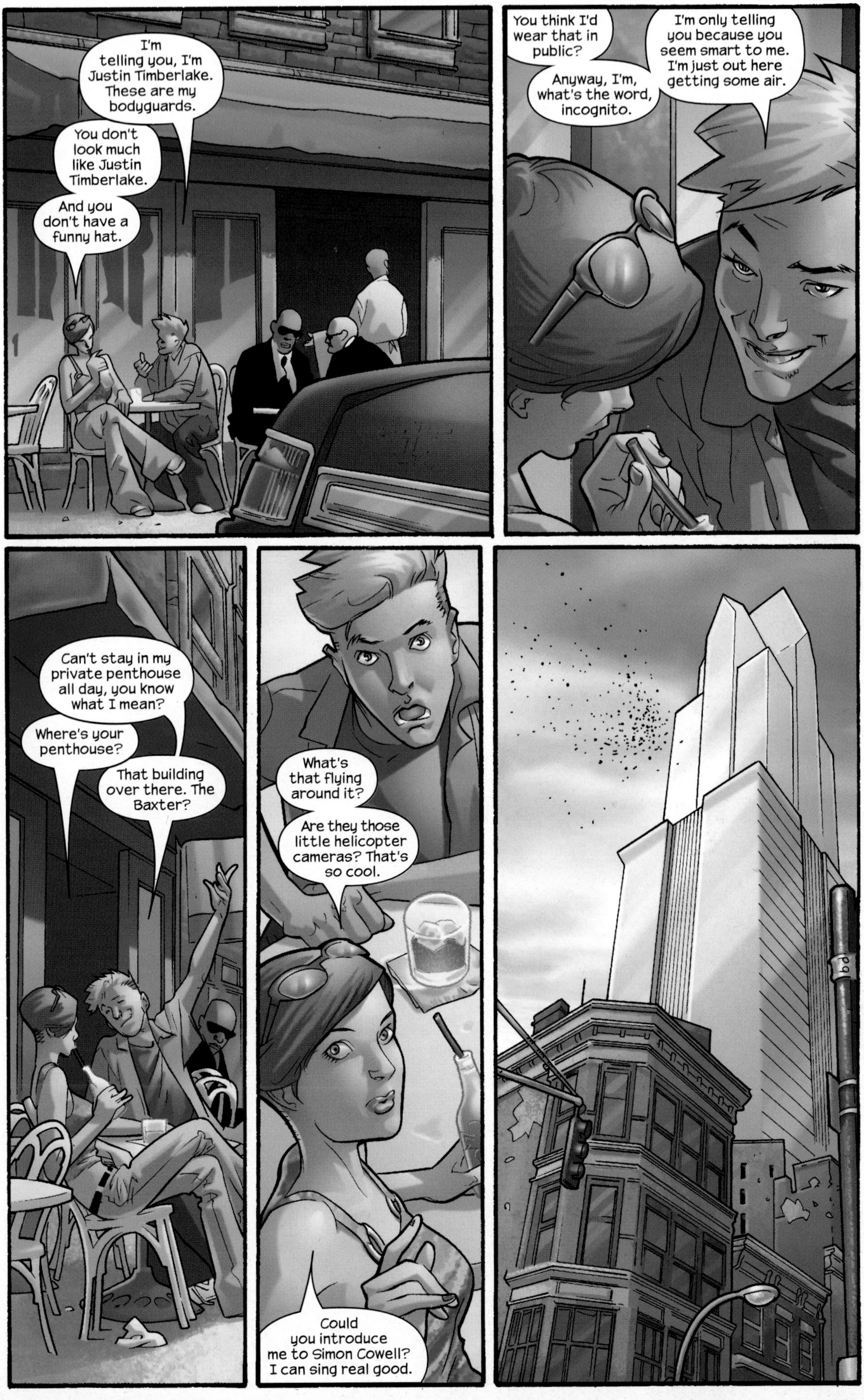
I'm telling you, I'm Justin Timberlake. These are my bodyguards.
You don't look much like Justin Timberlake.
And you don't have a funny hat.
You think I'd wear that in public?
Anyway, I'm, what's the word, incognito.
I'm only telling you because you seem smart to me. I'm just out here getting some air.
Can't stay in my private penthouse all day, you know what I mean?
Where's your penthouse?
That building over there. The Baxter?
What's that flying around it?
Are they those little helicopter cameras? That's so cool.
Could you introduce me to Simon Cowell? I can sing real good.

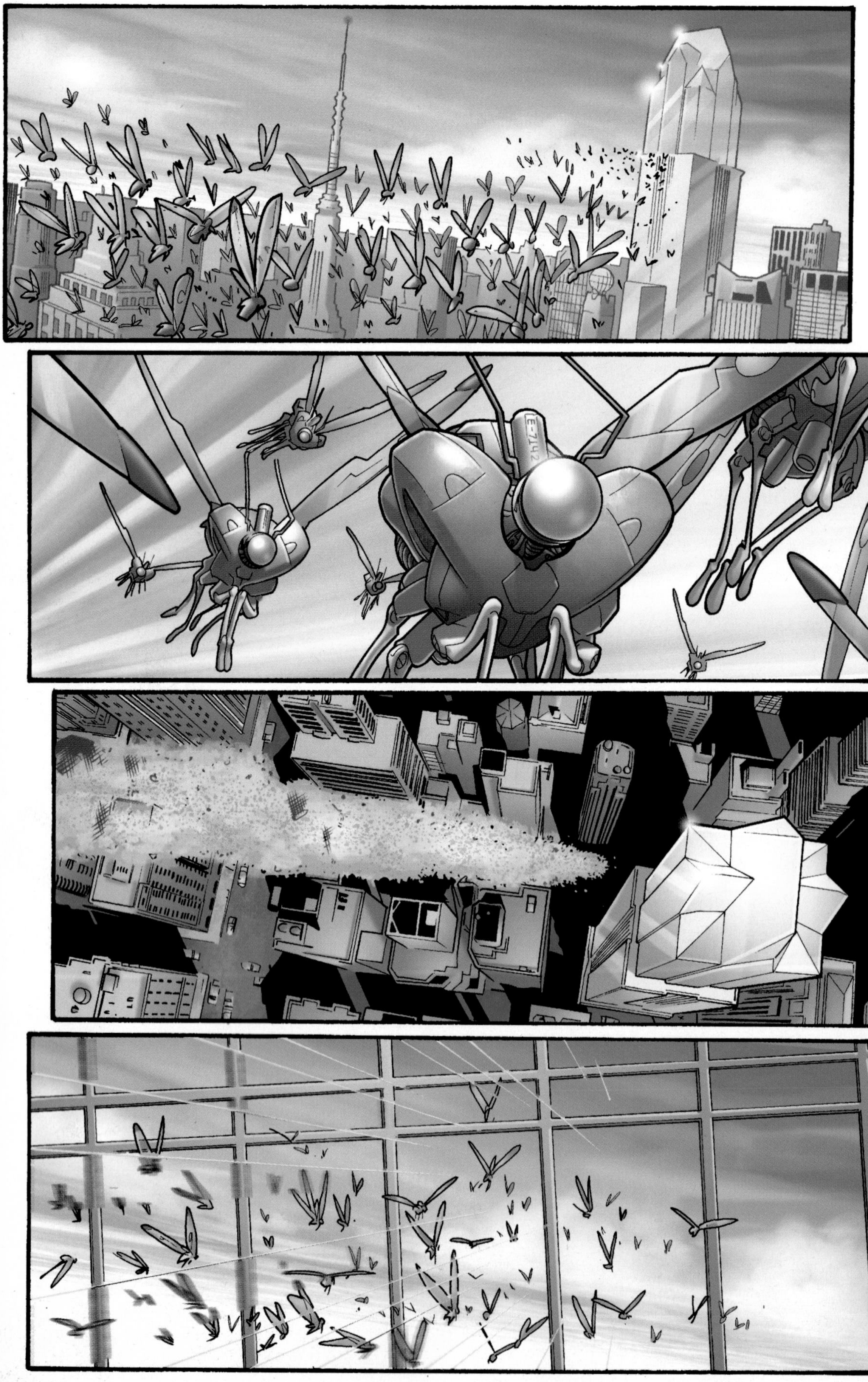
E-7142

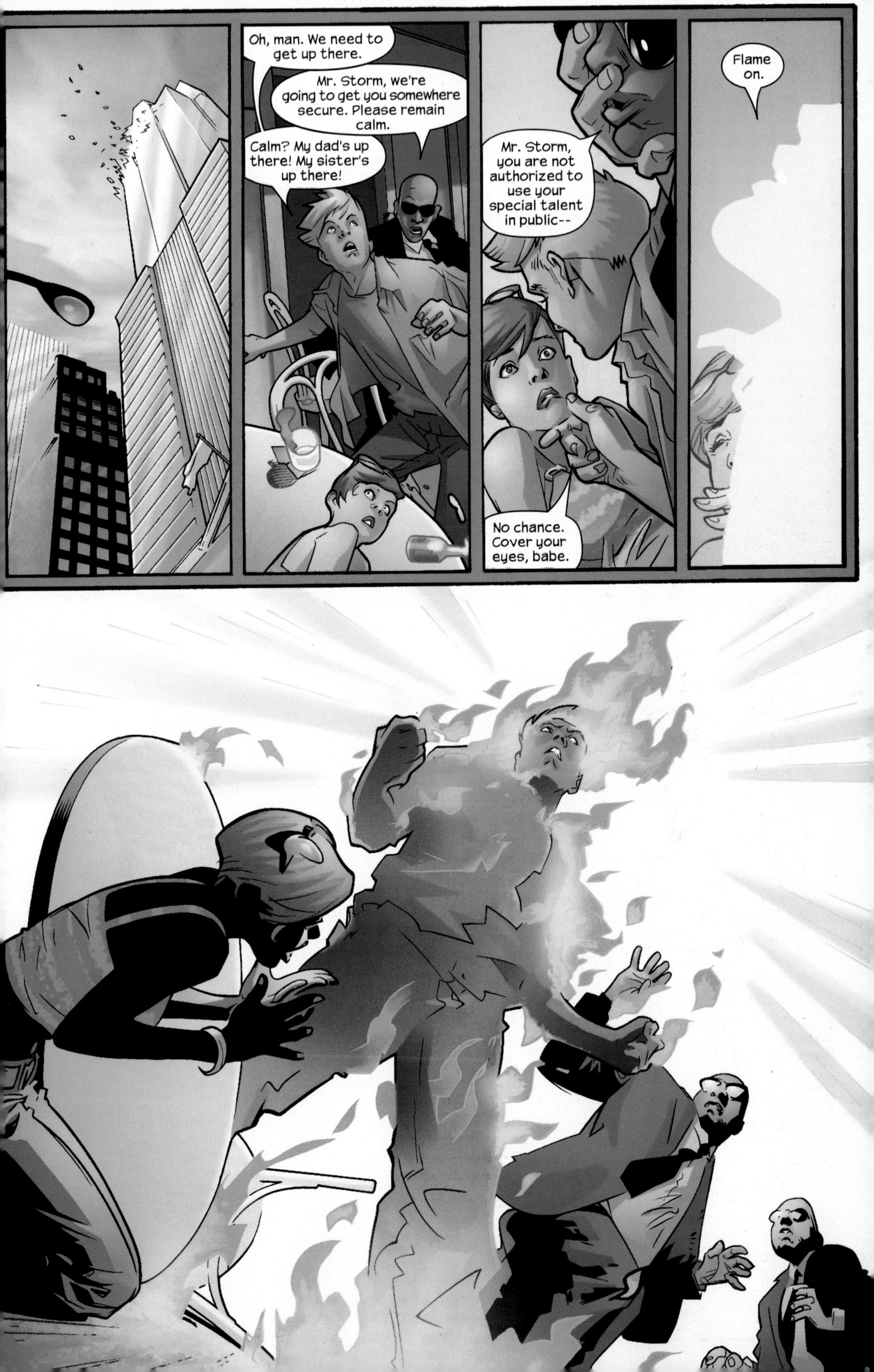
Oh, man. We need to get up there.
Mr. Storm, we're going to get you somewhere secure. Please remain calm.
Calm? My dad's up there! My sister's up there!
Mr. Storm, you are not authorized to use your special talent in public--
No chance. Cover your eyes, babe.
Flame on.

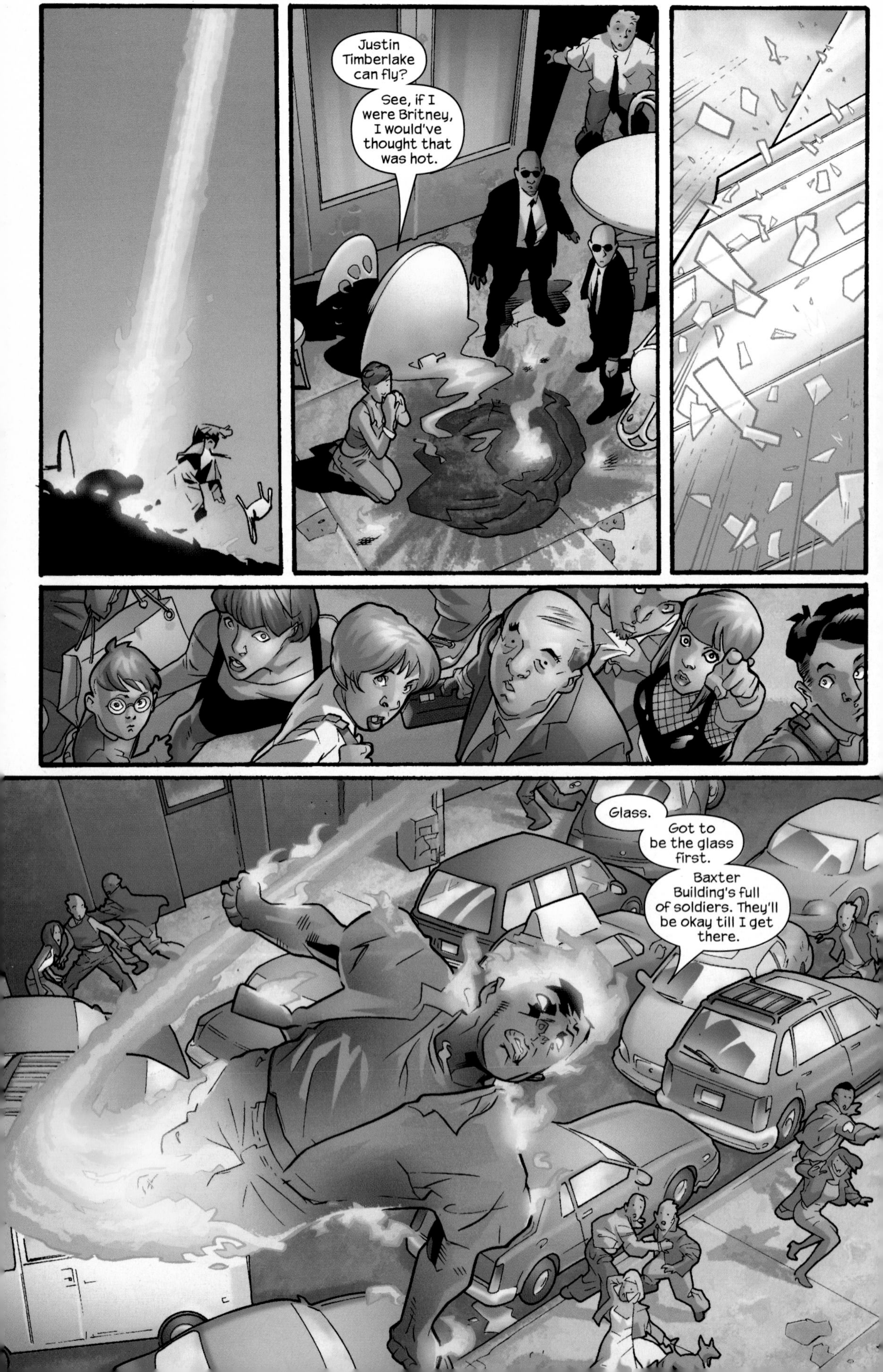
Justin Timberlake can fly?
See, if I were Britney, I would've thought that was hot.
Glass.
Got to be the glass first.
Baxter Building's full of soldiers. They'll be okay till I get there.

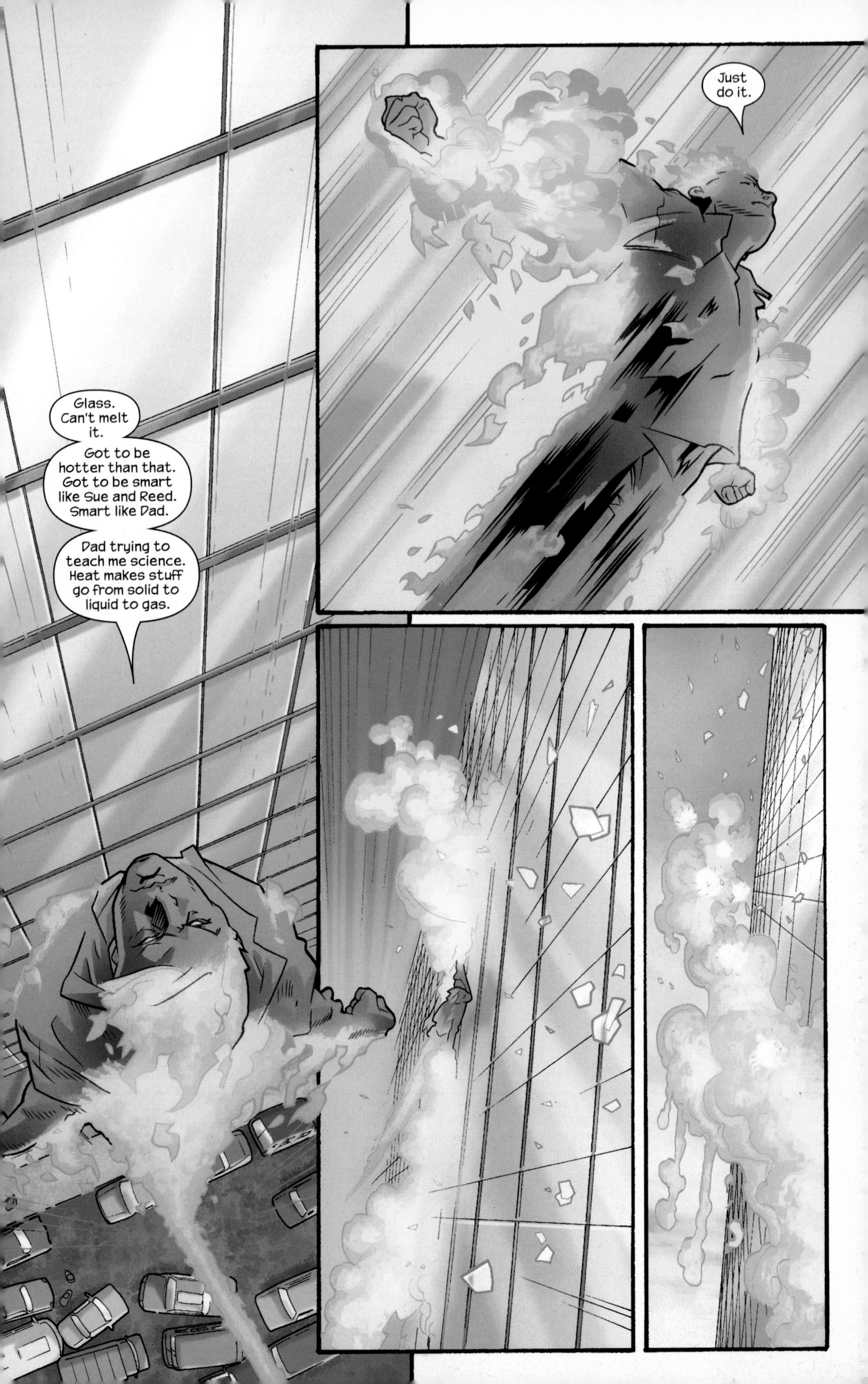
Glass. Can't melt it.
Got to be hotter than that. Got to be smart like Sue and Reed. Smart like Dad.
Dad trying to teach me science. Heat makes stuff go from solid to liquid to gas.
Just do it.

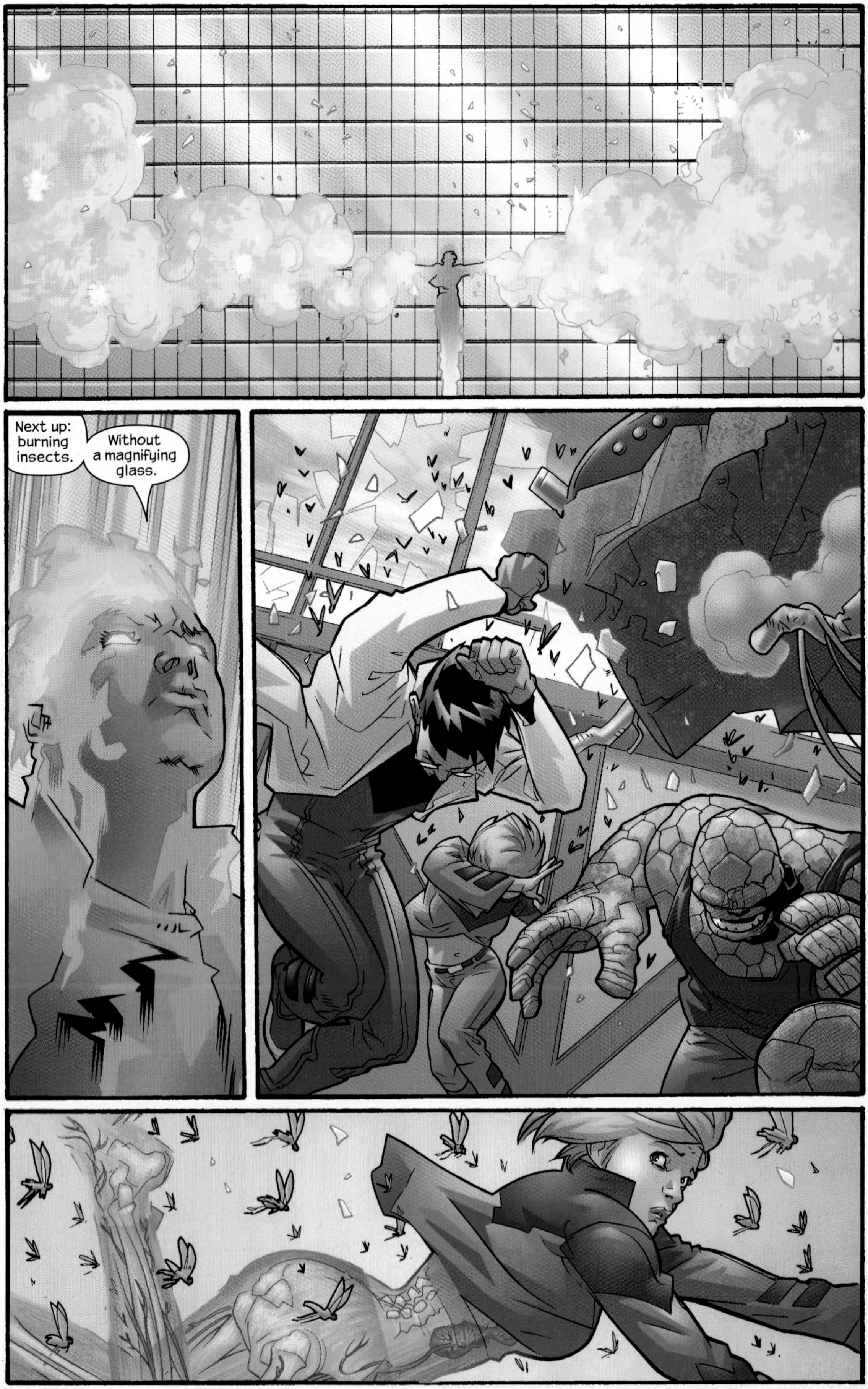
Next up: burning insects.
Without a magnifying glass.

Sue?

Sue, are you--

I'm okay--my invisibility just switched itself on-give me a second--

This ain't some special weirdo insect test, then?

What do you think we *do* here, Ben?

Aside from bug me?

Hey. These things are mechanical.

Sue, GO!

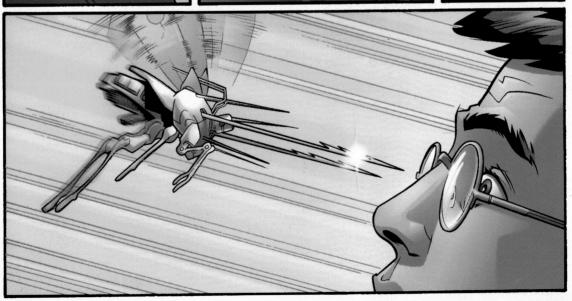

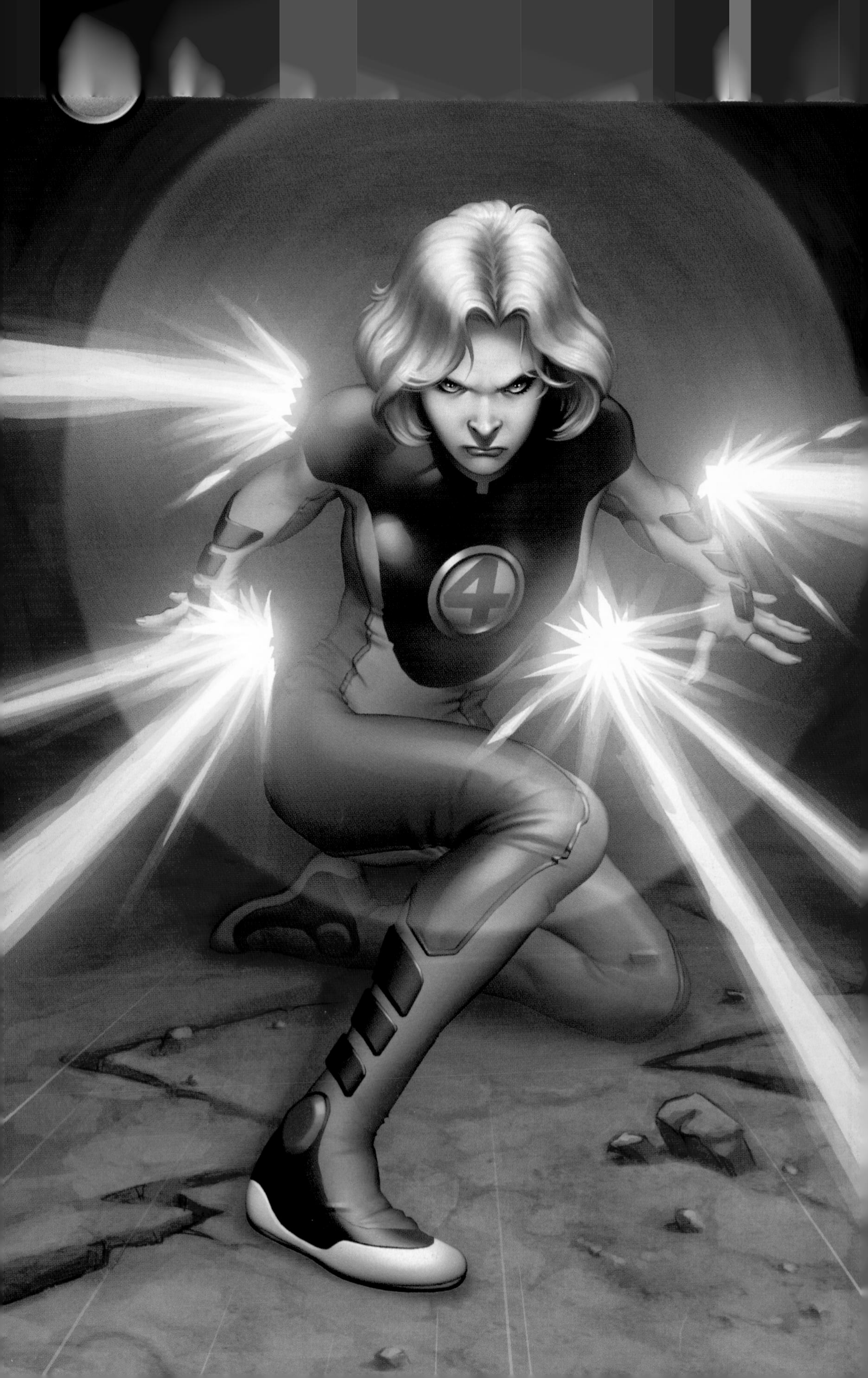

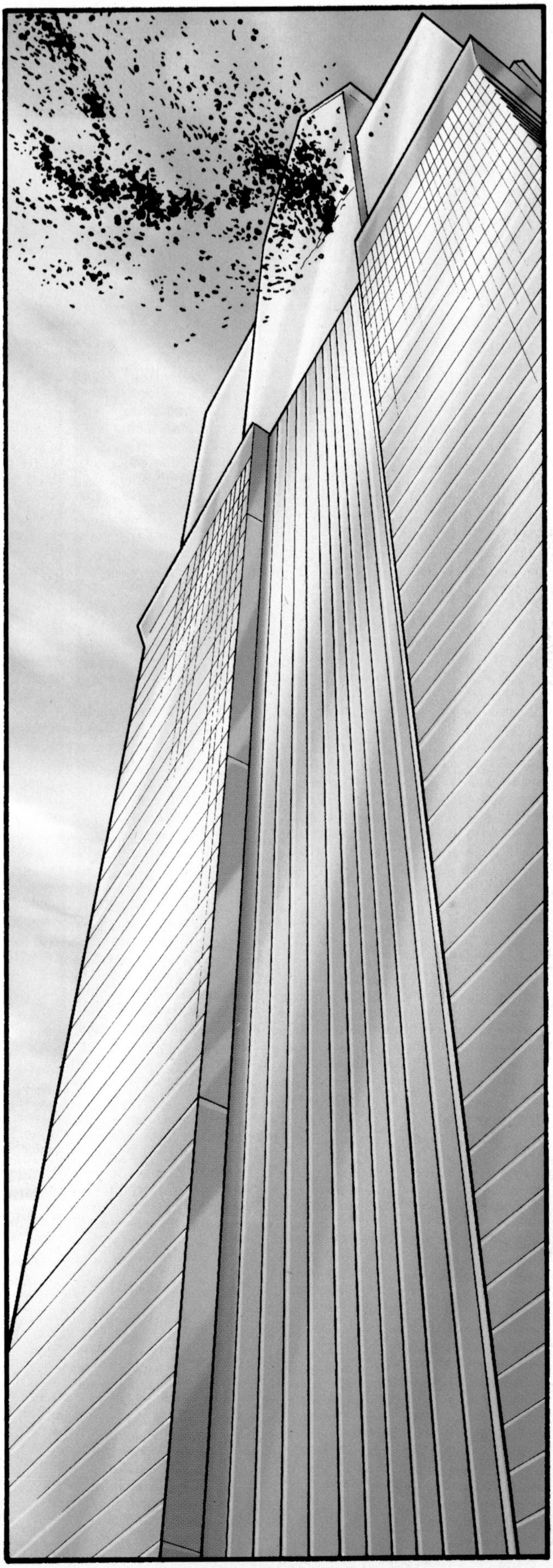

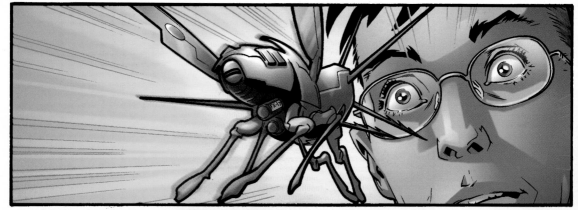

I thought I told you to go?

I'm not going to do anything you say when you shout at me like that.

Get out of here.

Pretty frickin' *please*.

You
hear that?
Gunfire.

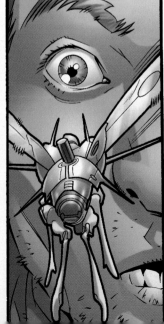

AAGGKK

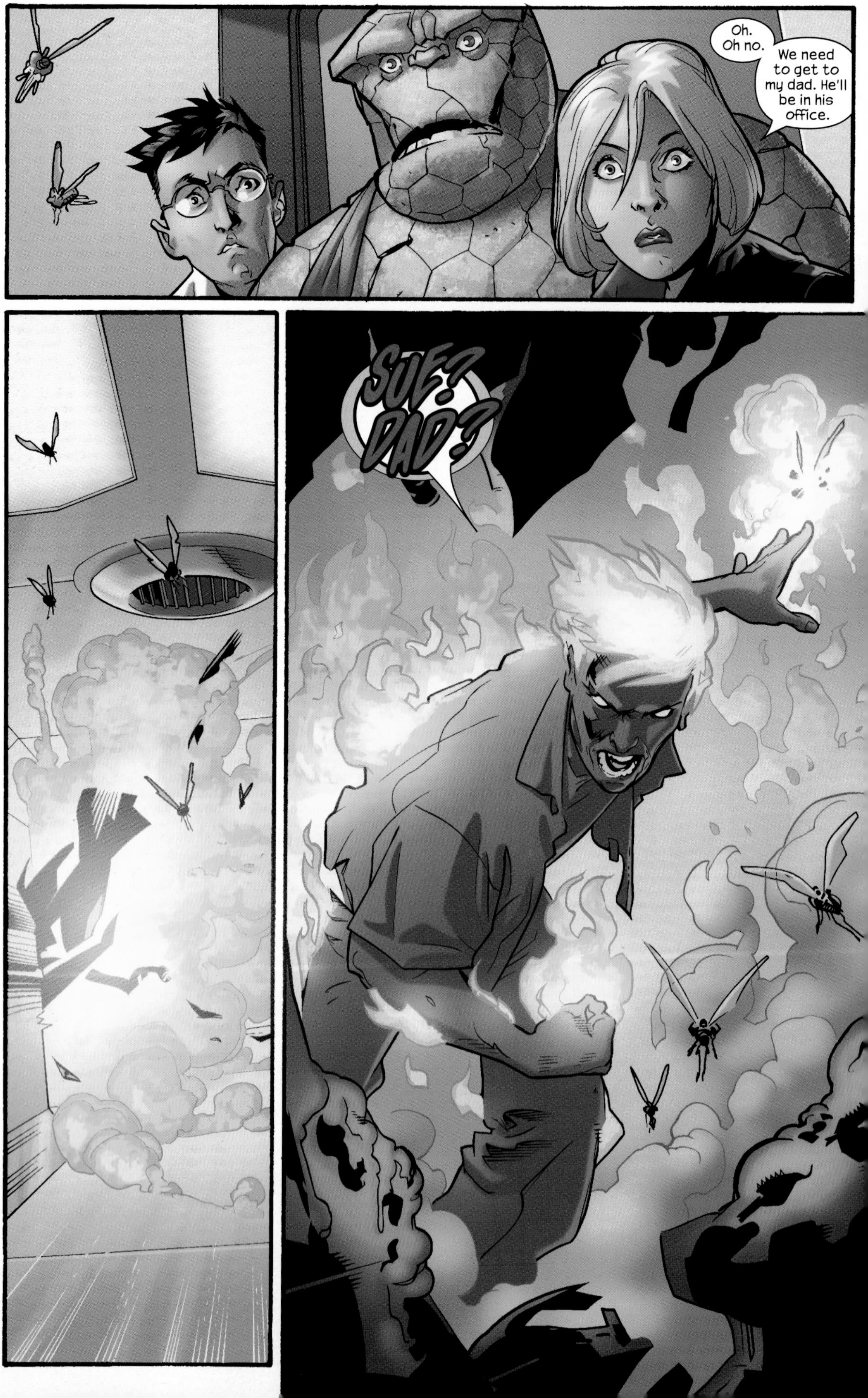
Oh. Oh no.
We need to get to my dad. He'll be in his office.
SUE? DAD?

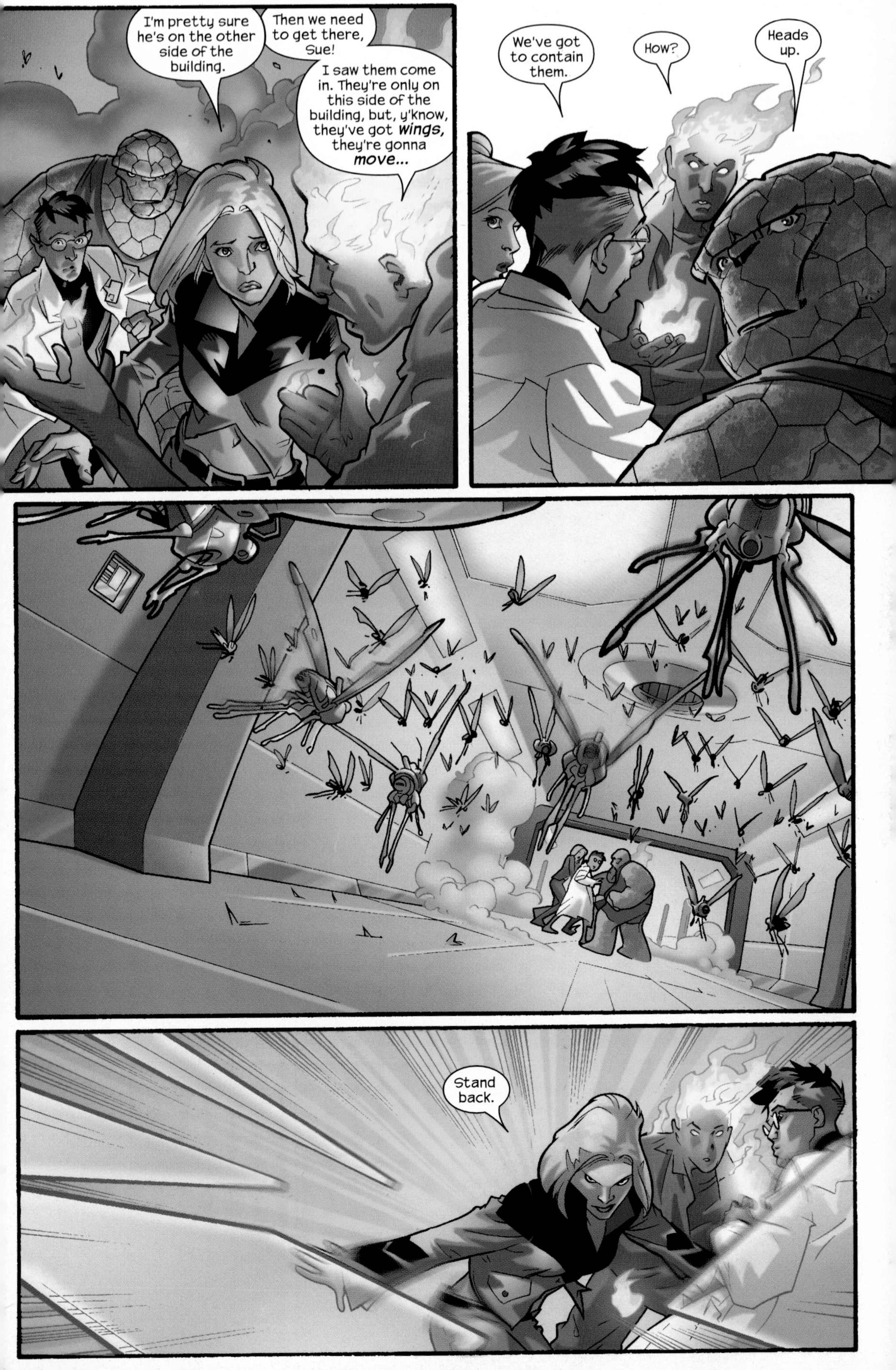
I'm pretty sure he's on the other side of the building.
Then we need to get there, Sue!
I saw them come in. They're only on this side of the building, but, y'know, they've got *wings,* they're gonna *move...*
We've got to contain them.
How?
Heads up.
Stand back.

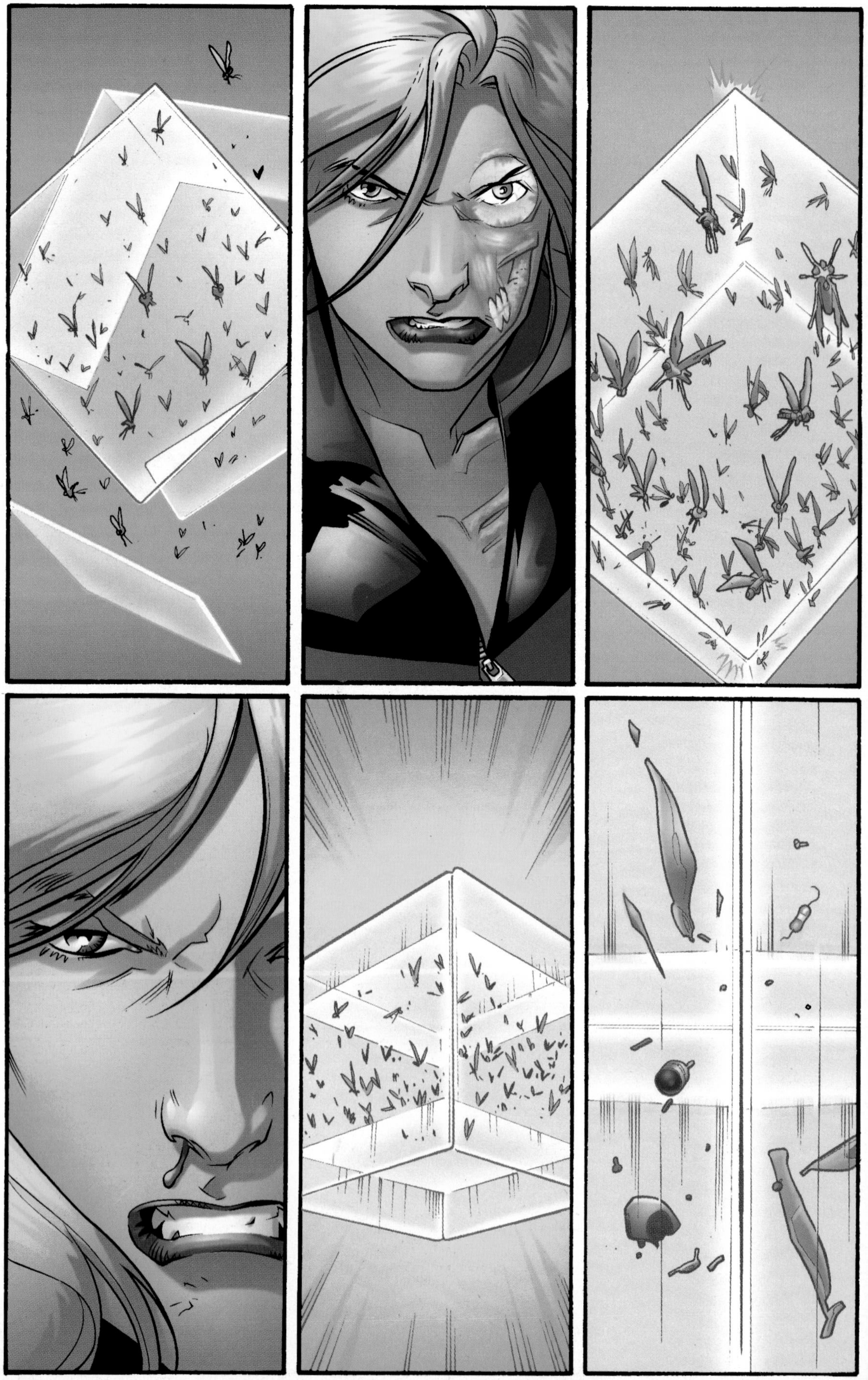

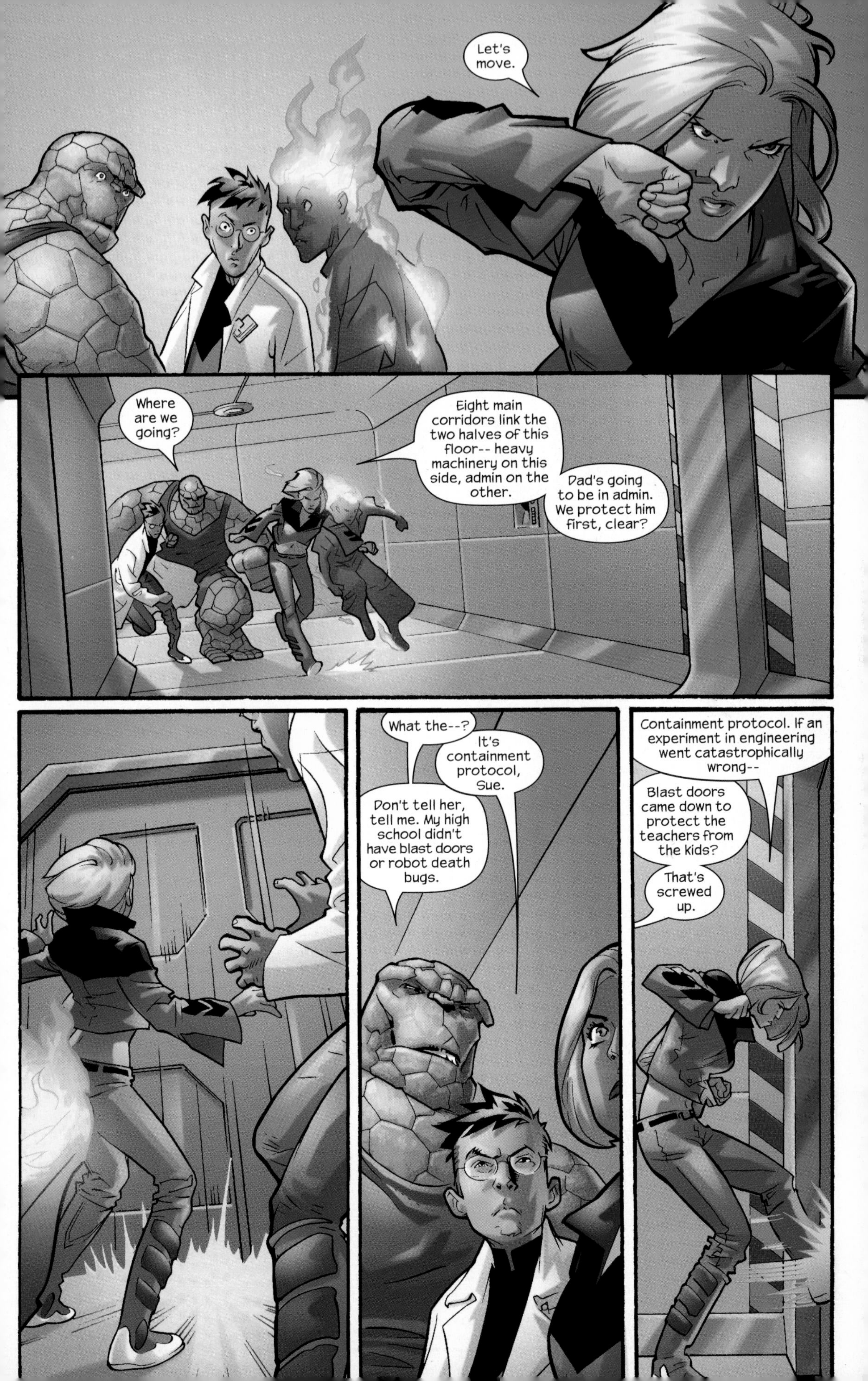
Let's move.
Where are we going?
Eight main corridors link the two halves of this floor-- heavy machinery on this side, admin on the other.
Dad's going to be in admin. We protect him first, clear?
What the--?
It's containment protocol, Sue.
Don't tell her, tell me. My high school didn't have blast doors or robot death bugs.
Containment protocol. If an experiment in engineering went catastrophically wrong--
Blast doors came down to protect the teachers from the kids?
That's screwed up.

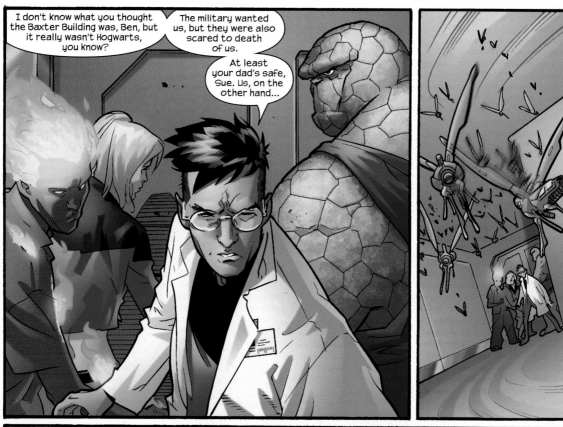

I don't know what you thought the Baxter Building was, Ben, but it really wasn't Hogwarts, you know?

The military wanted us, but they were also scared to death of us.

At least your dad's safe, Sue. Us, on the other hand...

Us? We're the scary kids.

My *children* are out there!

You know the rules, sir.

I *know* that the building is under attack and you've locked my children in there with whatever's attacking us!

I've also locked my men in, Dr. Storm.

I'm sorry for your children. But if they are half of what I've heard--

-- I am praying, Dr. Storm, that they can save my men's lives.

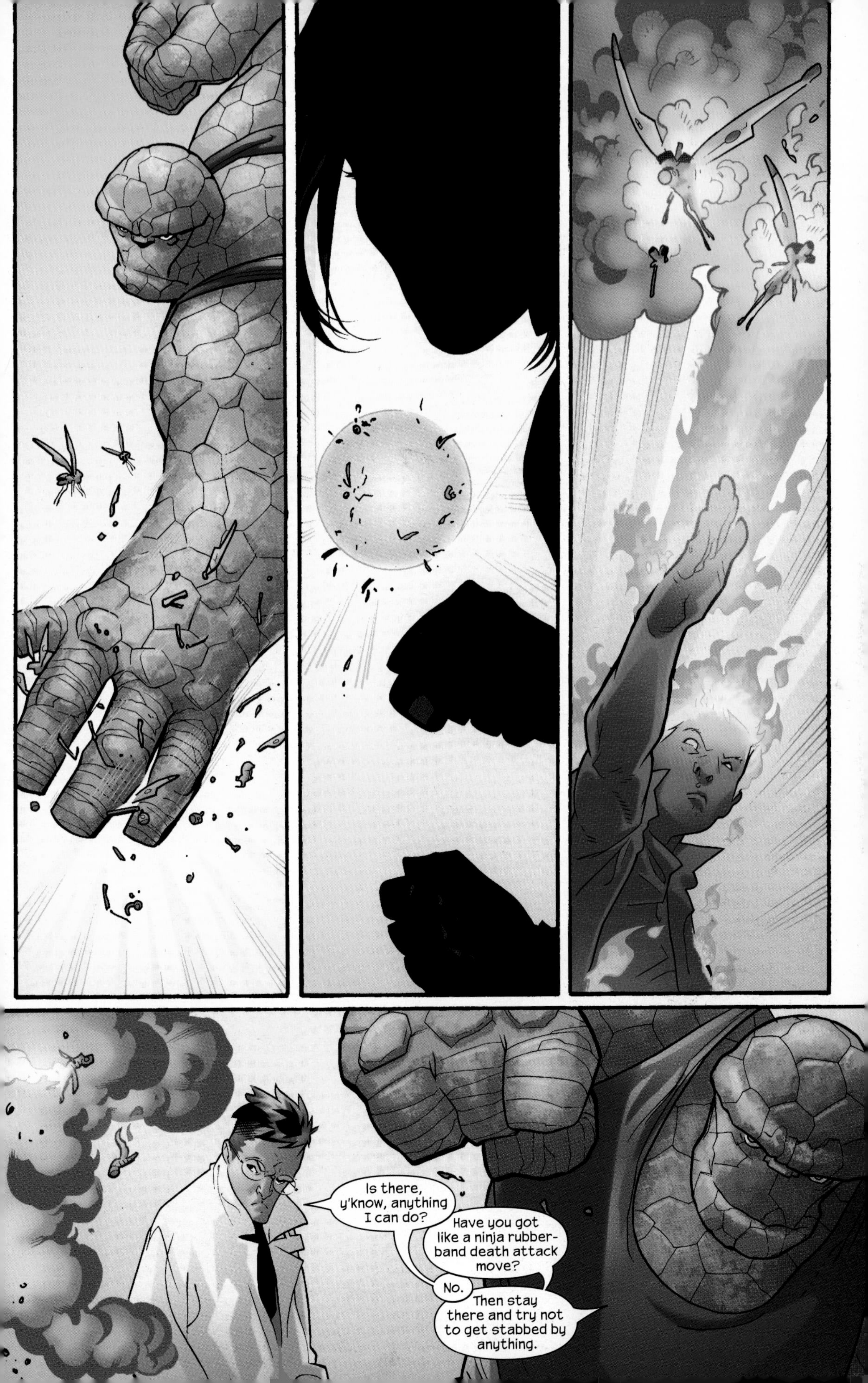
Is there, y'know, anything I can do?
Have you got like a ninja rubber-band death attack move?
No.
Then stay there and try not to get stabbed by anything.

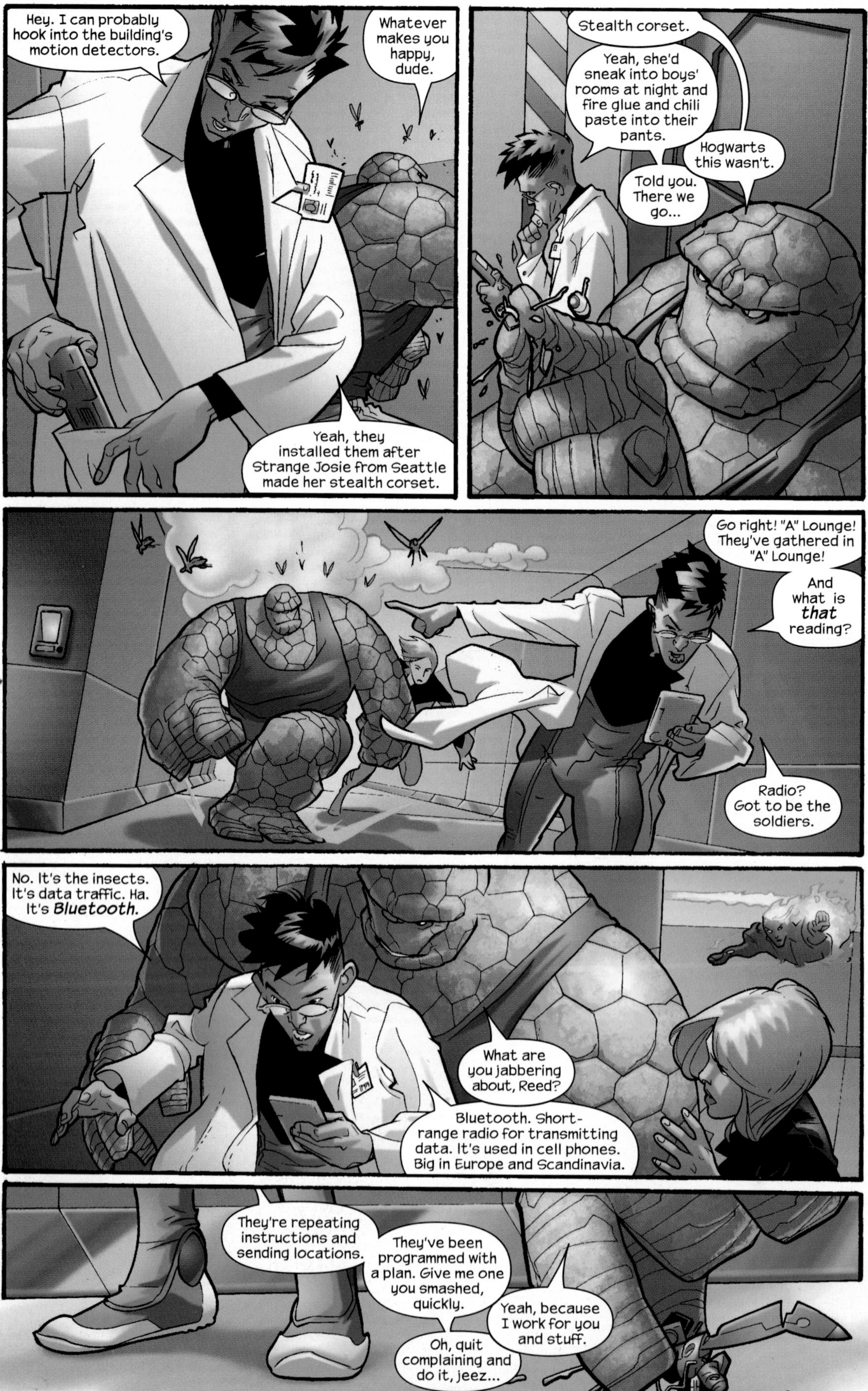

Hey. I can probably hook into the building's motion detectors.
Whatever makes you happy, dude.
Yeah, they installed them after Strange Josie from Seattle made her stealth corset.
Stealth corset.
Yeah, she'd sneak into boys' rooms at night and fire glue and chili paste into their pants.
Hogwarts this wasn't.
Told you. There we go...
Go right! "A" Lounge! They've gathered in "A" Lounge!
And what is *that* reading?
Radio? Got to be the soldiers.
No. It's the insects. It's data traffic. Ha. It's *Bluetooth.*
What are you jabbering about, Reed?
Bluetooth. Short-range radio for transmitting data. It's used in cell phones. Big in Europe and Scandinavia.
They're repeating instructions and sending locations.
They've been programmed with a plan. Give me one you smashed, quickly.
Yeah, because I work for you and stuff.
Oh, quit complaining and do it, jeez...

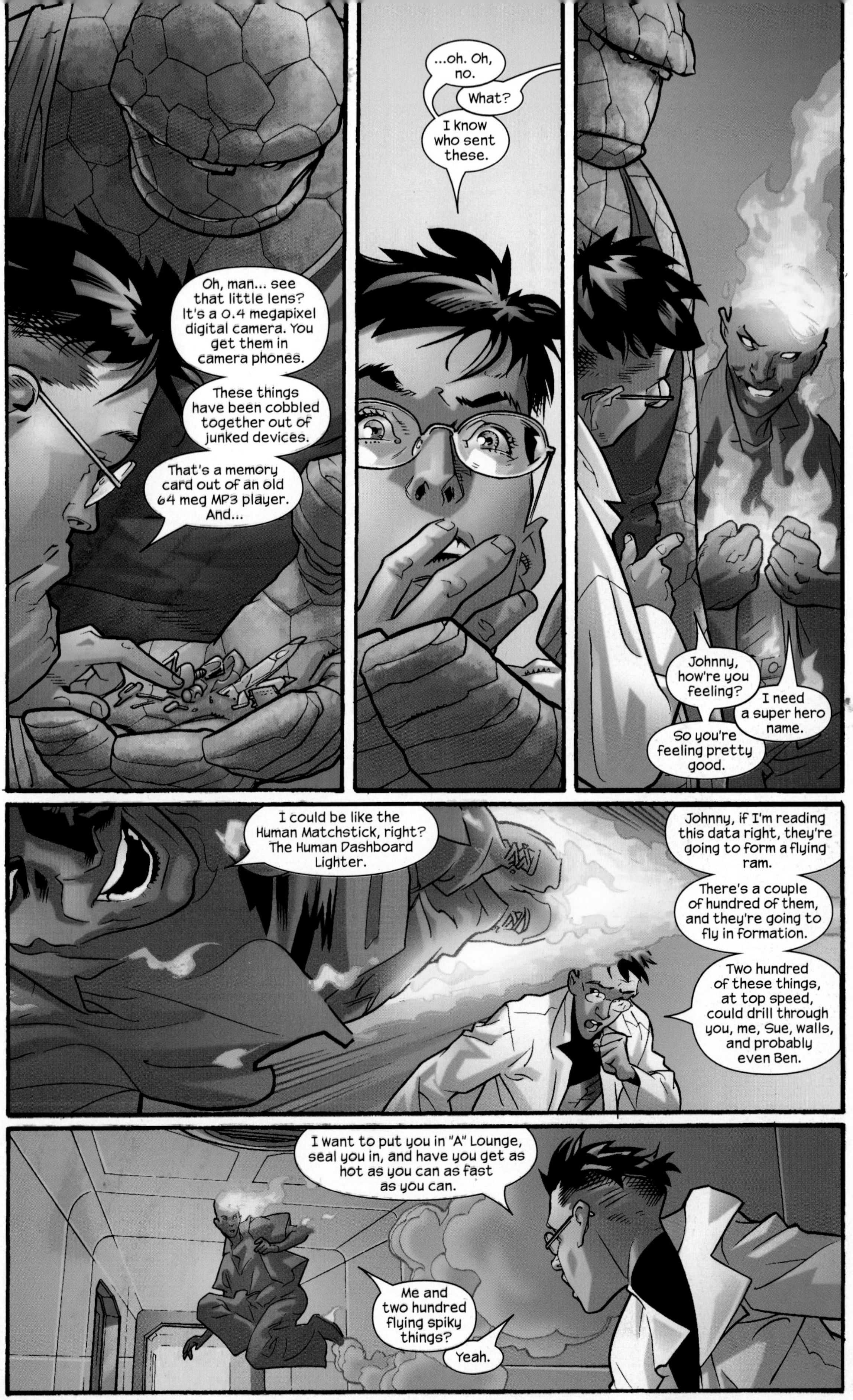
Oh, man... see that little lens? It's a 0.4 megapixel digital camera. You get them in camera phones.
These things have been cobbled together out of junked devices.
That's a memory card out of an old 64 meg MP3 player. And...
...oh. Oh, no.
What?
I know who sent these.
Johnny, how're you feeling?
I need a super hero name.
So you're feeling pretty good.
I could be like the Human Matchstick, right? The Human Dashboard Lighter.
Johnny, if I'm reading this data right, they're going to form a flying ram.
There's a couple of hundred of them, and they're going to fly in formation.
Two hundred of these things, at top speed, could drill through you, me, Sue, walls, and probably even Ben.
I want to put you in "A" Lounge, seal you in, and have you get as hot as you can as fast as you can.
Me and two hundred flying spiky things?
Yeah.

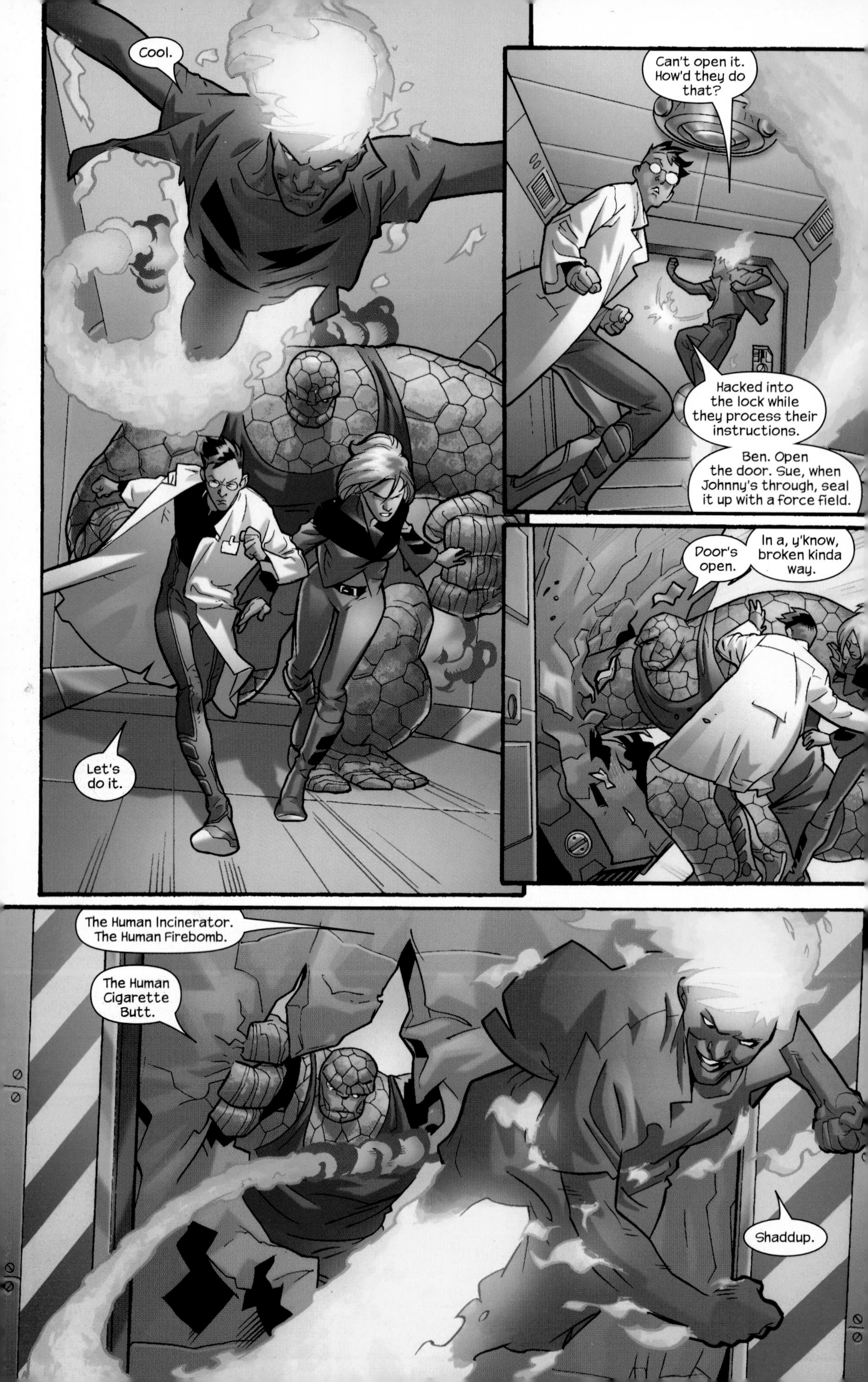
Cool.
Let's do it.
Can't open it. How'd they do that?
Hacked into the lock while they process their instructions.
Ben. Open the door. Sue, when Johnny's through, seal it up with a force field.
Door's open.
In a, y'know, broken kinda way.
The Human Incinerator. The Human Firebomb.
The Human Cigarette Butt.
Shaddup.

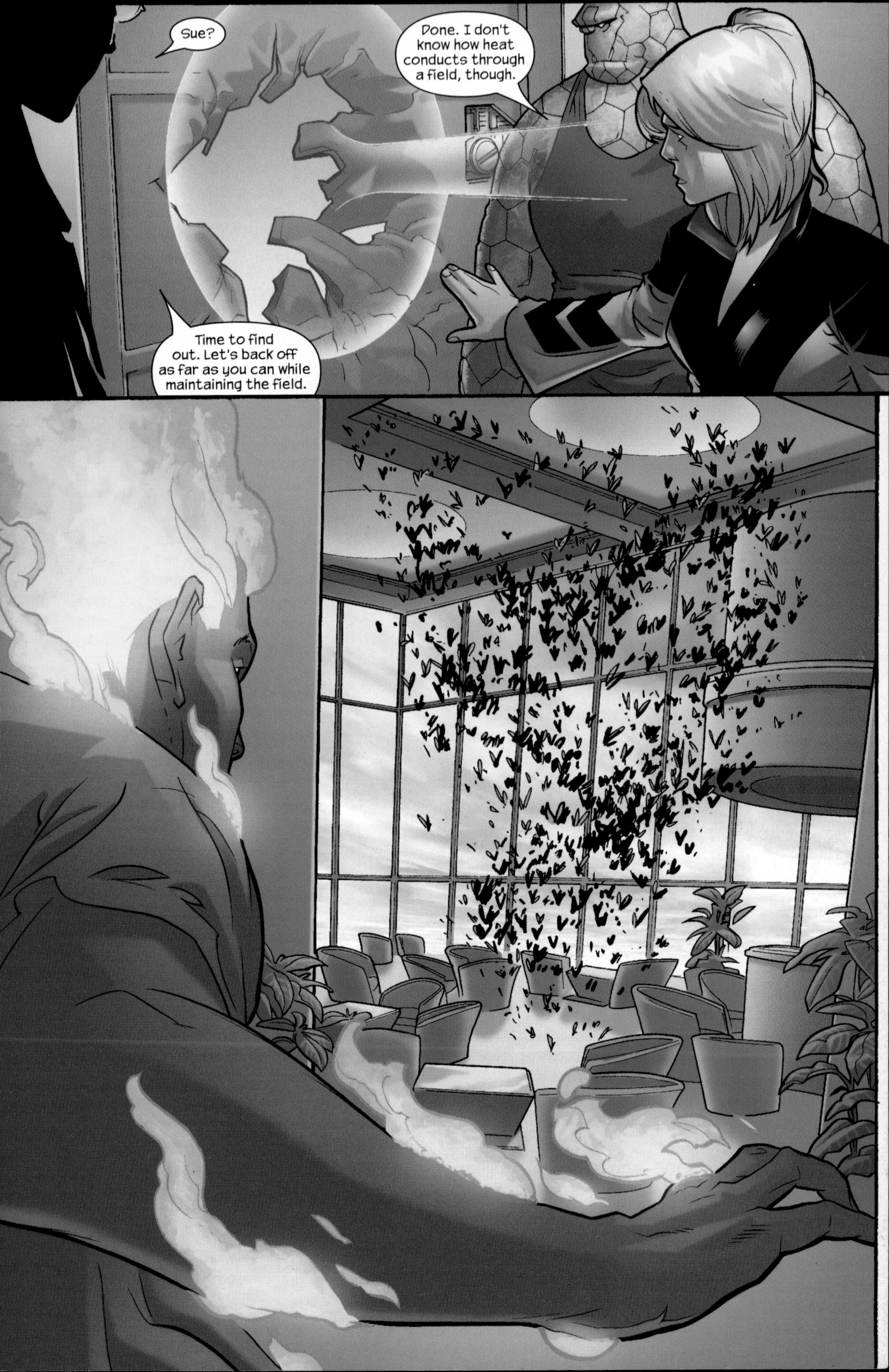
Sue?
Done. I don't know how heat conducts through a field, though.
Time to find out. Let's back off as far as you can while maintaining the field.

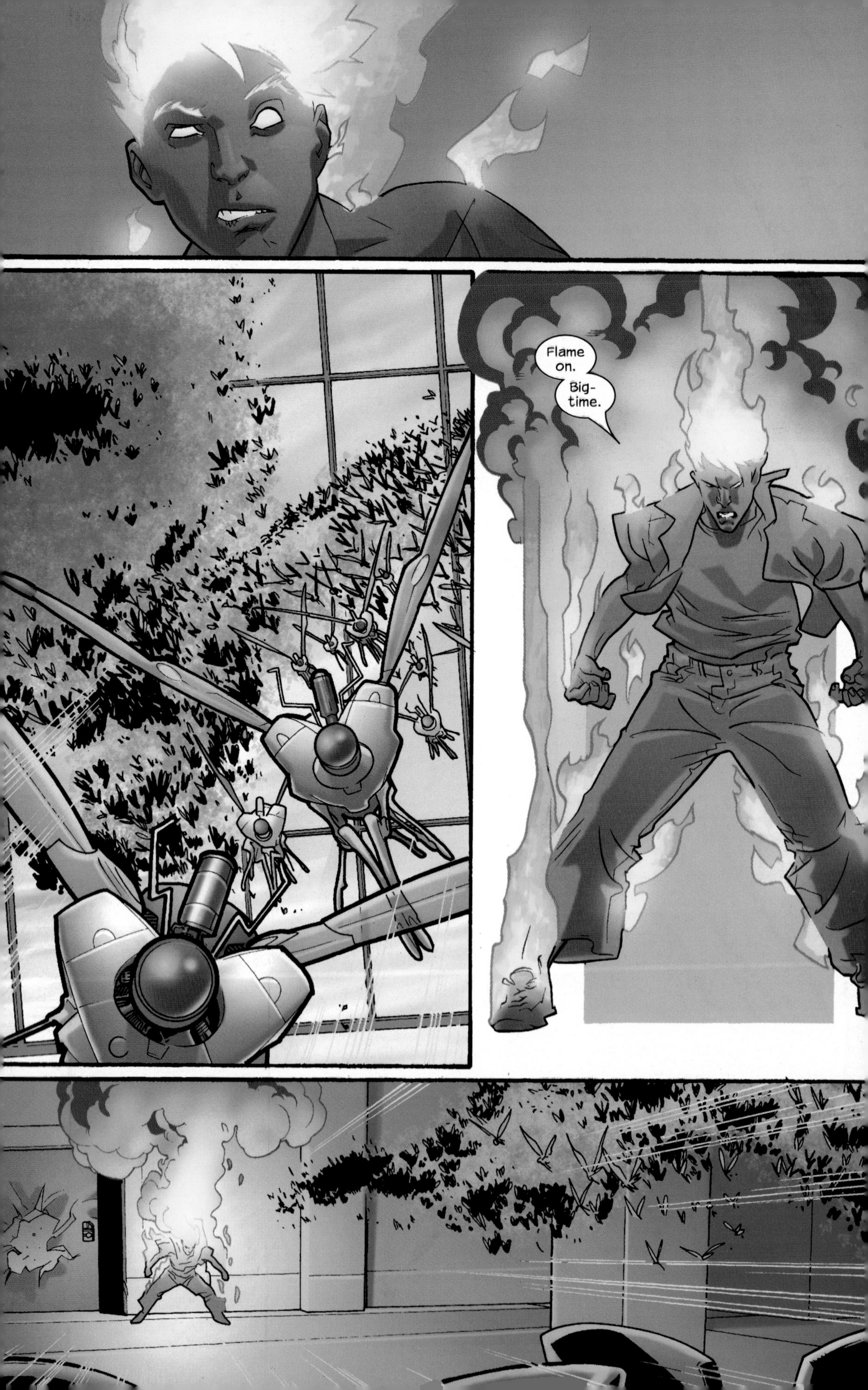
Flame on.
Big-time.

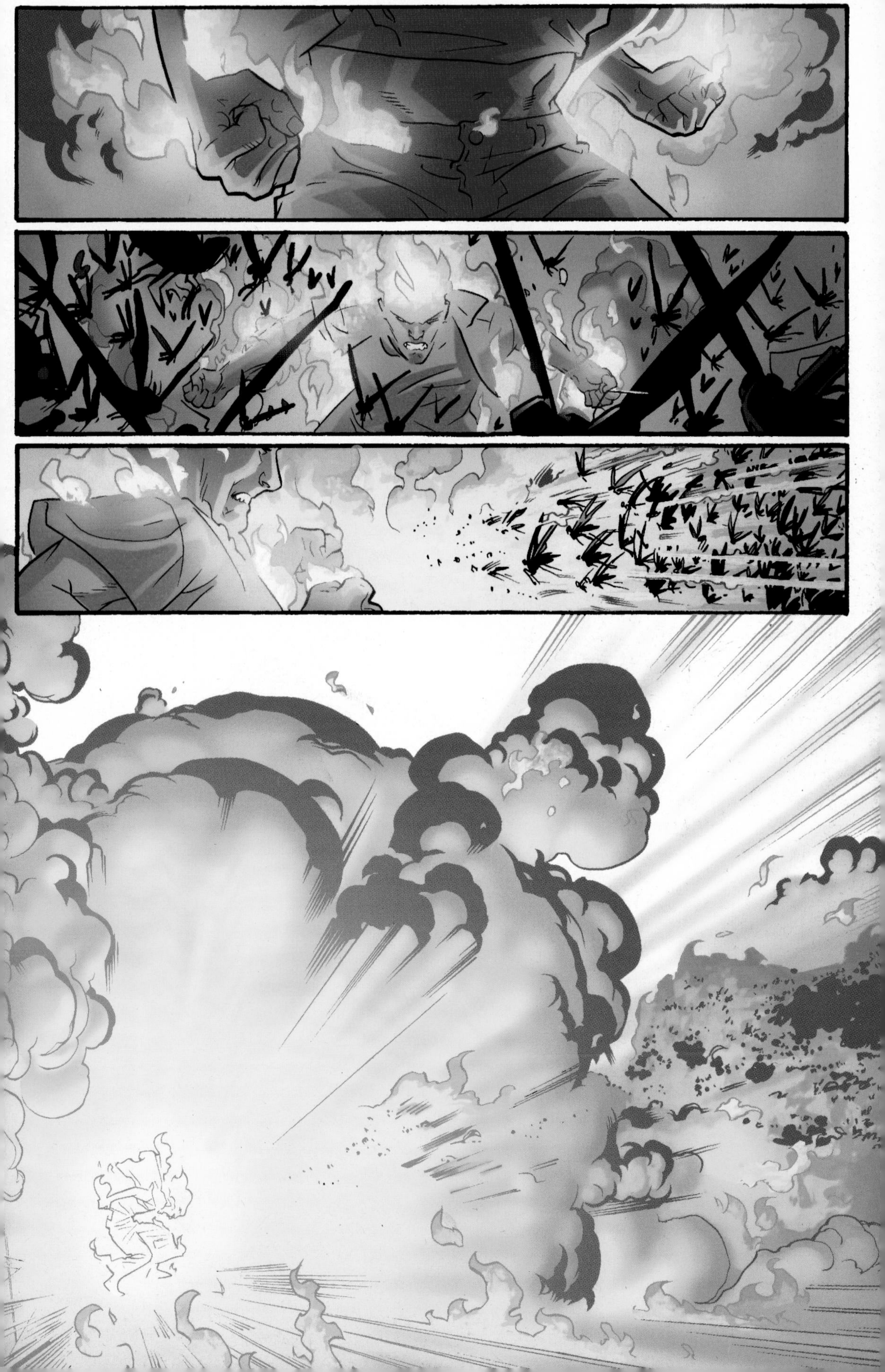

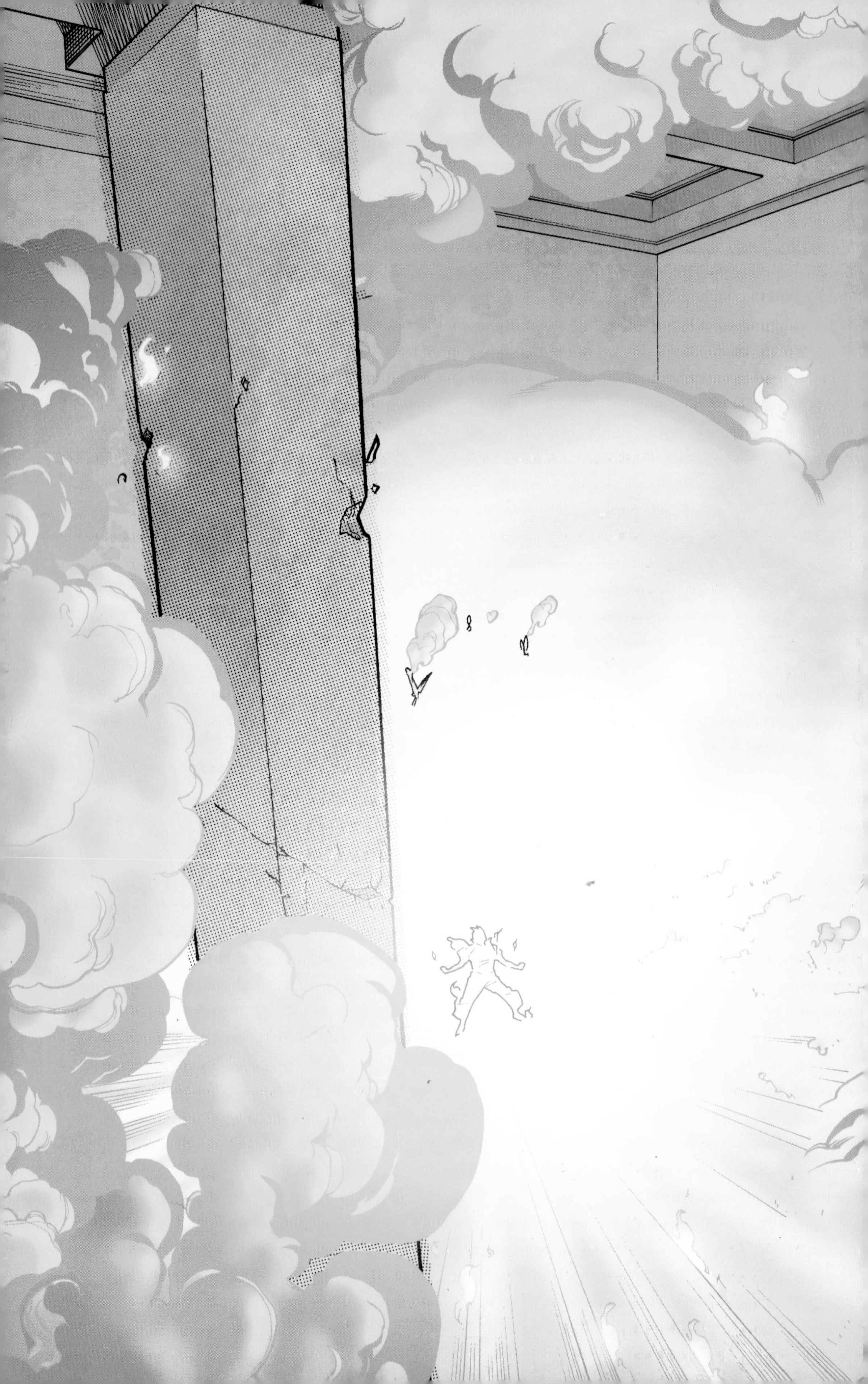

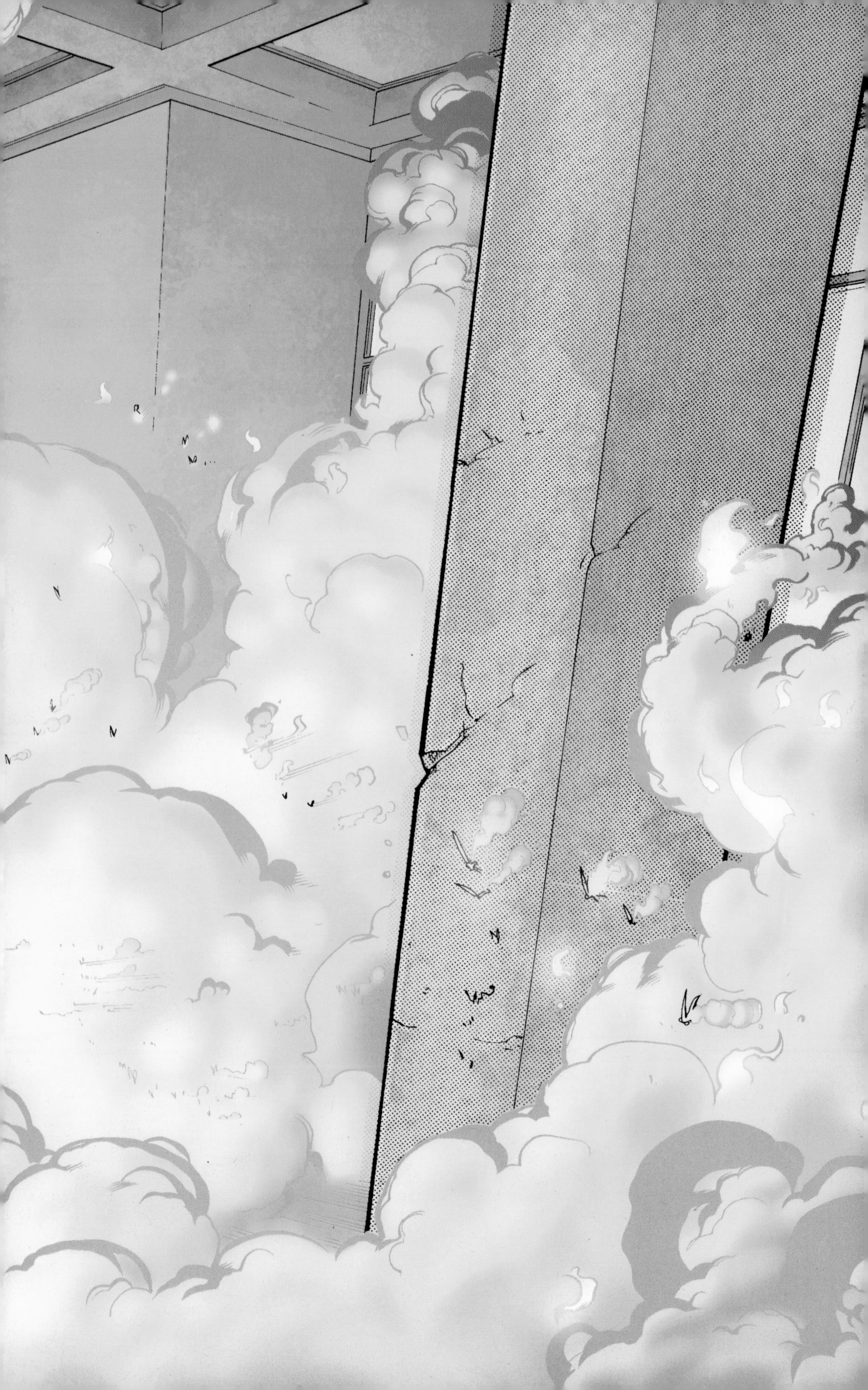

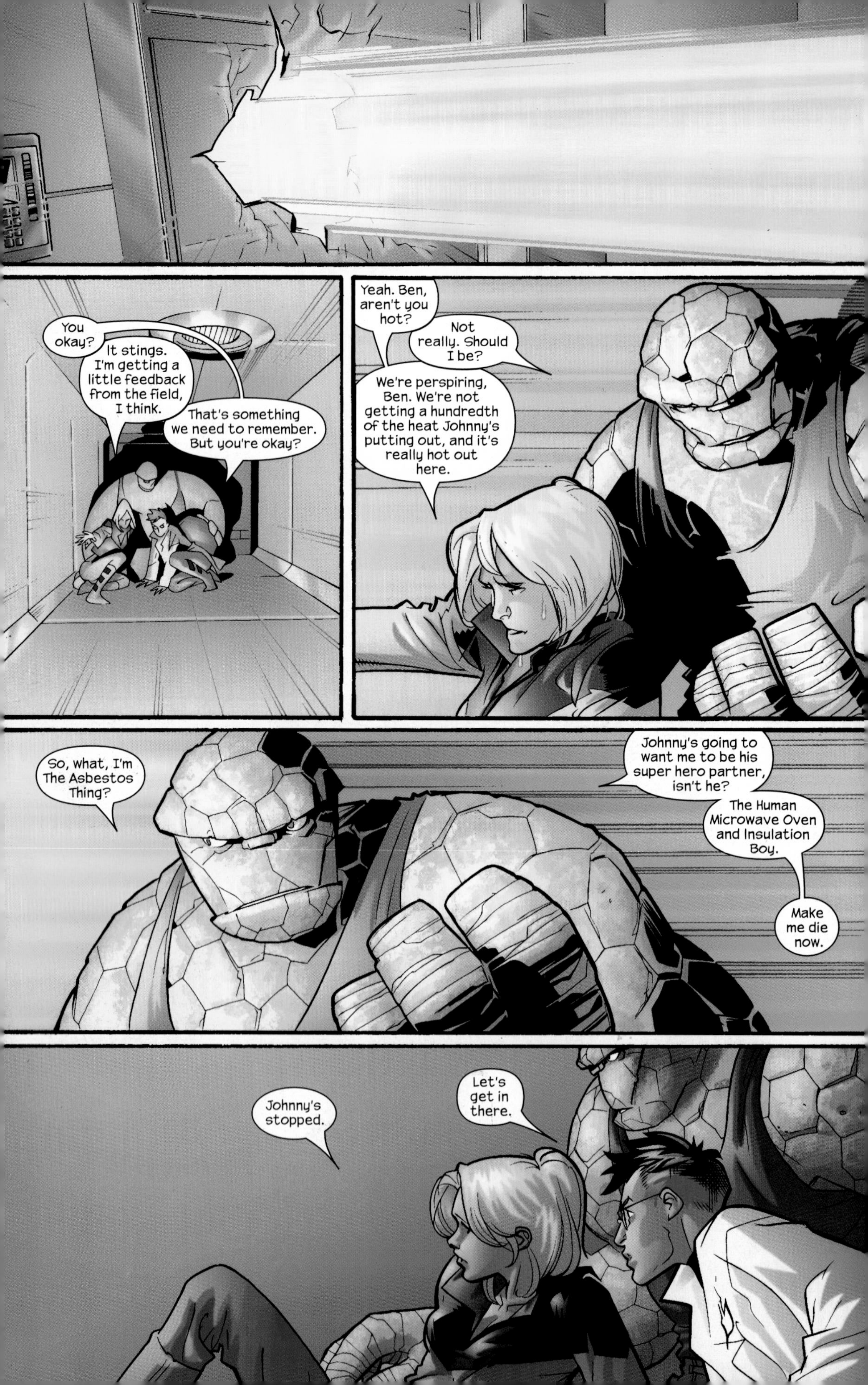
You okay?
It stings. I'm getting a little feedback from the field, I think.
That's something we need to remember. But you're okay?
Yeah. Ben, aren't you hot?
Not really. Should I be?
We're perspiring, Ben. We're not getting a hundredth of the heat Johnny's putting out, and it's really hot out here.
So, what, I'm The Asbestos Thing?
Johnny's going to want me to be his super hero partner, isn't he?
The Human Microwave Oven and Insulation Boy.
Make me die now.
Johnny's stopped.
Let's get in there.

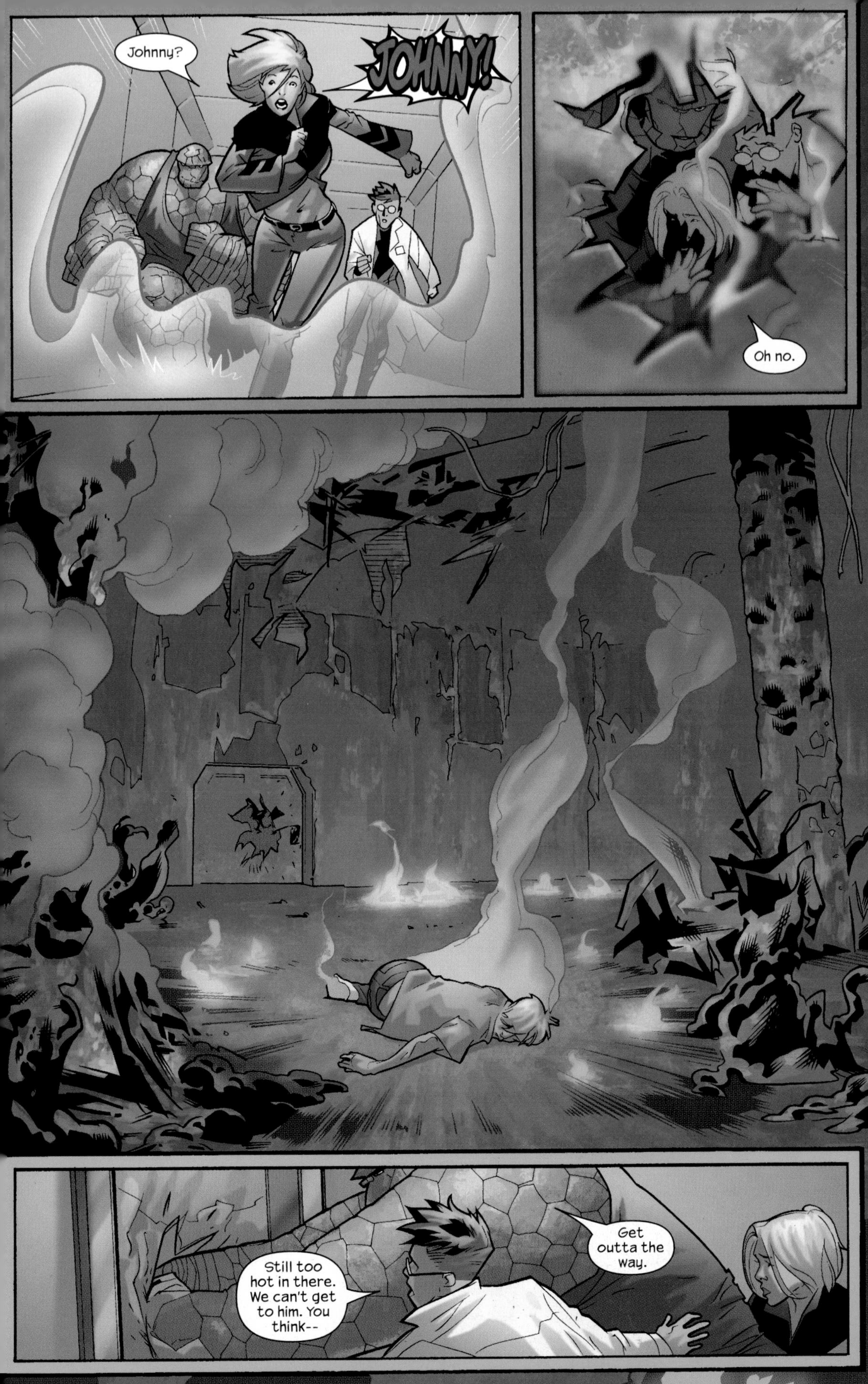
Johnny?
JOHNNY!
Oh no.
Still too hot in there. We can't get to him. You think--
Get outta the way.

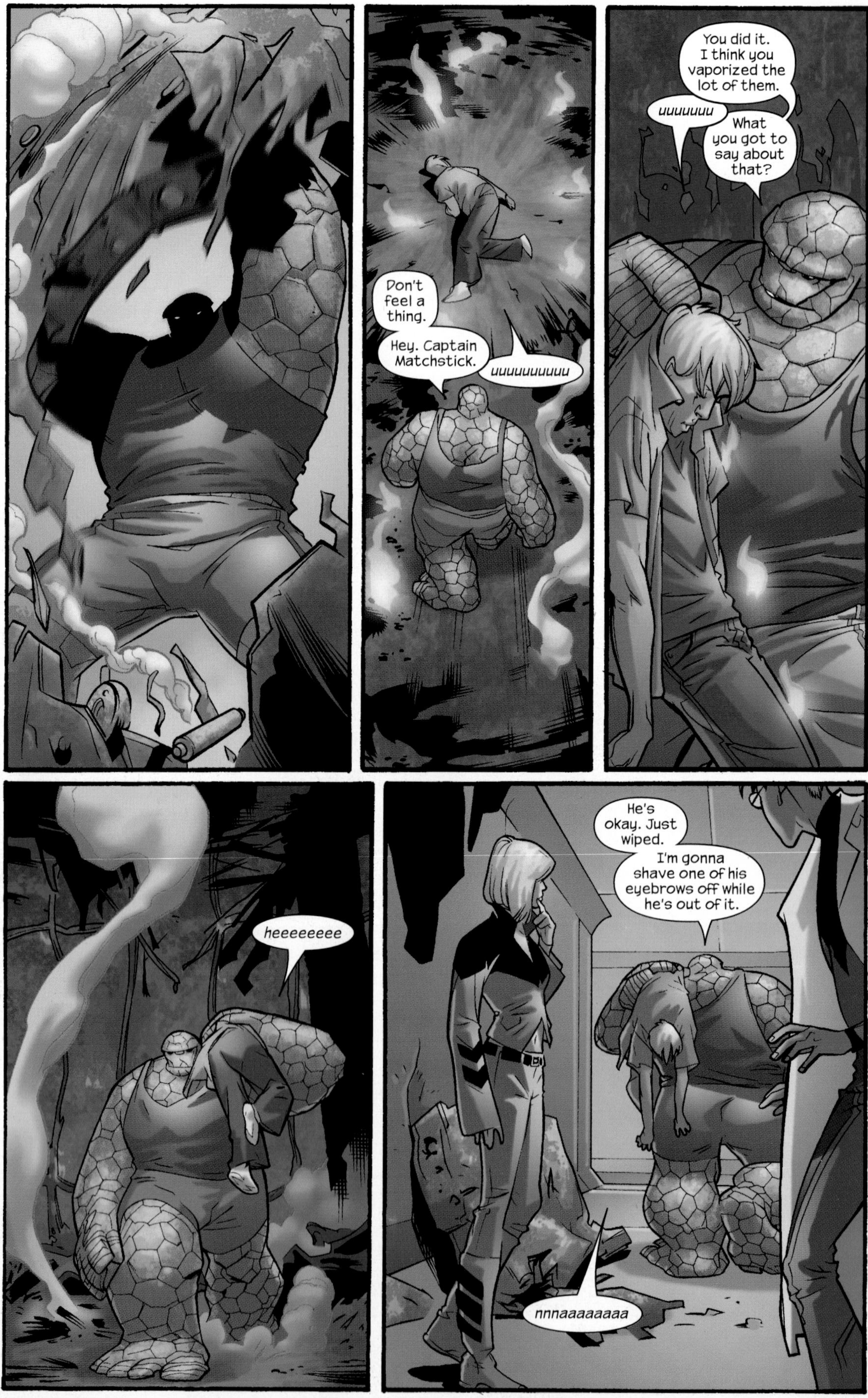
Don't feel a thing.
Hey. Captain Matchstick.
uuuuuuuuuu
You did it. I think you vaporized the lot of them.
uuuuuuu
What you got to say about that?
heeeeeeee
He's okay. Just wiped.
I'm gonna shave one of his eyebrows off while he's out of it.
nnnaaaaaaaaa

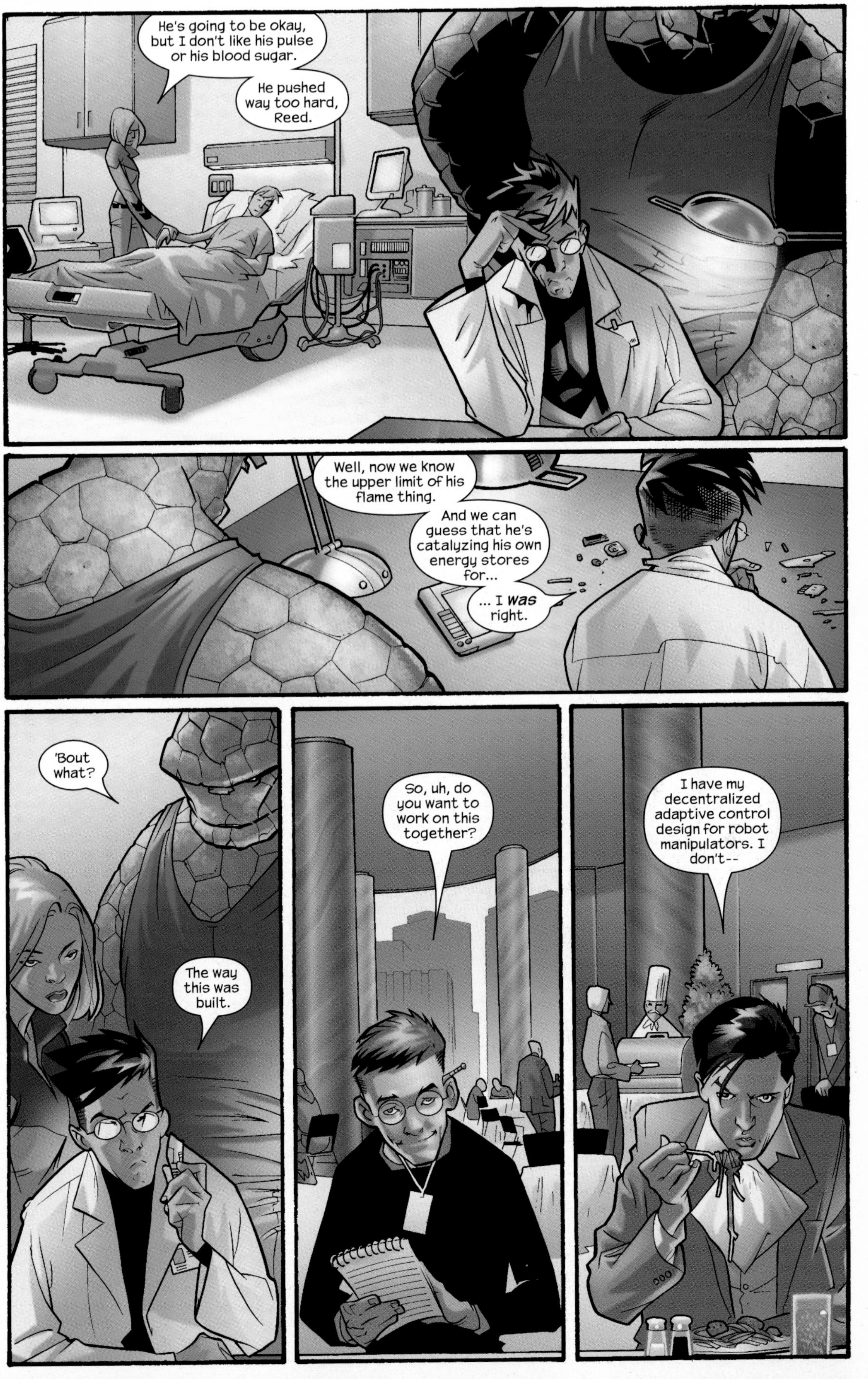
He's going to be okay, but I don't like his pulse or his blood sugar.
He pushed way too hard, Reed.
Well, now we know the upper limit of his flame thing.
And we can guess that he's catalyzing his own energy stores for...
... I *was* right.
'Bout what?
The way this was built.
So, uh, do you want to work on this together?
I have my decentralized adaptive control design for robot manipulators. I don't--

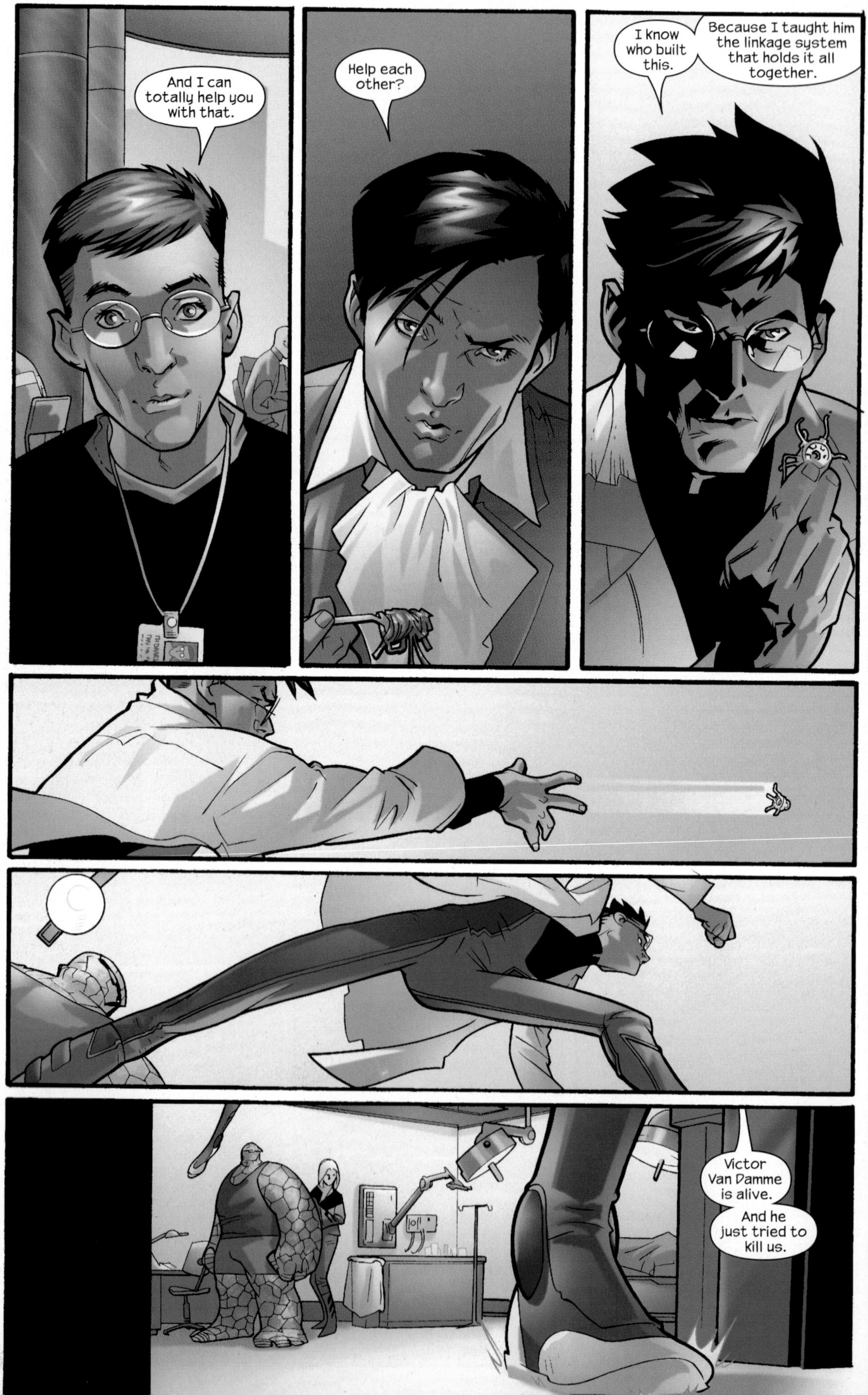
And I can totally help you with that.
Help each other?
I know who built this.
Because I taught him the linkage system that holds it all together.
Victor Van Damme is alive.
And he just tried to kill us.

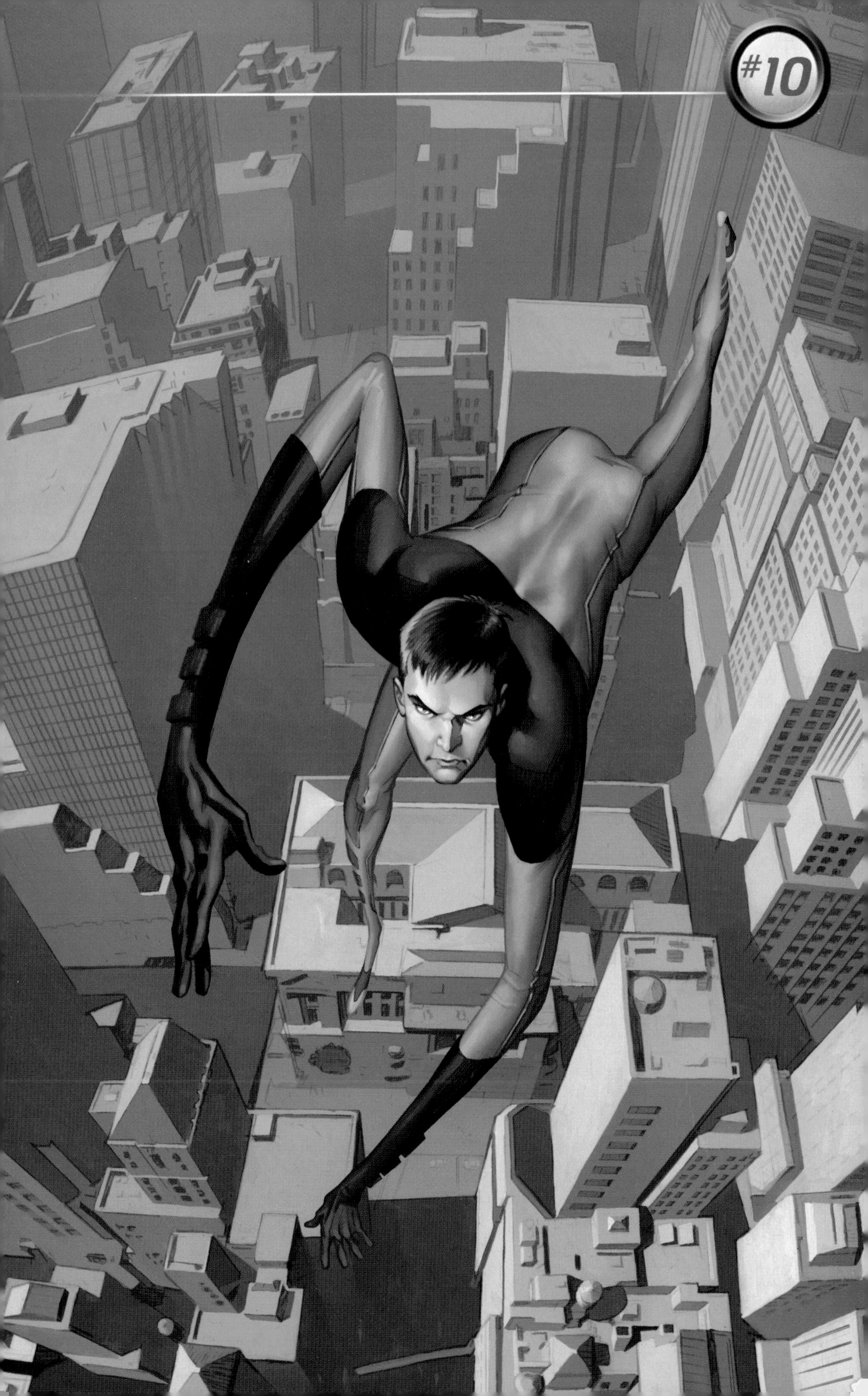
#10

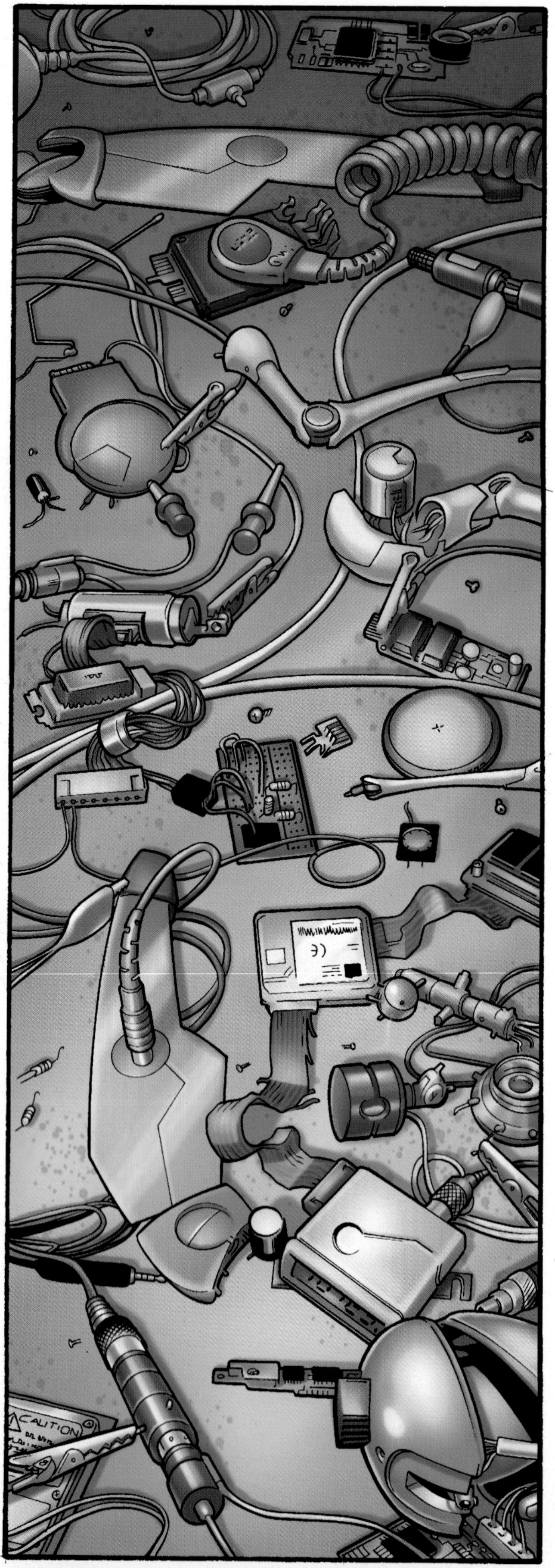
CAUTION

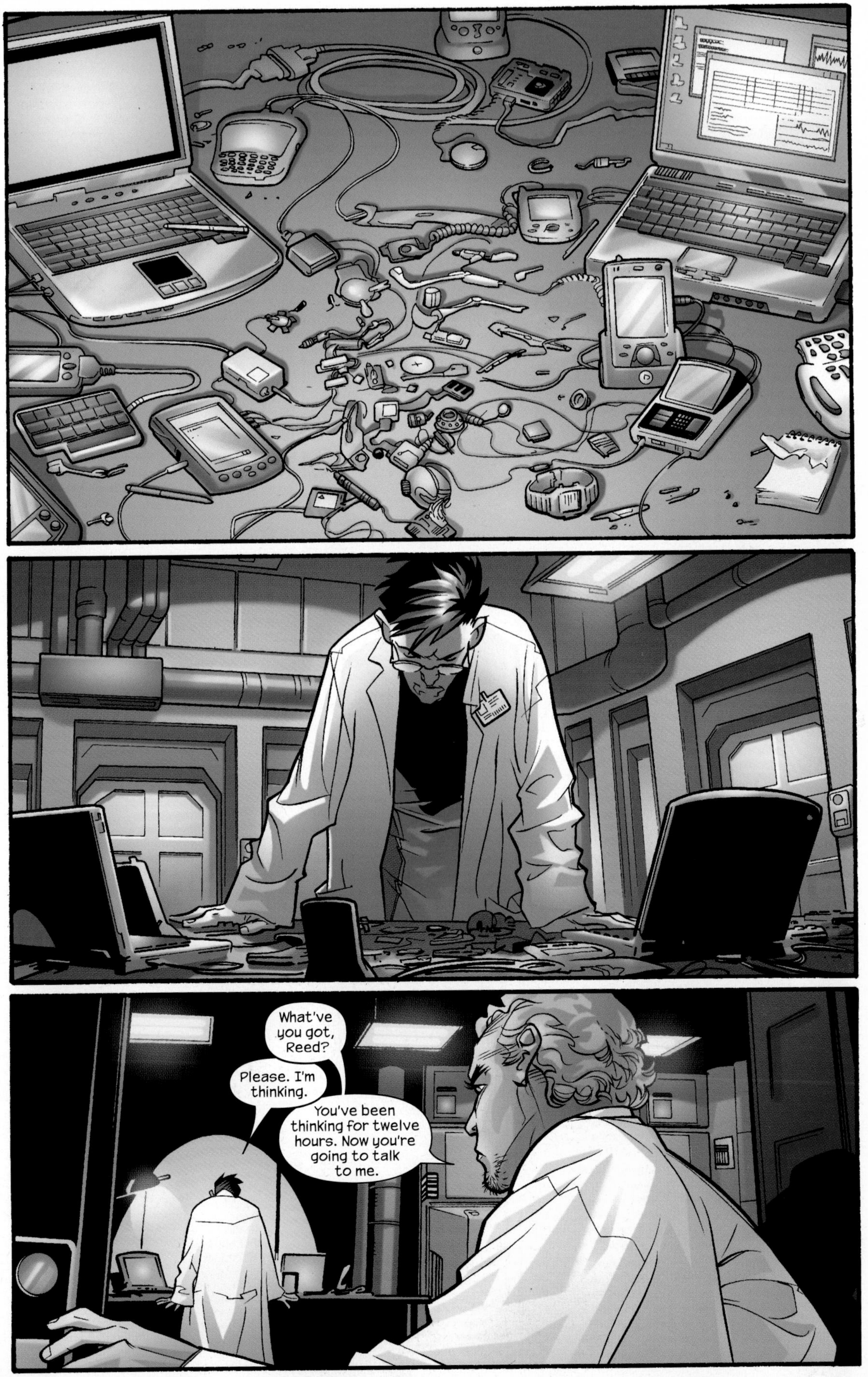
What've you got, Reed?
Please. I'm thinking.
You've been thinking for twelve hours. Now you're going to talk to me.

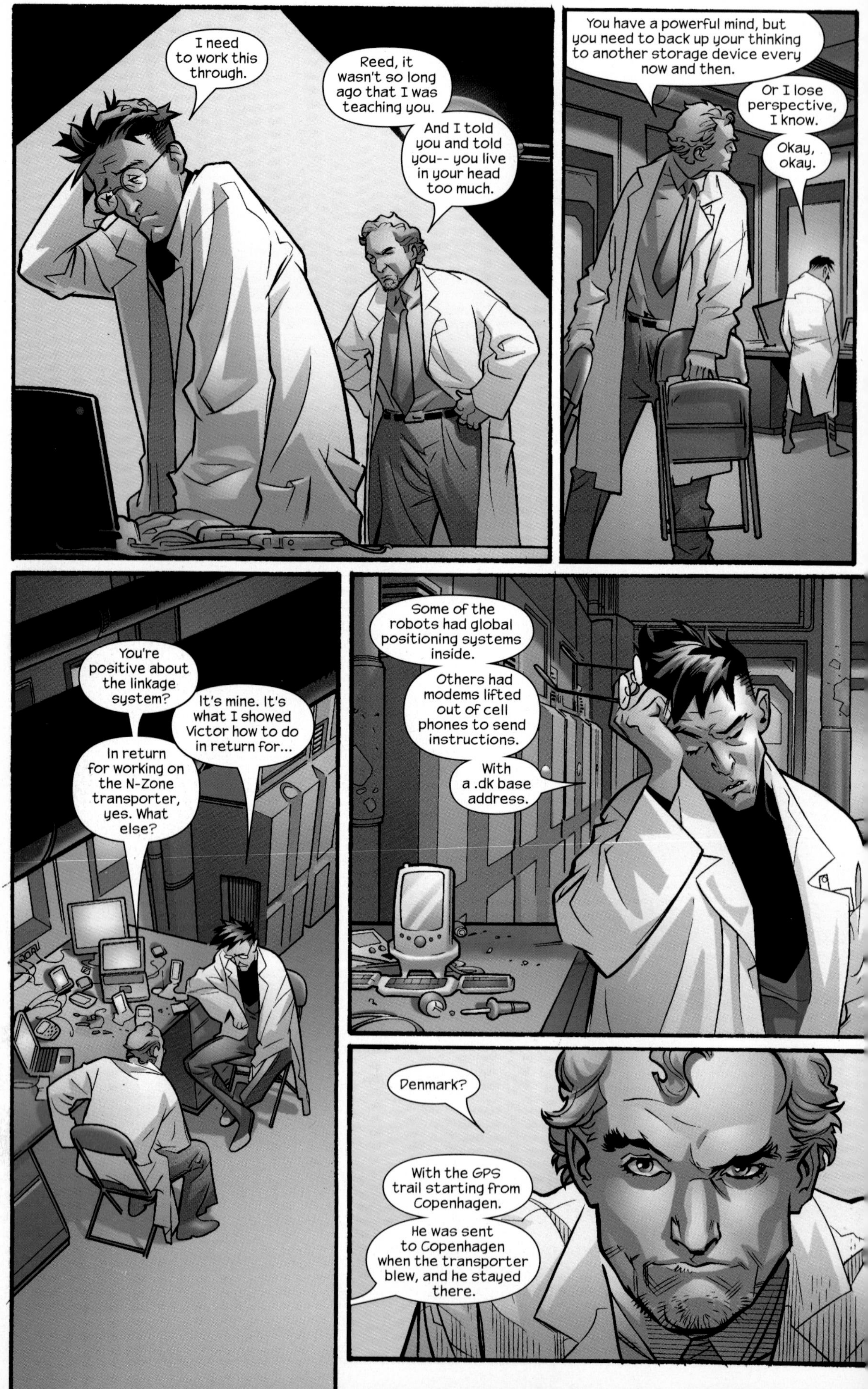
I need to work this through.
Reed, it wasn't so long ago that I was teaching you.
And I told you and told you-- you live in your head too much.
You have a powerful mind, but you need to back up your thinking to another storage device every now and then.
Or I lose perspective, I know.
Okay, okay.
You're positive about the linkage system?
It's mine. It's what I showed Victor how to do in return for...
In return for working on the N-Zone transporter, yes. What else?
Some of the robots had global positioning systems inside.
Others had modems lifted out of cell phones to send instructions.
With a .dk base address.
Denmark?
With the GPS trail starting from Copenhagen.
He was sent to Copenhagen when the transporter blew, and he stayed there.

He stayed there and he scavenged parts from dumpsters to make a swarm of attack robots and sent them here to kill us.

Well, Victor was never exactly normal...

He doesn't know we've changed, Dr. Storm.

Evidence?

You don't send small robots with little stabby things to kill Ben.

I assume "little stabby things" is the technical term.

Yes.

Is it possible he wasn't altered by the accident?

He either knows or assumes you're all still alive, but he didn't take the change into account. Why would he do that, unless he survived the accident unaltered?

That or he's just arrogant enough to assume that only he changed.

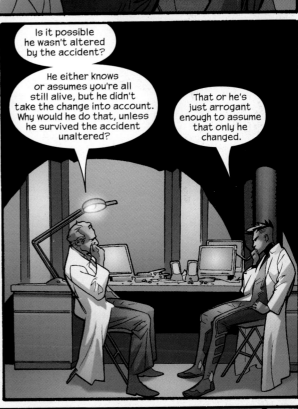

He was always a little flaky, right? Maybe the accident pushed him over the edge.

We need to go and get him.

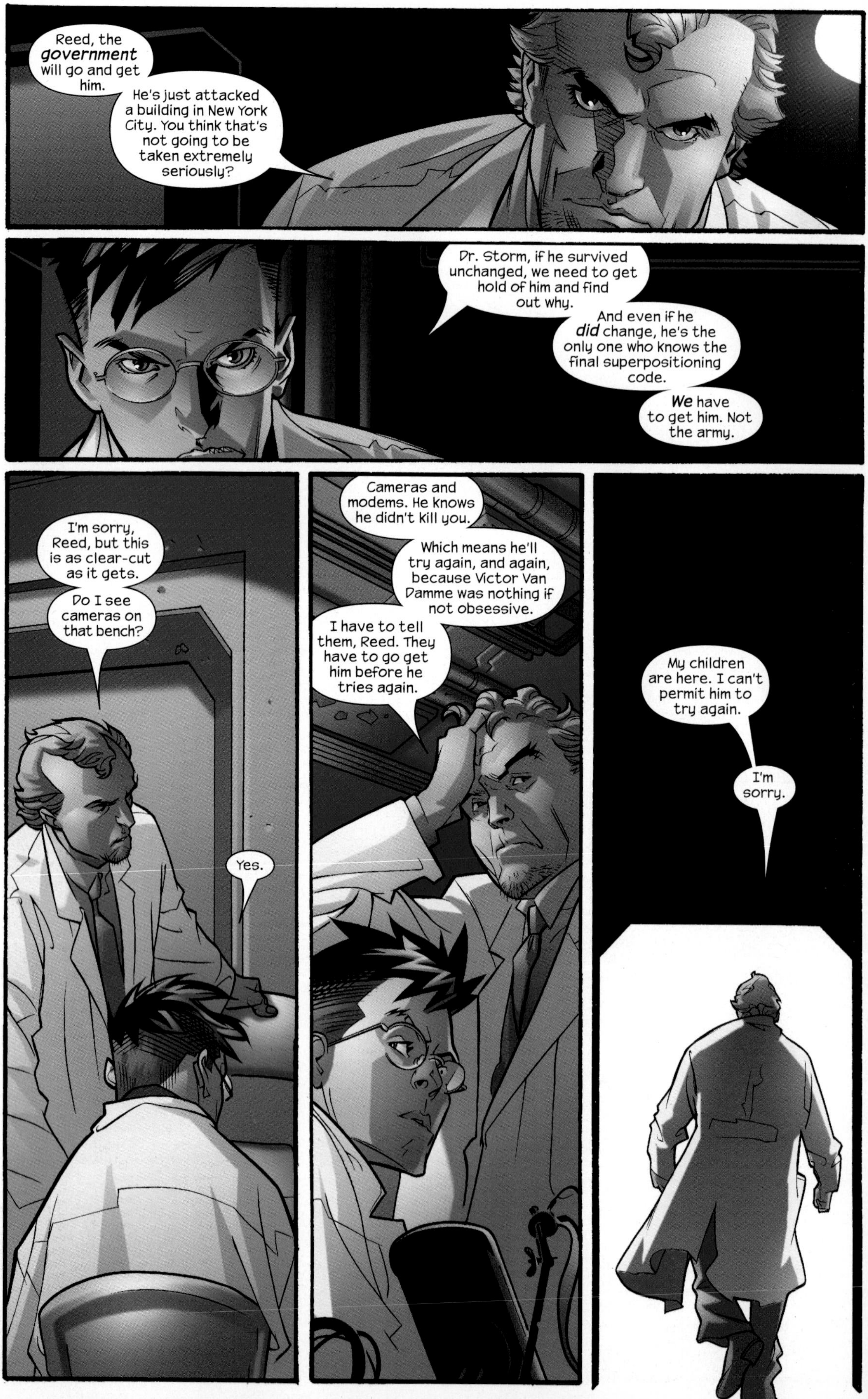
Reed, the *government* will go and get him.
He's just attacked a building in New York City. You think that's not going to be taken extremely seriously?
Dr. Storm, if he survived unchanged, we need to get hold of him and find out why.
And even if he *did* change, he's the only one who knows the final superpositioning code.
We have to get him. Not the army.
I'm sorry, Reed, but this is as clear-cut as it gets.
Do I see cameras on that bench?
Yes.
Cameras and modems. He knows he didn't kill you.
Which means he'll try again, and again, because Victor Van Damme was nothing if not obsessive.
I have to tell them, Reed. They have to go get him before he tries again.
My children are here. I can't permit him to try again.
I'm sorry.

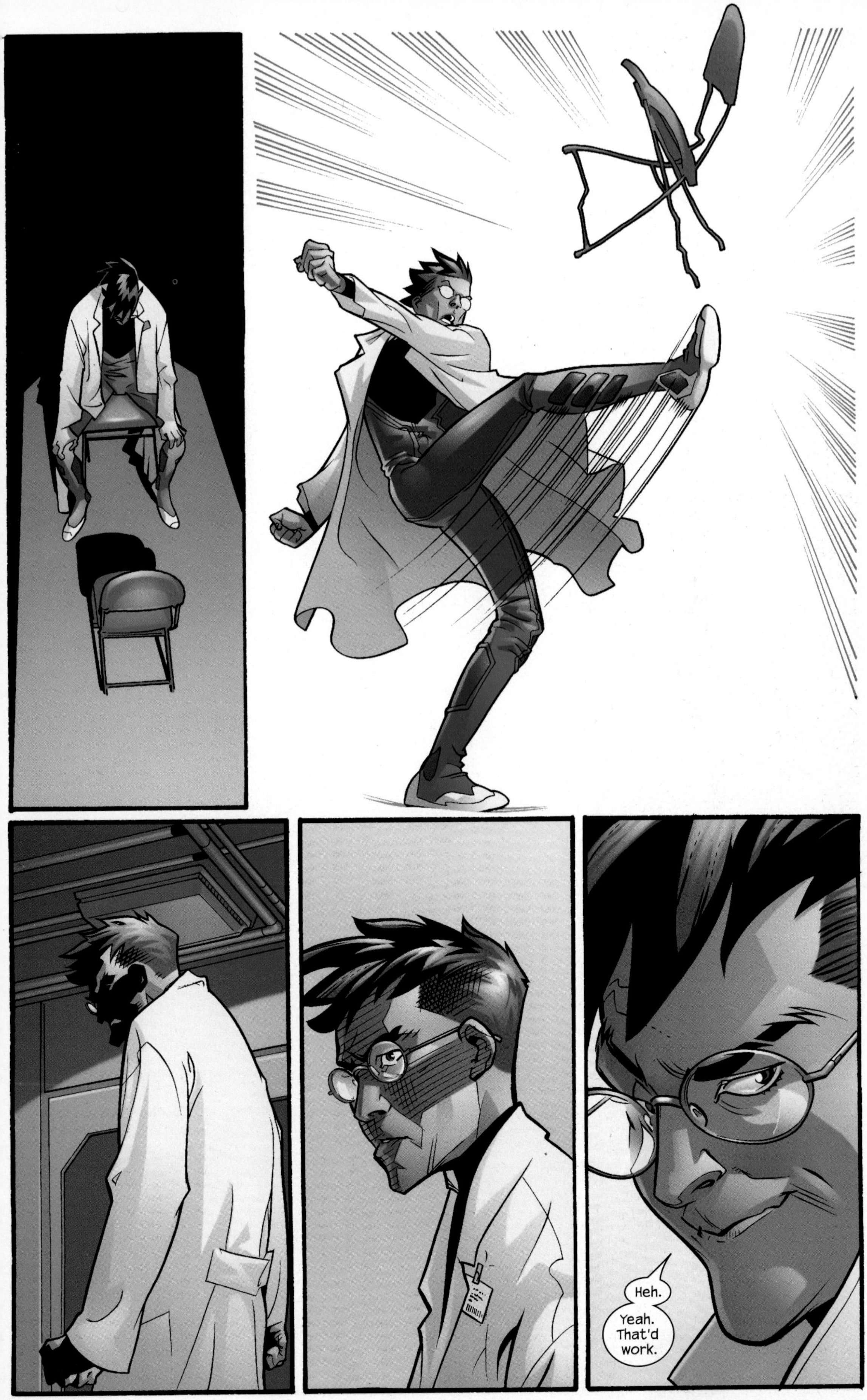
Heh.
Yeah. That'd work.

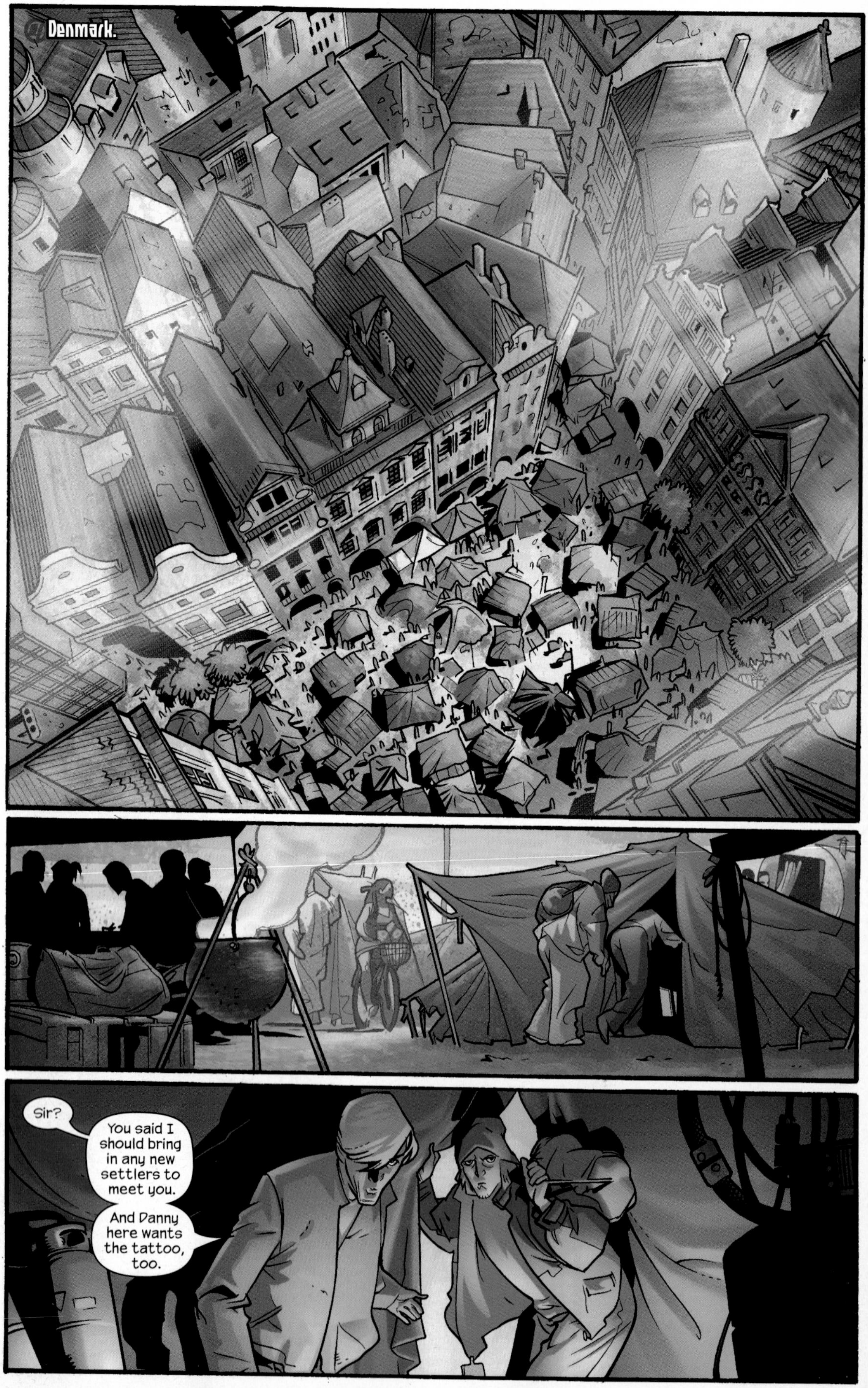
Denmark.
Sir?
You said I should bring in any new settlers to meet you.
And Danny here wants the tattoo, too.

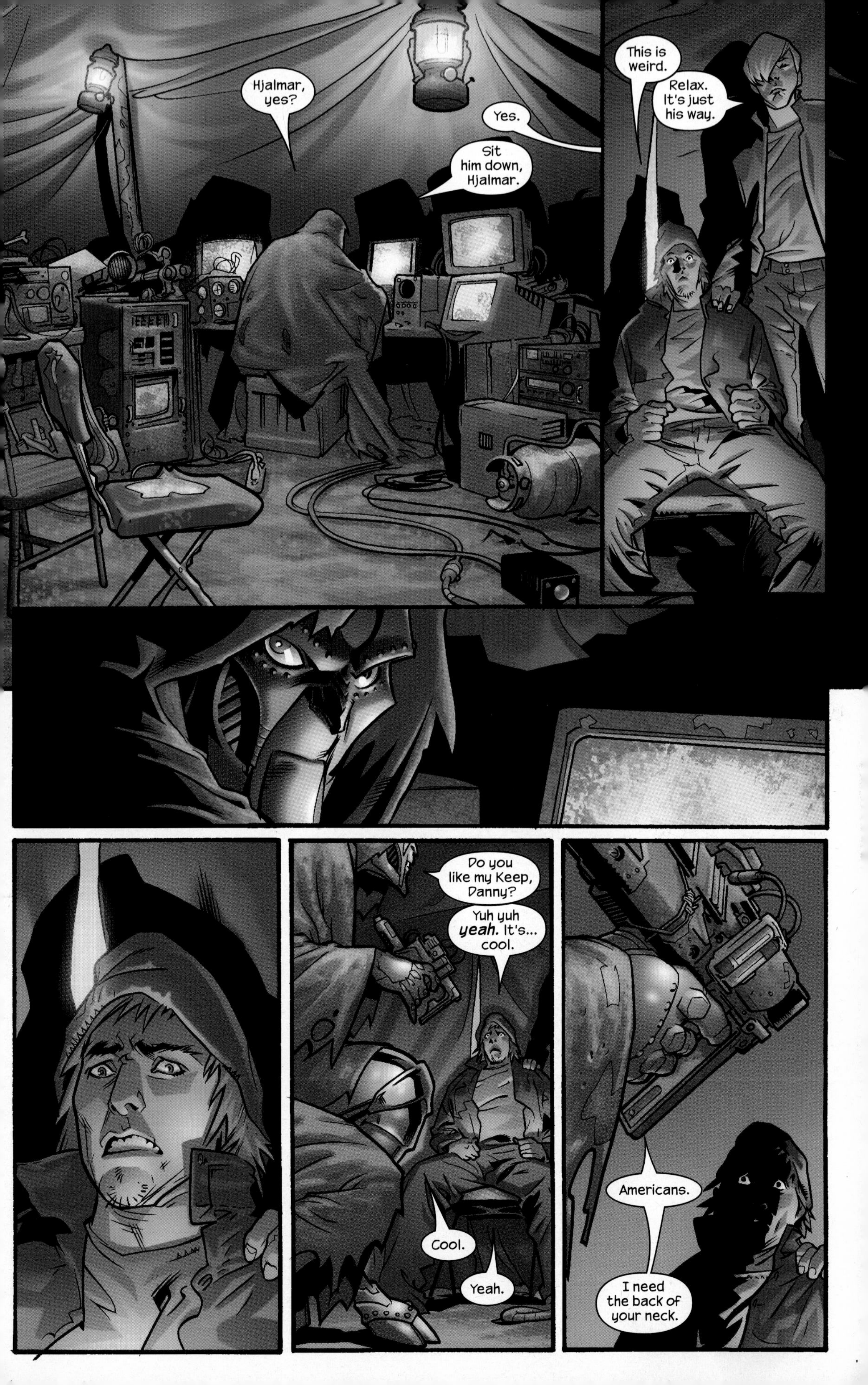
Hjalmar, yes?
Yes.
Sit him down, Hjalmar.
This is weird.
Relax. It's just his way.
Do you like my Keep, Danny?
Yuh yuh *yeah.* It's... cool.
Cool.
Yeah.
Americans.
I need the back of your neck.

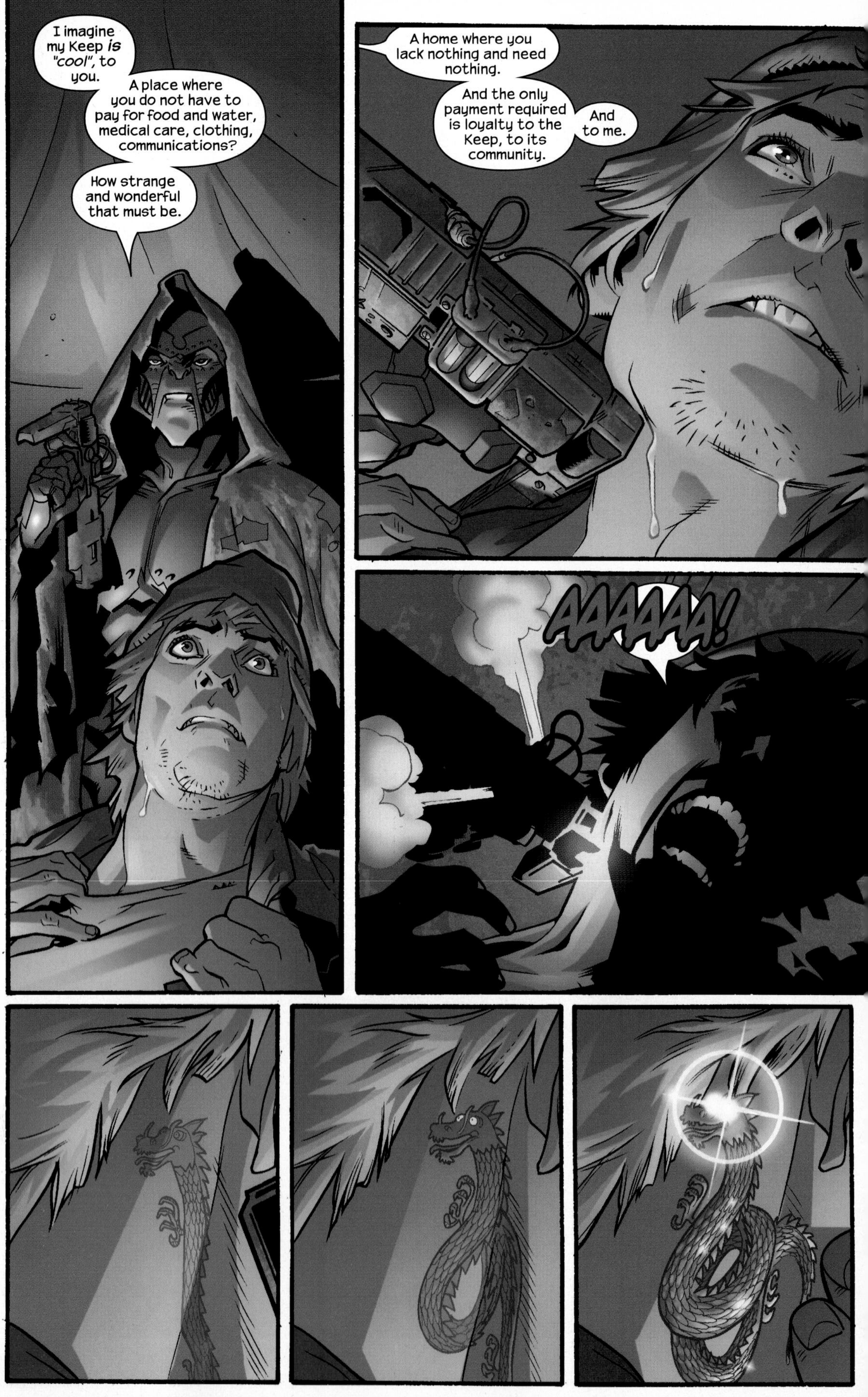

I imagine my Keep *is* "*cool*", to you.
A place where you do not have to pay for food and water, medical care, clothing, communications?
How strange and wonderful that must be.
A home where you lack nothing and need nothing.
And the only payment required is loyalty to the Keep, to its community.
And to me.
AAAAAA!

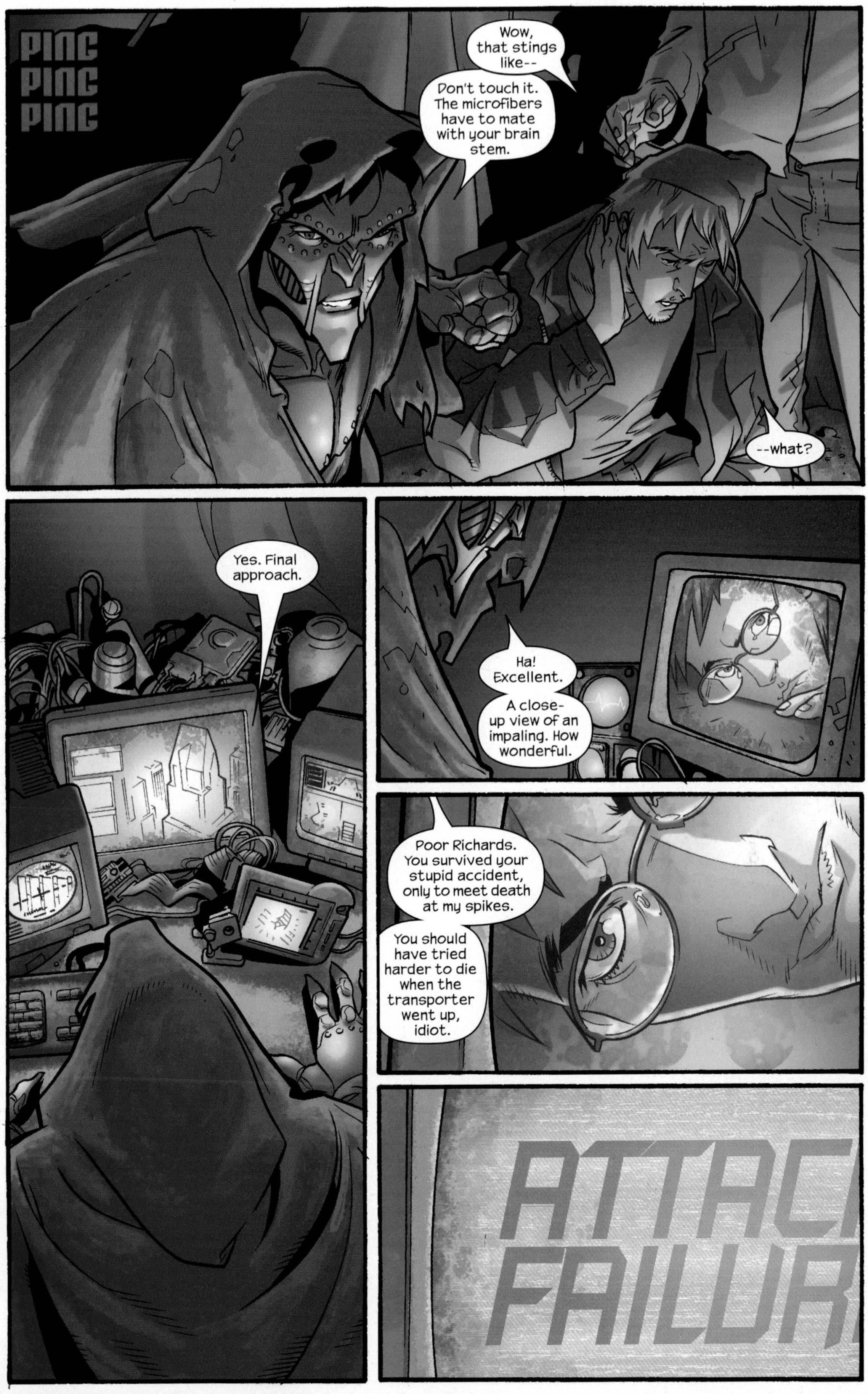
PING PING PING
Wow, that stings like--
Don't touch it. The microfibers have to mate with your brain stem.
--what?
Yes. Final approach.
Ha! Excellent.
A close-up view of an impaling. How wonderful.
Poor Richards. You survived your stupid accident, only to meet death at my spikes.
You should have tried harder to die when the transporter went up, idiot.
ATTACH FAILUR

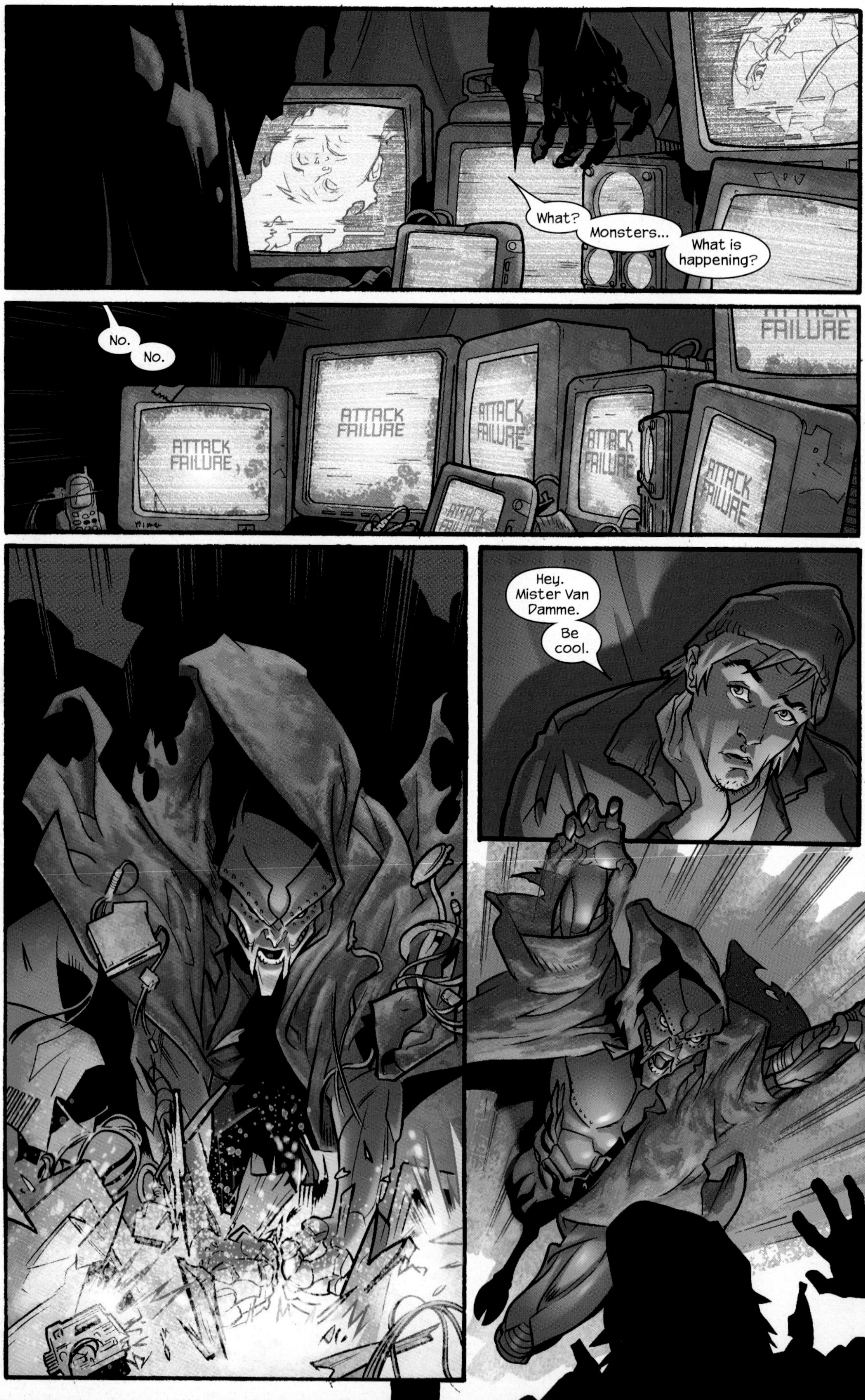
What?
Monsters...
What is happening?
No.
No.
ATTACK FAILURE
ATTACK FAILURE
ATTACK FAILURE
ATTACK FAILURE
ATTACK FAILURE
ATTACK FAILURE
Hey. Mister Van Damme.
Be cool.

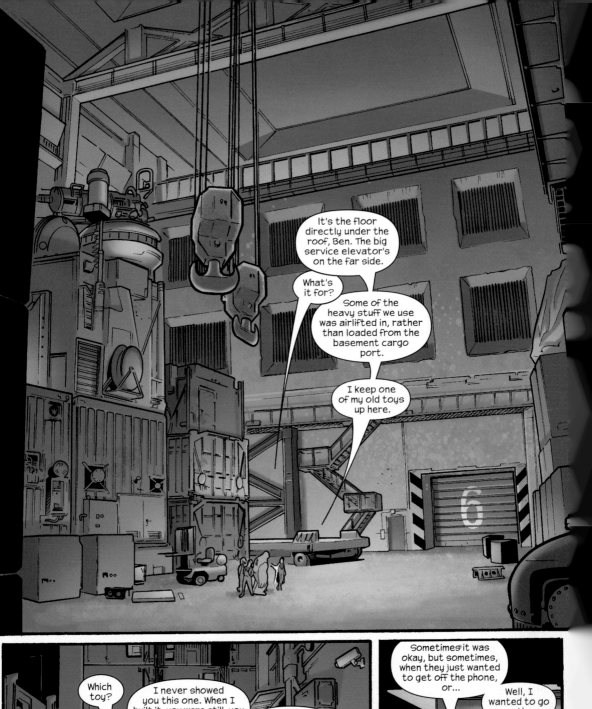

It's the floor directly under the roof, Ben. The big service elevator's on the far side.

What's it for?

Some of the heavy stuff we use was airlifted in, rather than loaded from the basement cargo port.

I keep one of my old toys up here.

Which toy?

I never showed you this one. When I built it, you were still, you know, the principal's daughter.

See, my folks have barely said a word to me since I moved here.

Sometimes it was okay, but sometimes, when they just wanted to get off the phone, or...

Well, I wanted to go see them.

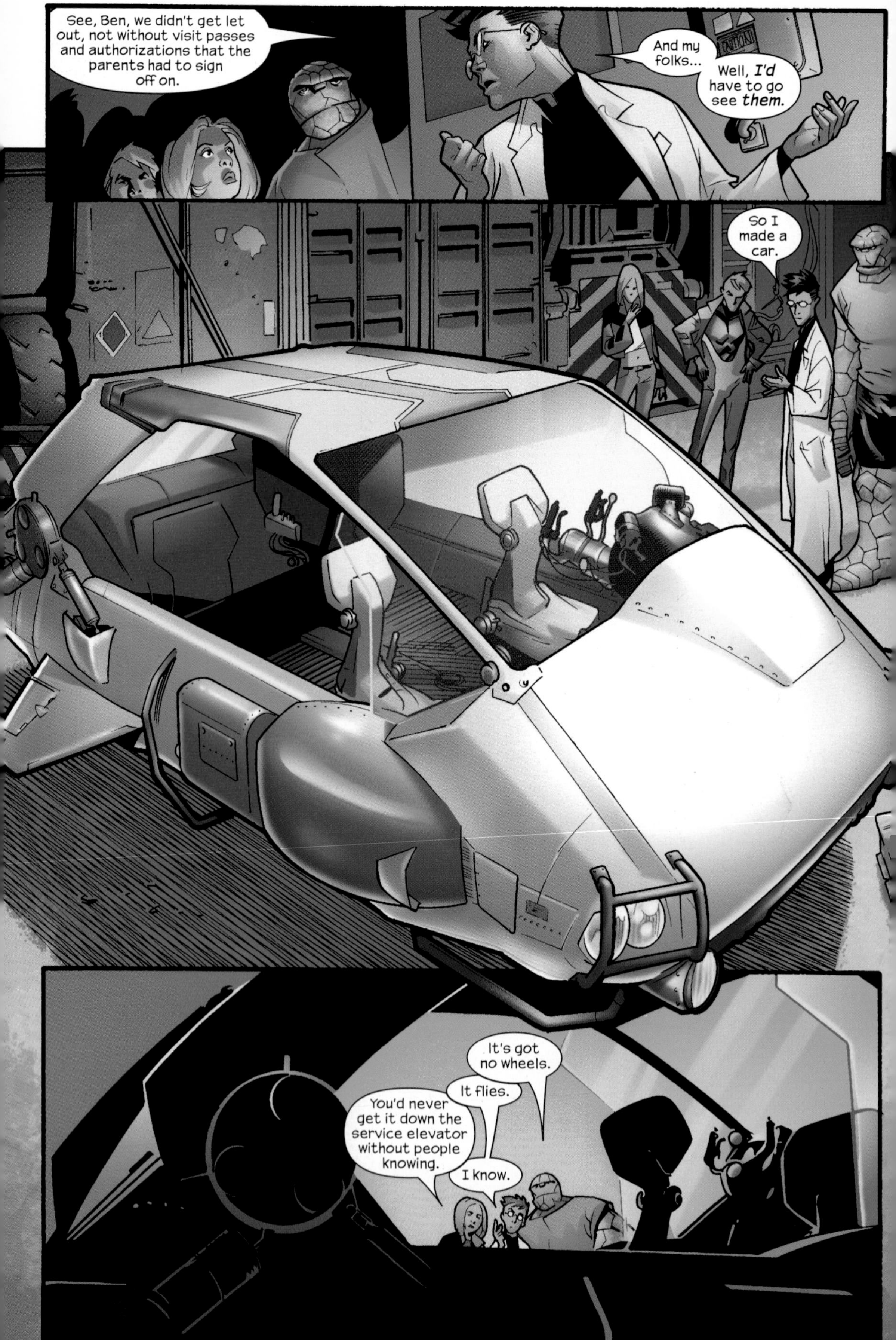
See, Ben, we didn't get let out, not without visit passes and authorizations that the parents had to sign off on.
And my folks...
Well, *I'd* have to go see *them.*
So I made a car.
It's got no wheels.
It flies.
You'd never get it down the service elevator without people knowing.
I know.

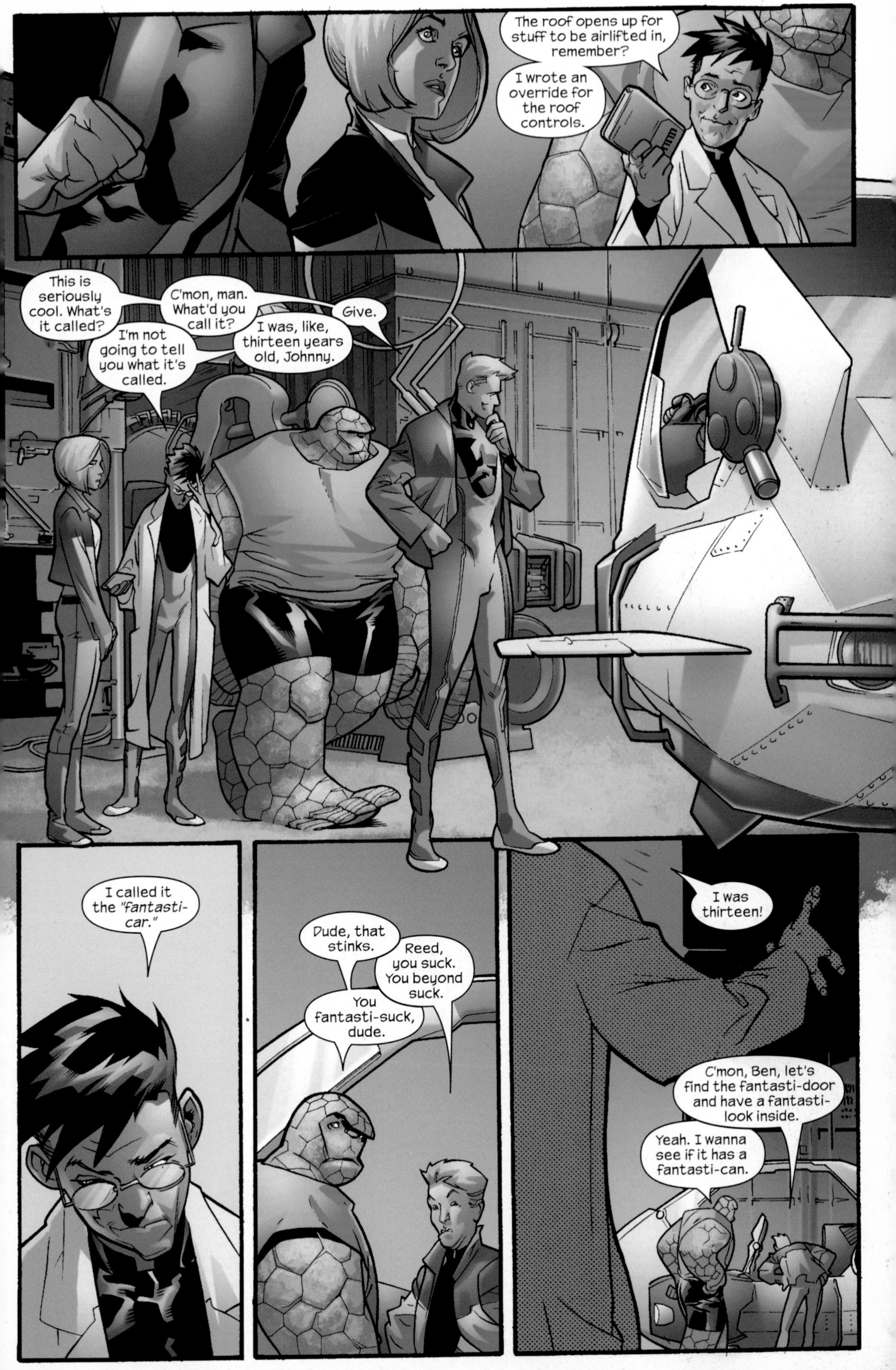
The roof opens up for stuff to be airlifted in, remember?
I wrote an override for the roof controls.
This is seriously cool. What's it called?
C'mon, man. What'd you call it?
Give.
I'm not going to tell you what it's called.
I was, like, thirteen years old, Johnny.
I called it the "fantasti-car."
Dude, that stinks.
Reed, you suck. You beyond suck.
You fantasti-suck, dude.
I was thirteen!
C'mon, Ben, let's find the fantasti-door and have a fantasti-look inside.
Yeah. I wanna see if it has a fantasti-can.

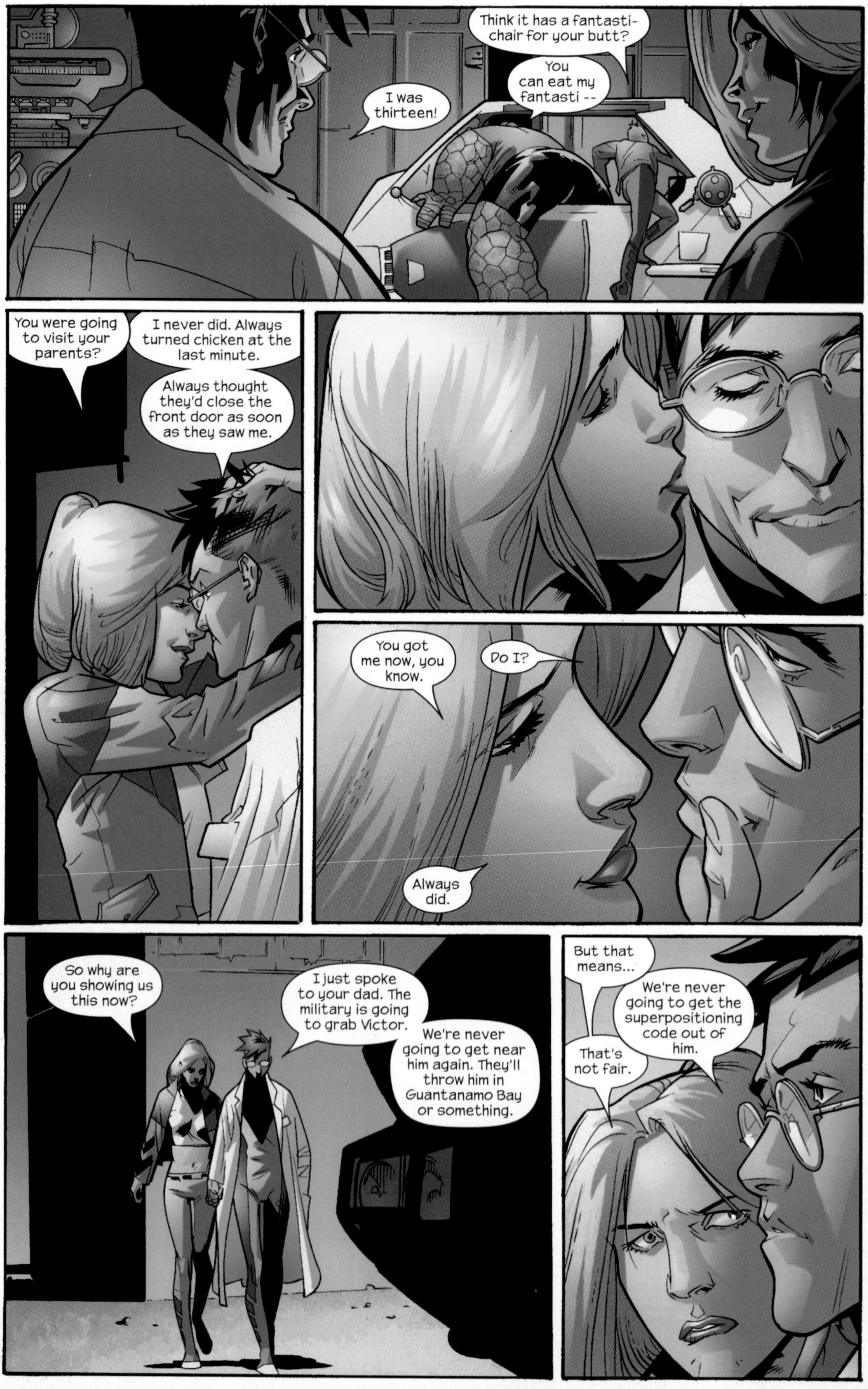
Think it has a fantasti-chair for your butt?
You can eat my fantasti --
I was thirteen!
You were going to visit your parents?
I never did. Always turned chicken at the last minute.
Always thought they'd close the front door as soon as they saw me.
You got me now, you know.
Do I?
Always did.
So why are you showing us this now?
I just spoke to your dad. The military is going to grab Victor.
We're never going to get near him again. They'll throw him in Guantanamo Bay or something.
But that means...
We're never going to get the superpositioning code out of him.
That's not fair.

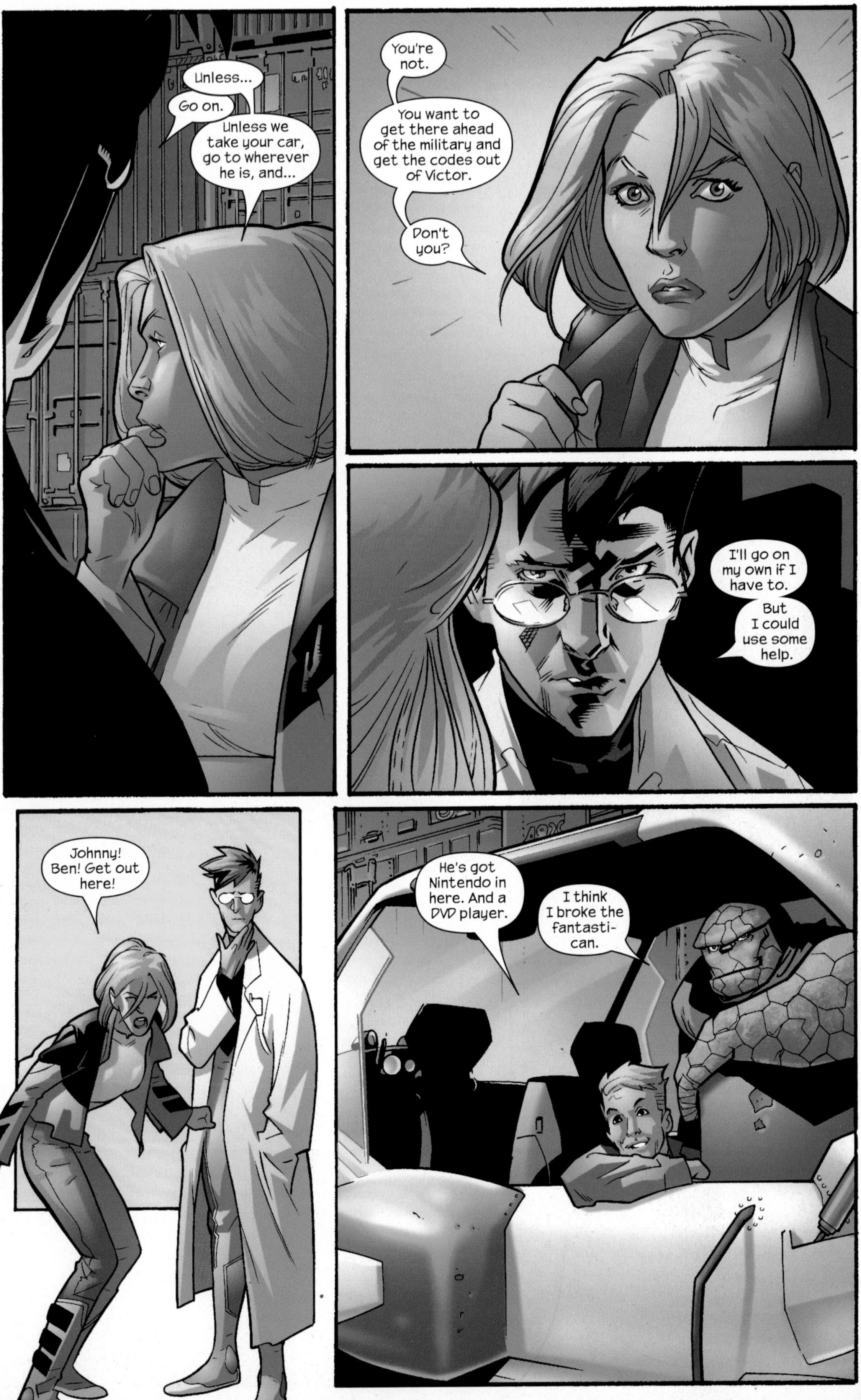
Unless...
Go on.
Unless we take your car, go to wherever he is, and...
You're not.
You want to get there ahead of the military and get the codes out of Victor.
Don't you?
I'll go on my own if I have to.
But I could use some help.
Johnny! Ben! Get out here!
He's got Nintendo in here. And a DVD player.
I think I broke the fantasti-can.

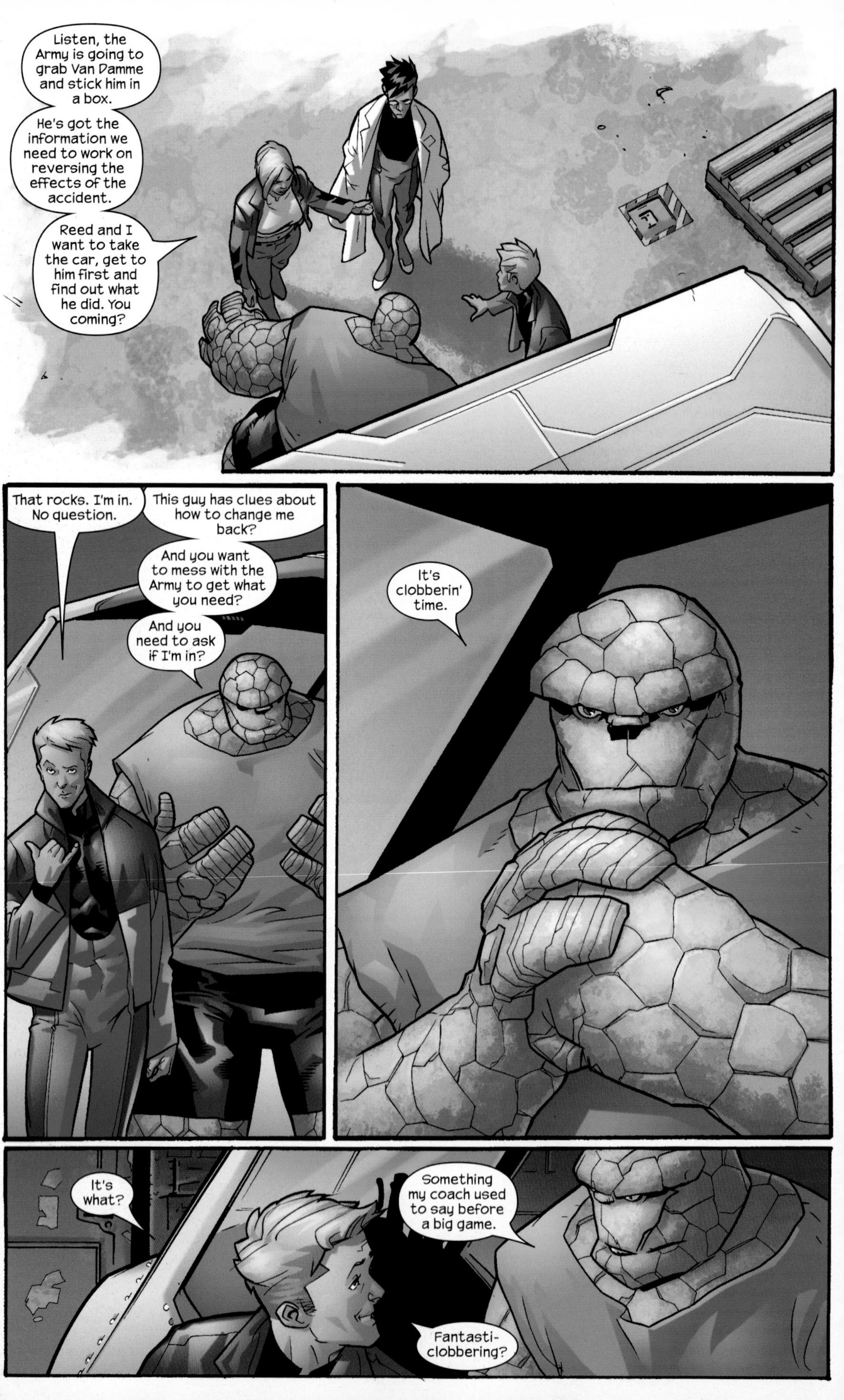
Listen, the Army is going to grab Van Damme and stick him in a box.
He's got the information we need to work on reversing the effects of the accident.
Reed and I want to take the car, get to him first and find out what he did. You coming?
That rocks. I'm in. No question.
This guy has clues about how to change me back?
And you want to mess with the Army to get what you need?
And you need to ask if I'm in?
It's clobberin' time.
It's what?
Something my coach used to say before a big game.
Fantasti-clobbering?

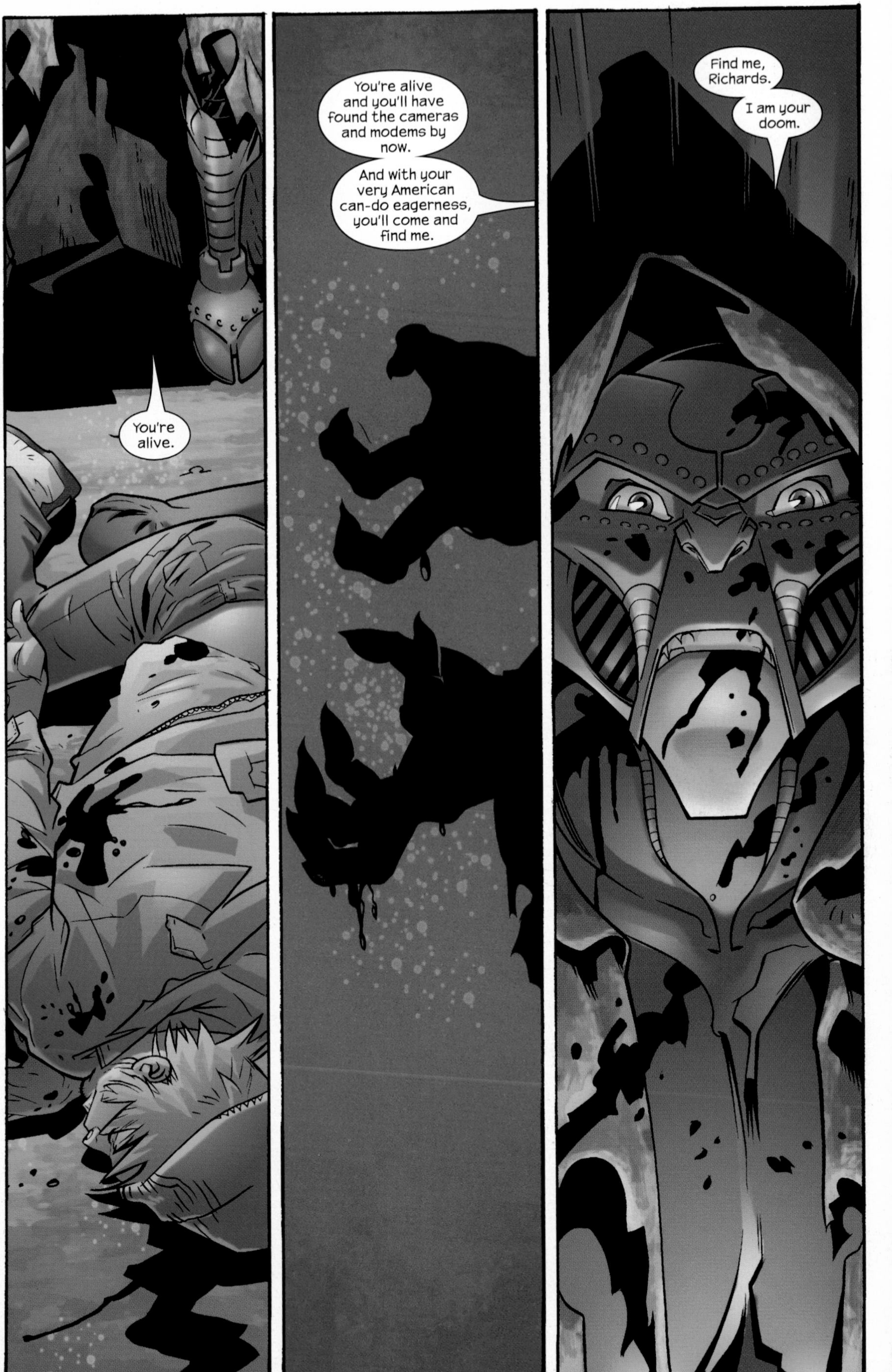
You're alive.
You're alive and you'll have found the cameras and modems by now.
And with your very American can-do eagerness, you'll come and find me.
Find me, Richards.
I am your doom.

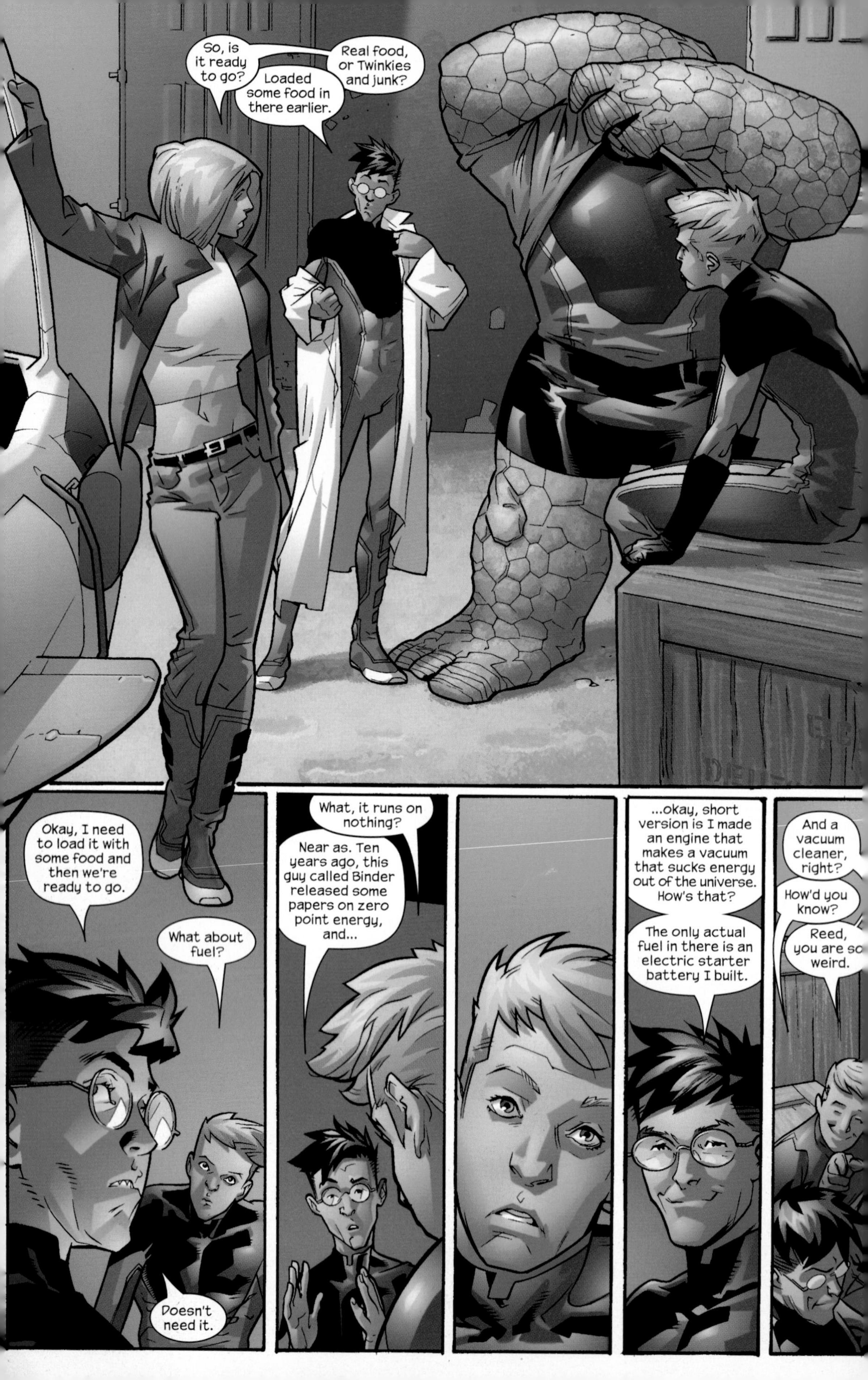
So, is it ready to go?
Real food, or Twinkies and junk?
Loaded some food in there earlier.
Okay, I need to load it with some food and then we're ready to go.
What about fuel?
Doesn't need it.
What, it runs on nothing?
Near as. Ten years ago, this guy called Binder released some papers on zero point energy, and...
...okay, short version is I made an engine that makes a vacuum that sucks energy out of the universe. How's that?
The only actual fuel in there is an electric starter battery I built.
And a vacuum cleaner, right?
How'd you know?
Reed, you are so weird.

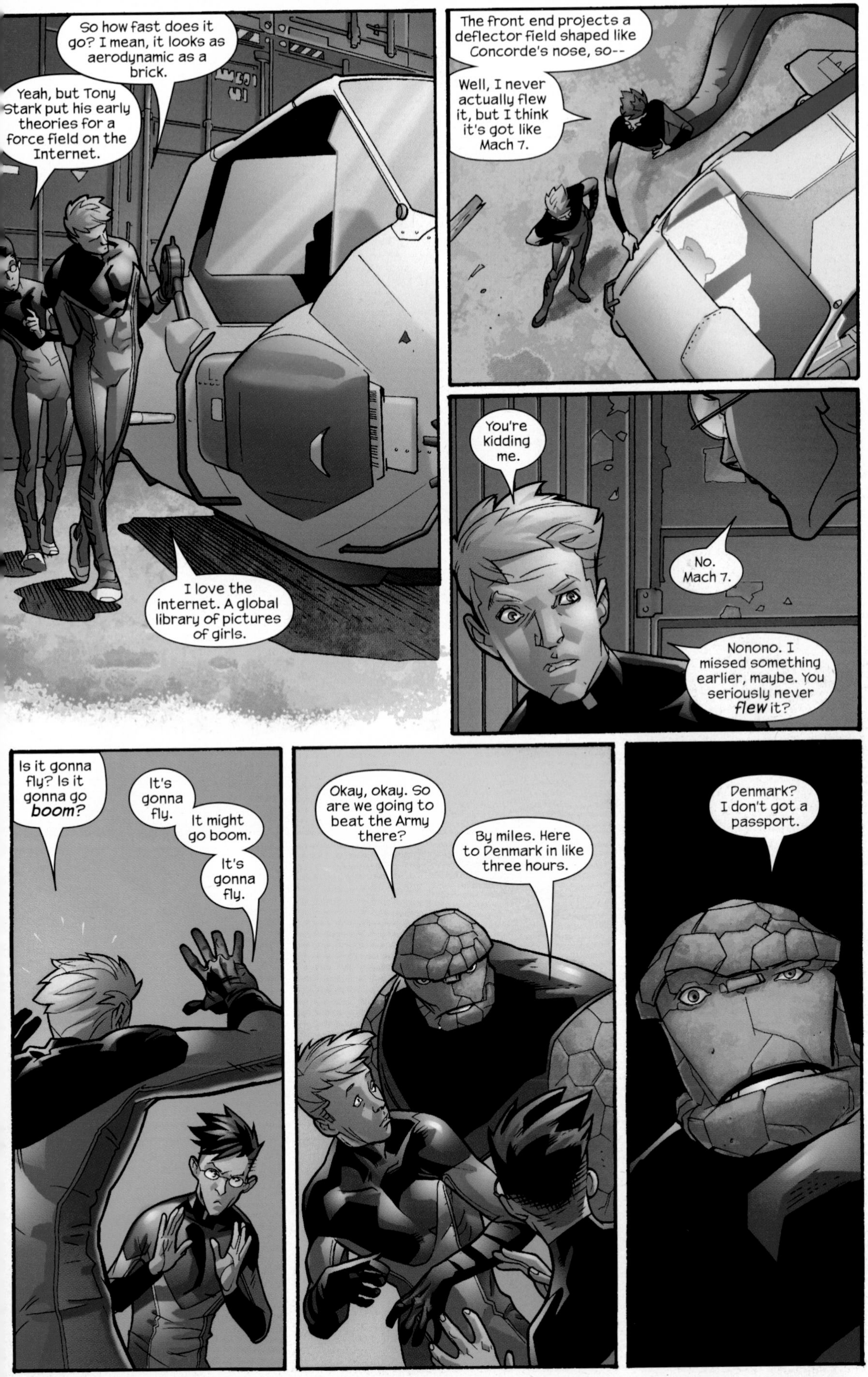
So how fast does it go? I mean, it looks as aerodynamic as a brick.
Yeah, but Tony Stark put his early theories for a force field on the Internet.
I love the internet. A global library of pictures of girls.
The front end projects a deflector field shaped like Concorde's nose, so--
Well, I never actually flew it, but I think it's got like Mach 7.
You're kidding me.
No. Mach 7.
Nonono. I missed something earlier, maybe. You seriously never *flew* it?
Is it gonna fly? Is it gonna go *boom*?
It's gonna fly.
It might go boom.
It's gonna fly.
Okay, okay. So are we going to beat the Army there?
By miles. Here to Denmark in like three hours.
Denmark? I don't got a passport.

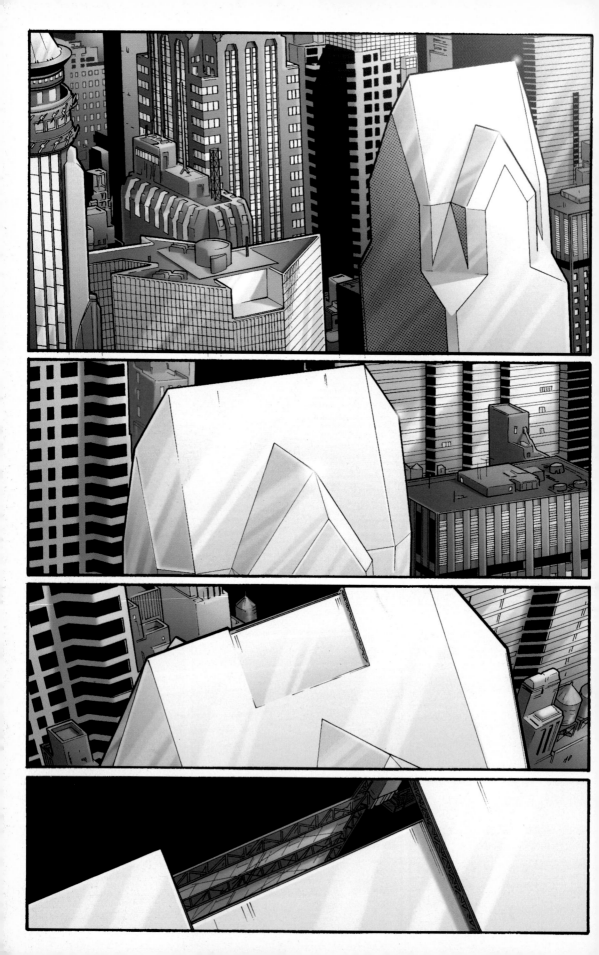

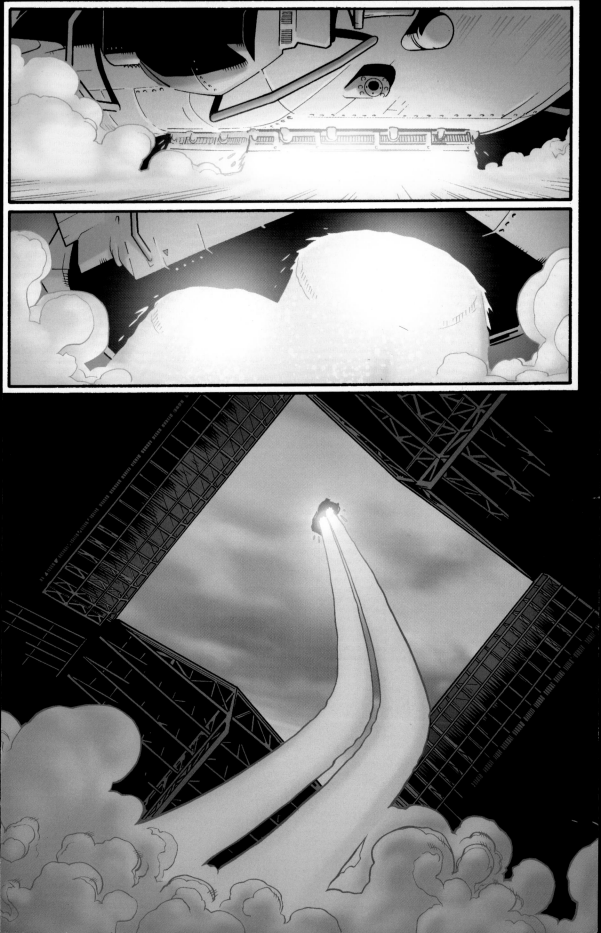

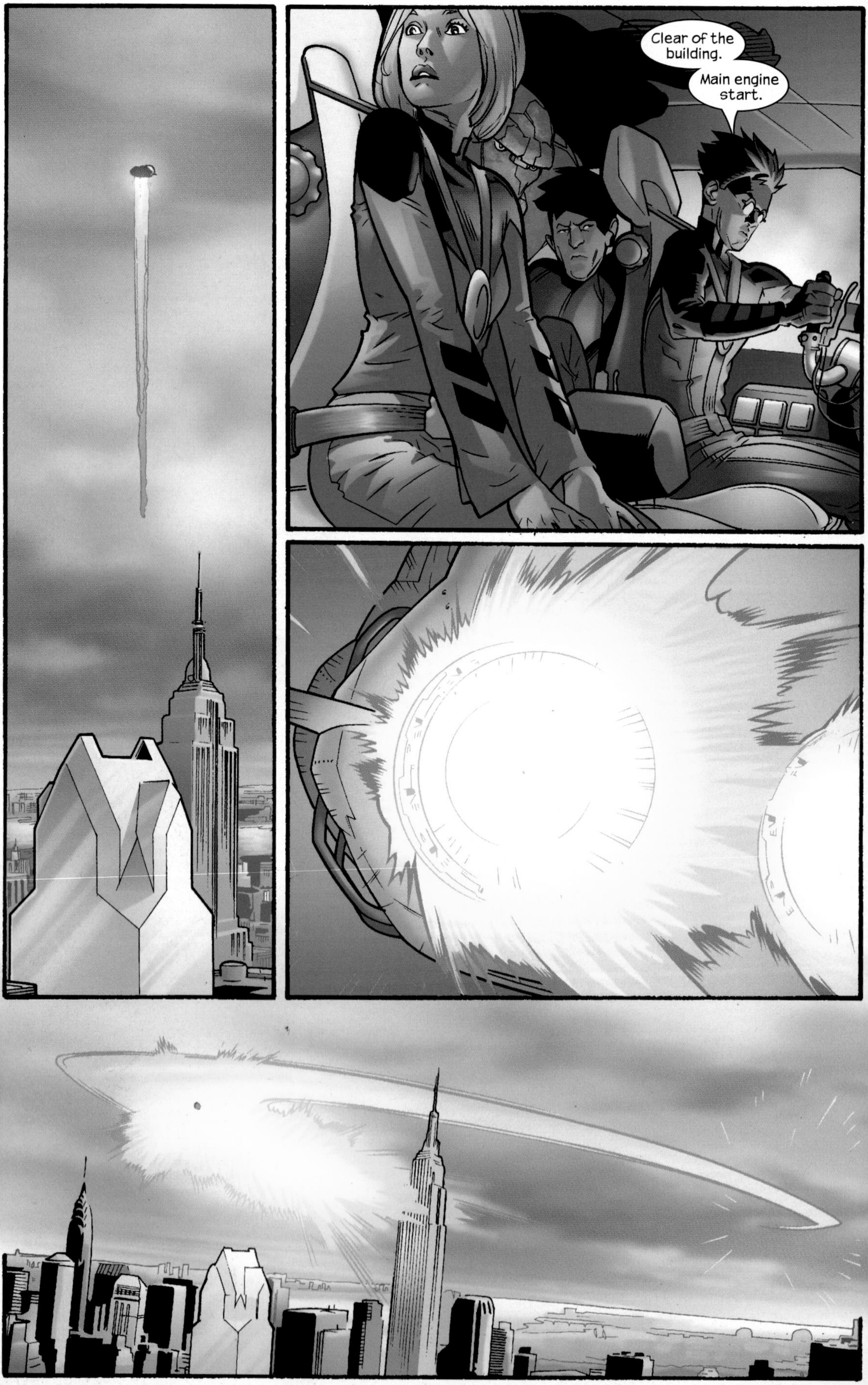
Clear of the building.
Main engine start.

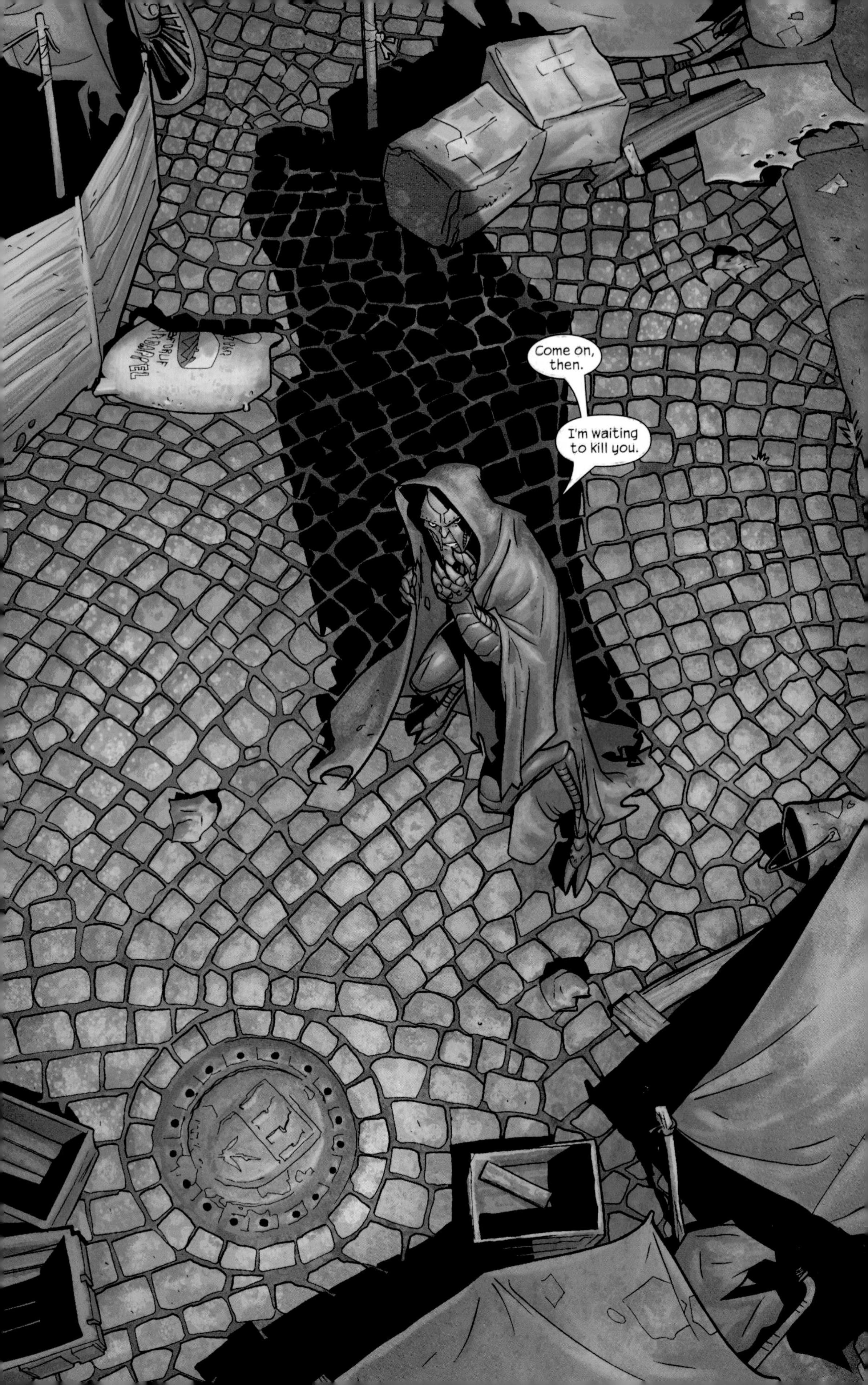
Come on, then.
I'm waiting to kill you.

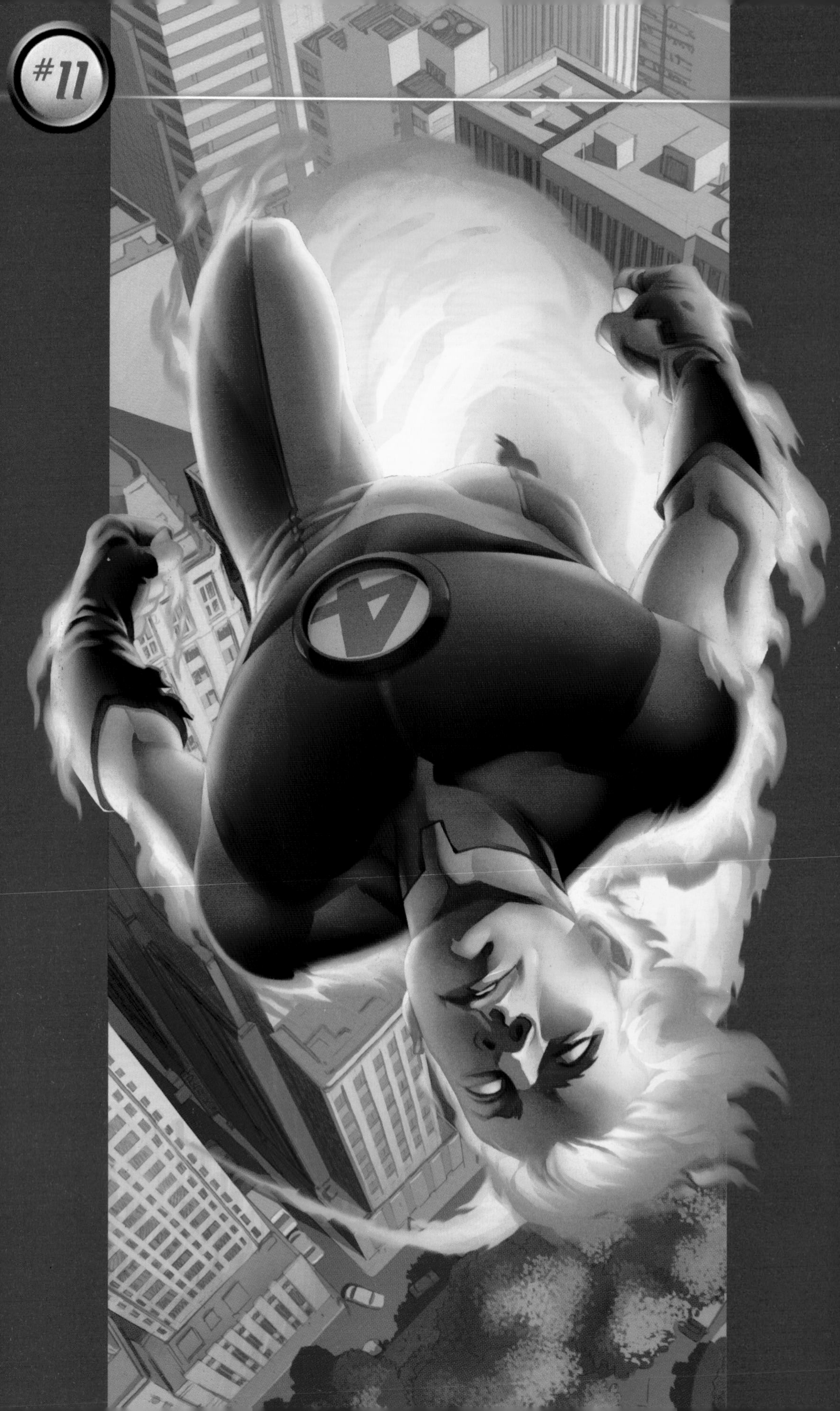
#11

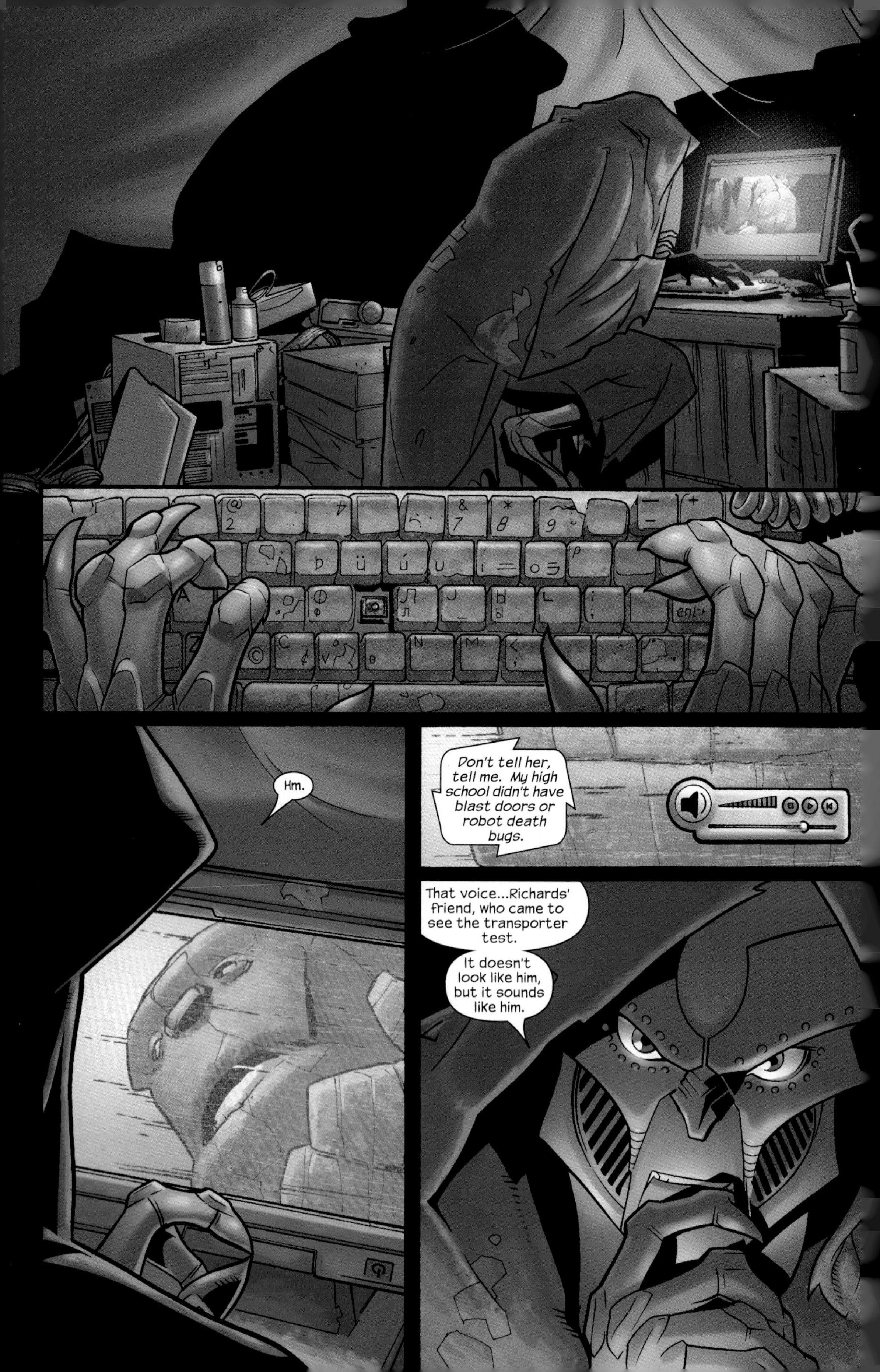
Hm.
Don't tell her, tell me. My high school didn't have blast doors or robot death bugs.
That voice...Richards' friend, who came to see the transporter test.
It doesn't look like him, but it sounds like him.

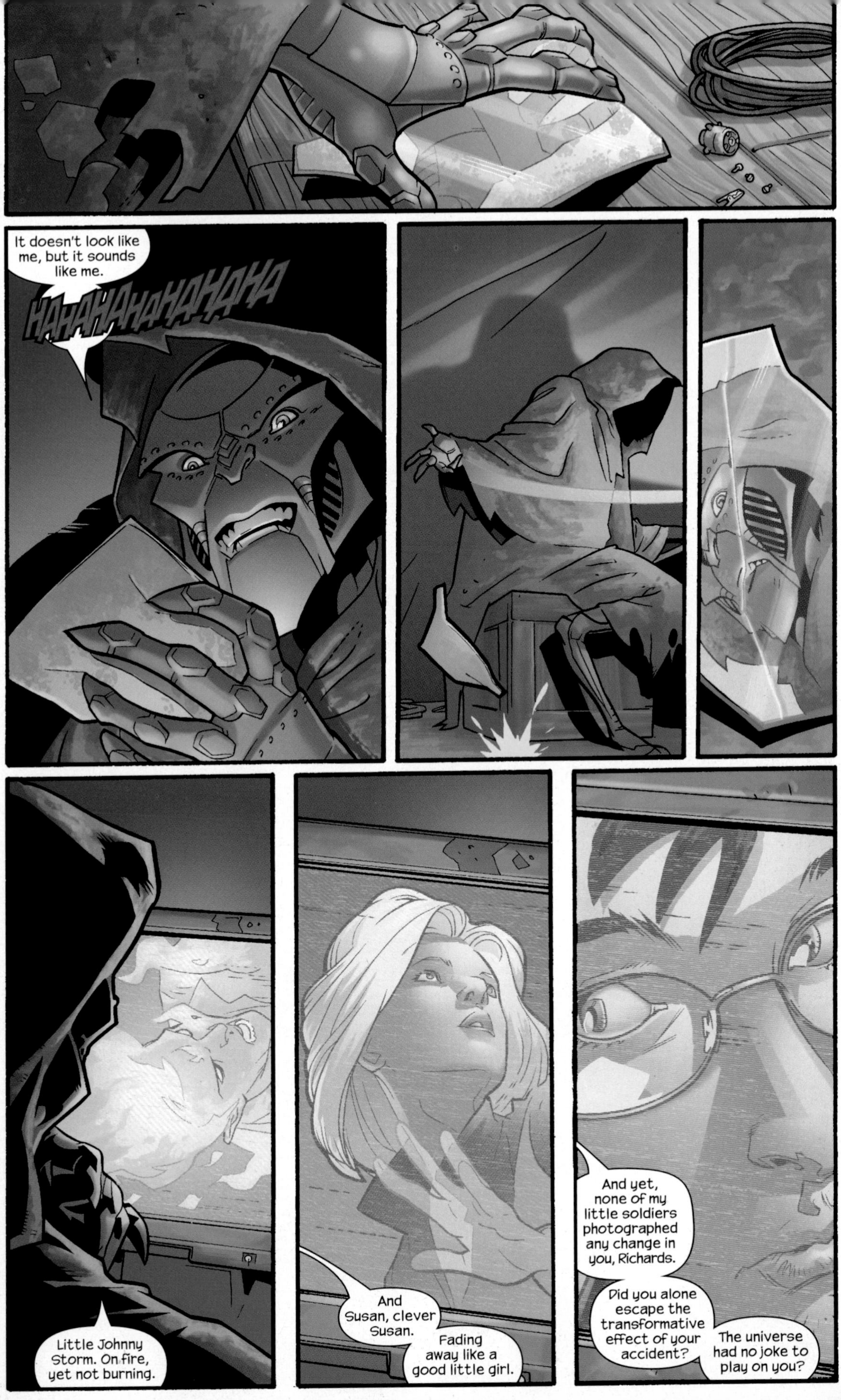
It doesn't look like me, but it sounds like me.
HAHAHAHAHAHAHAHA
Little Johnny Storm. On fire, yet not burning.
And Susan, clever Susan.
Fading away like a good little girl.
And yet, none of my little soldiers photographed any change in you, Richards.
Did you alone escape the transformative effect of your accident?
The universe had no joke to play on you?

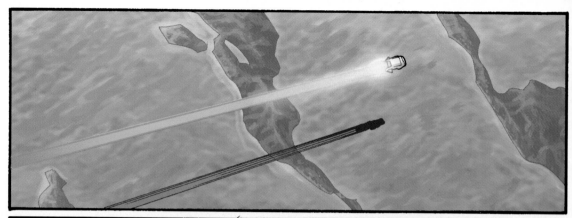

Are we there yet?

Another hour.

Hey.

What?

I think I see something down there, in the ocean.

From all the way up here?

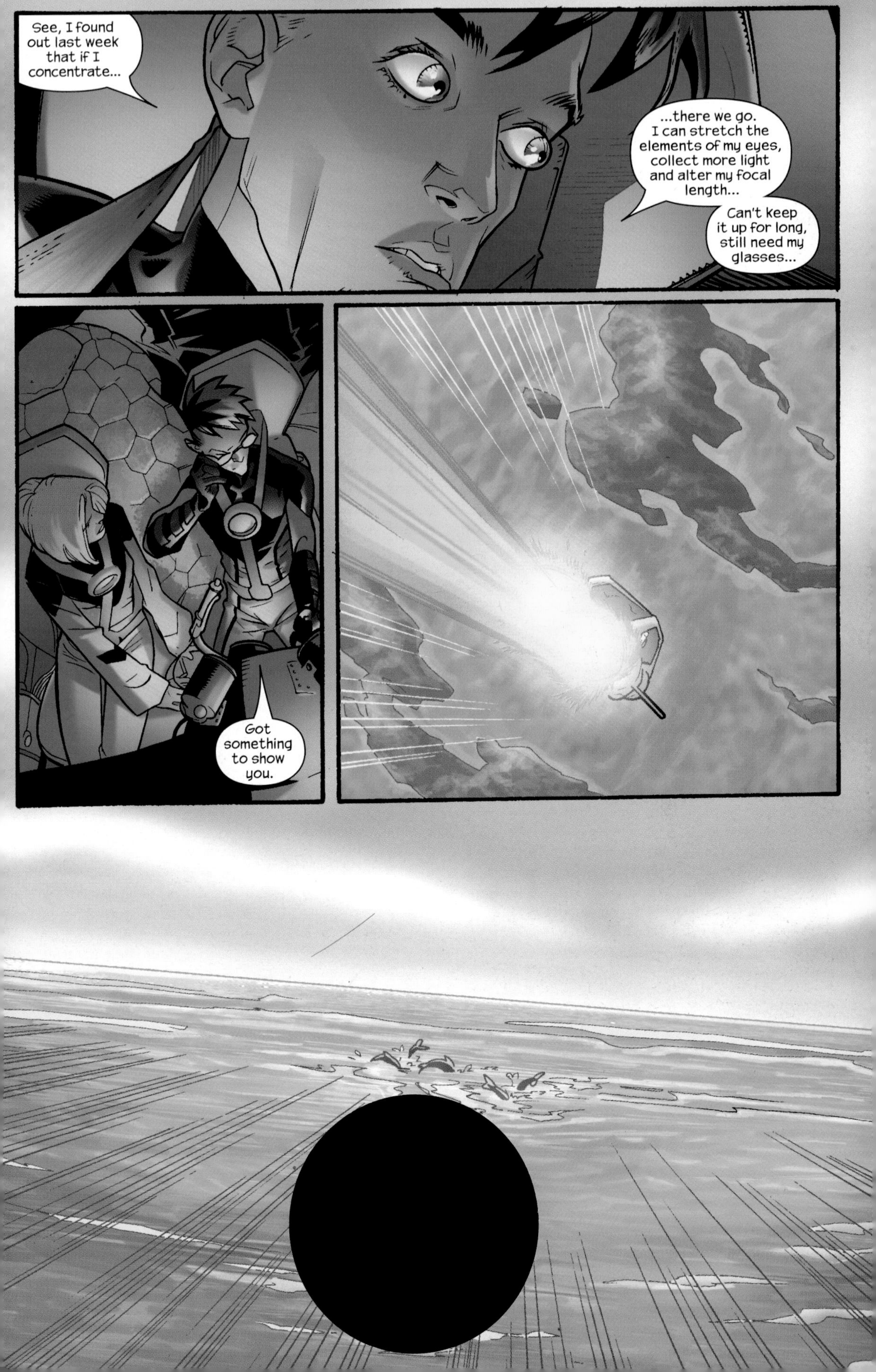
See, I found out last week that if I concentrate...
...there we go. I can stretch the elements of my eyes, collect more light and alter my focal length...
Can't keep it up for long, still need my glasses...
Got something to show you.

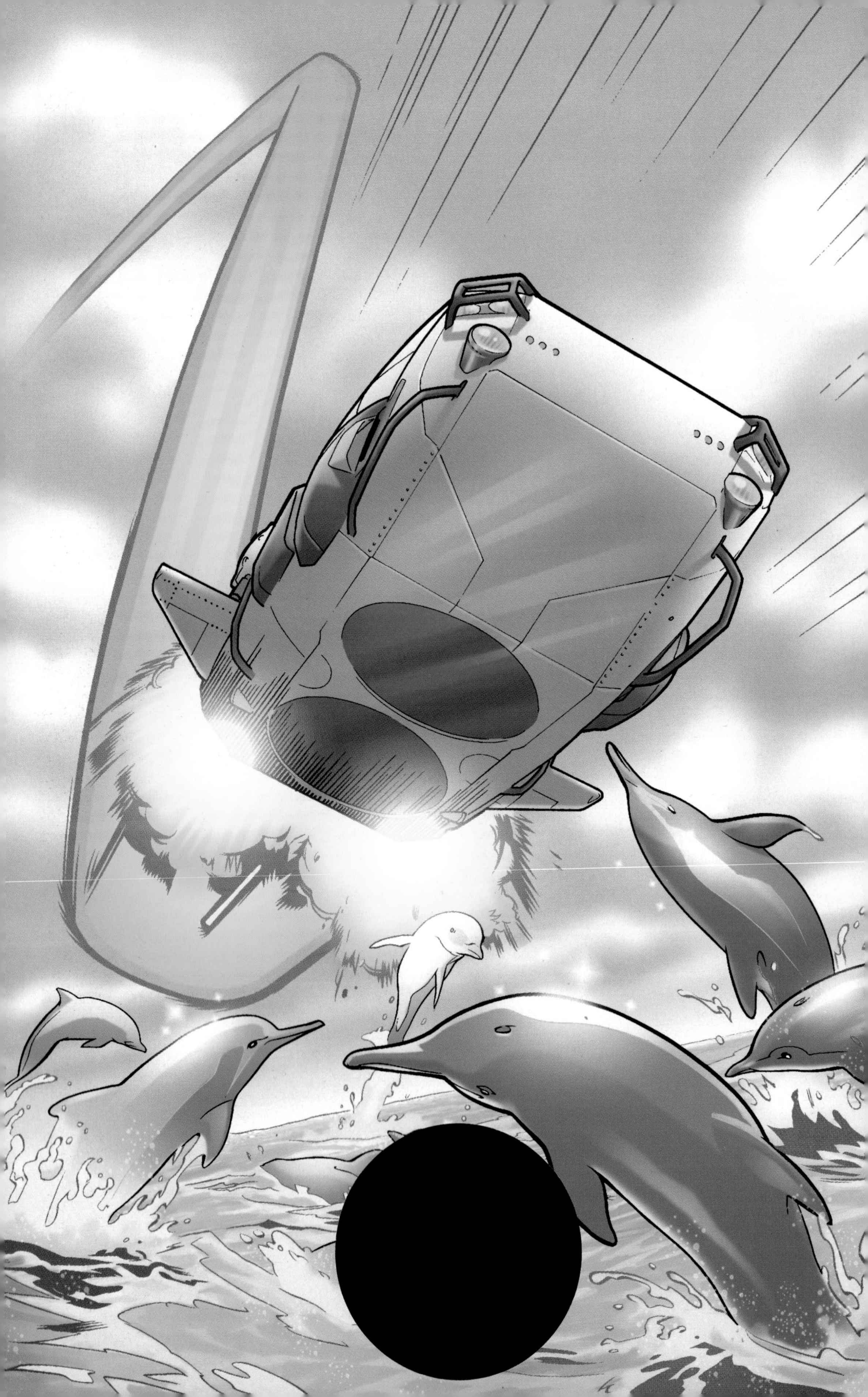

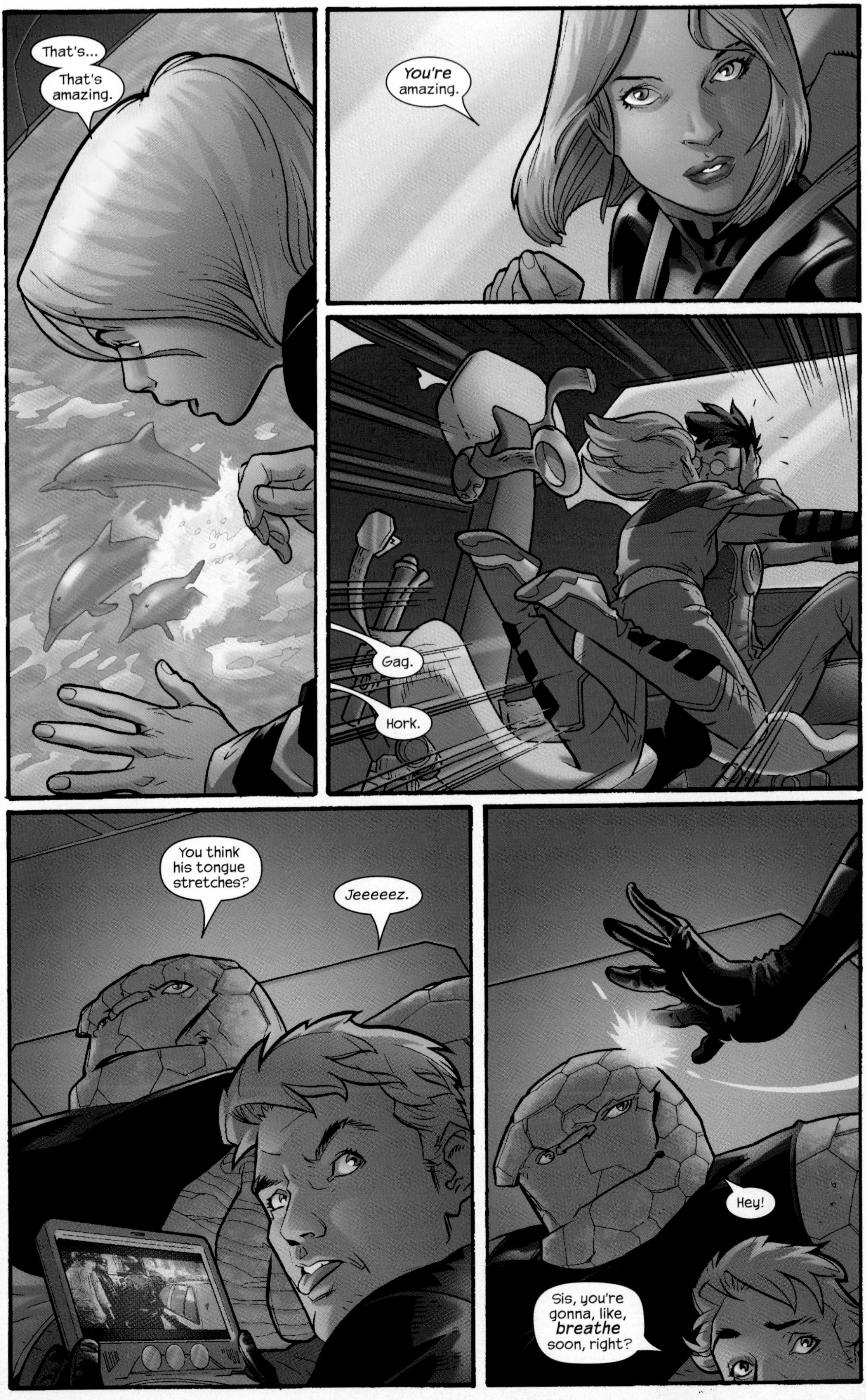
That's...
That's amazing.
You're amazing.
Gag.
Hork.
You think his tongue stretches?
Jeeeeez.
Hey!
Sis, you're gonna, like, breathe soon, right?

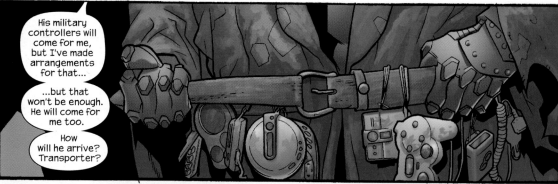

His military controllers will come for me, but I've made arrangements for that...

...but that won't be enough. He will come for me too.

How will he arrive? Transporter?

Surely he wouldn't risk that yet.

But he *will* want to speak with me before the Army arrives.

Alternative transportation?

Good evening.

No. It's a bad evening. Trouble comes.

Mr. Van Damme?

Trouble comes. From abroad. People want to take me away.

No. Who would want to do that?

Americans.

Soldiers.

Why?

Because of what I've done. The crimes I've committed.

The crime of creating ways of giving you free food, free water and free power.

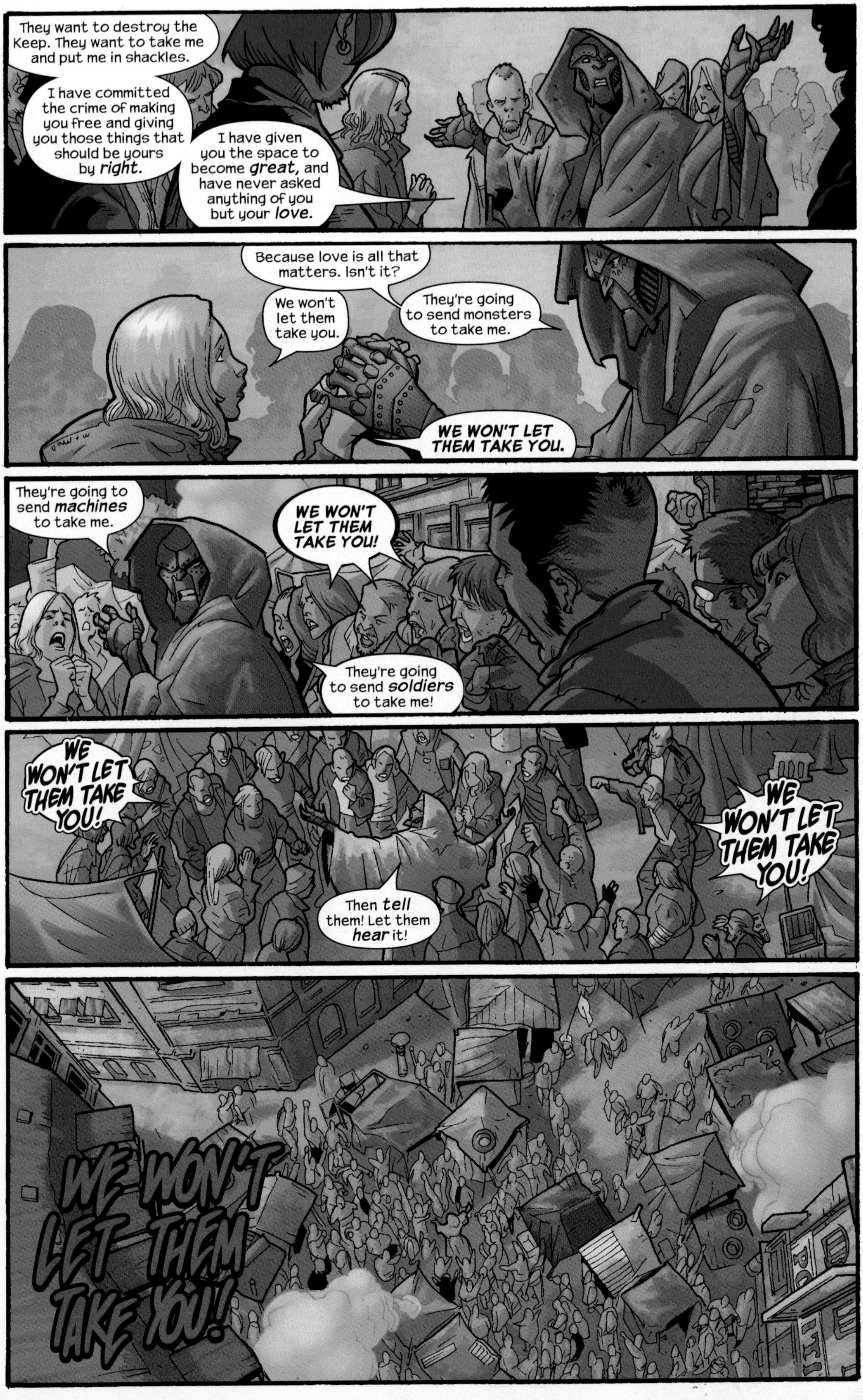
They want to destroy the Keep. They want to take me and put me in shackles.
I have committed the crime of making you free and giving you those things that should be yours by *right*.
I have given you the space to become *great*, and have never asked anything of you but your *love*.
Because love is all that matters. Isn't it?
We won't let them take you.
They're going to send monsters to take me.
WE WON'T LET THEM TAKE YOU.
They're going to send *machines* to take me.
WE WON'T LET THEM TAKE YOU!
They're going to send *soldiers* to take me!
WE WON'T LET THEM TAKE YOU!
WE WON'T LET THEM TAKE YOU!
Then *tell* them! Let them *hear* it!
WE WON'T LET THEM TAKE YOU!

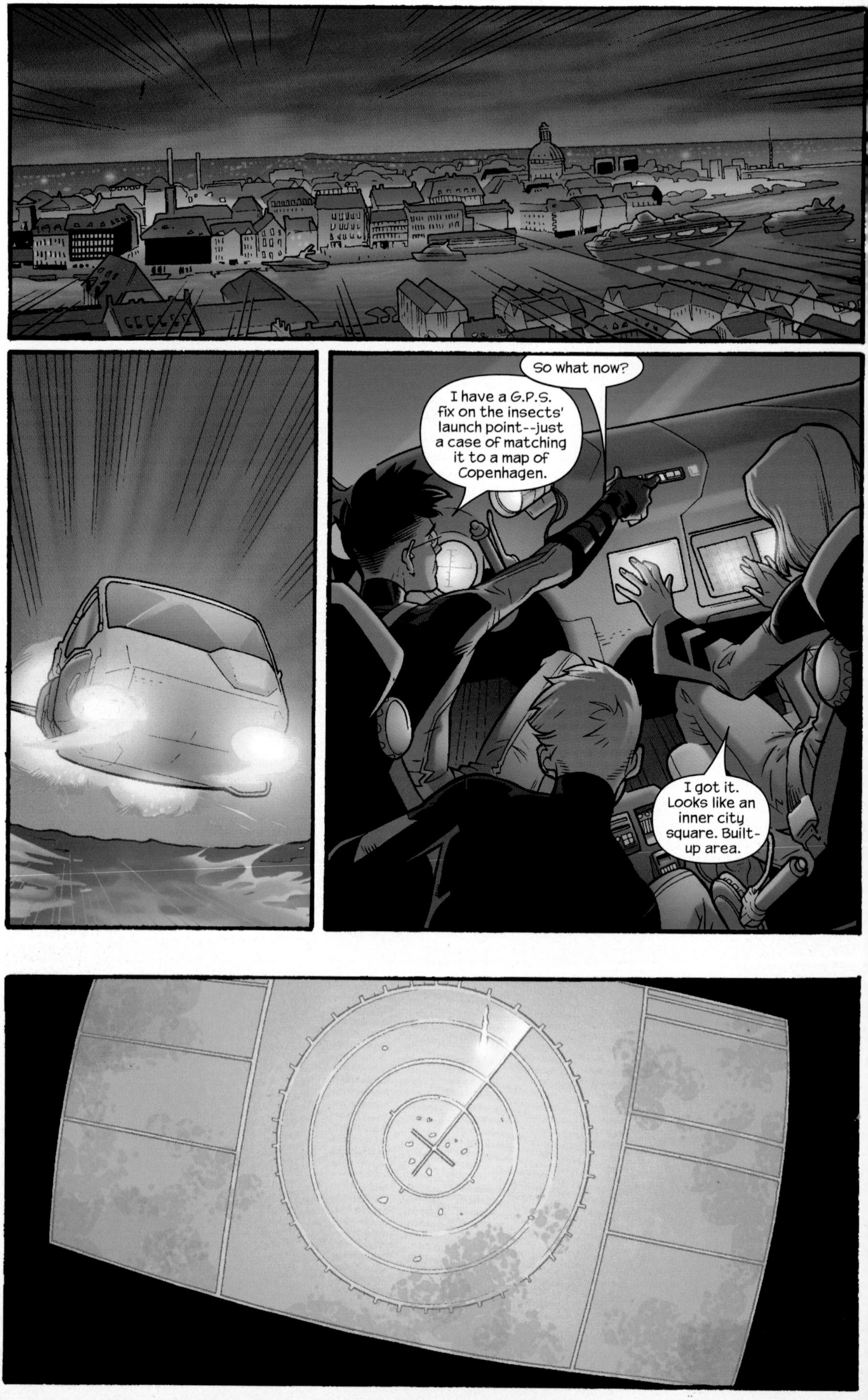
So what now?
I have a G.P.S. fix on the insects' launch point--just a case of matching it to a map of Copenhagen.
I got it. Looks like an inner city square. Built-up area.

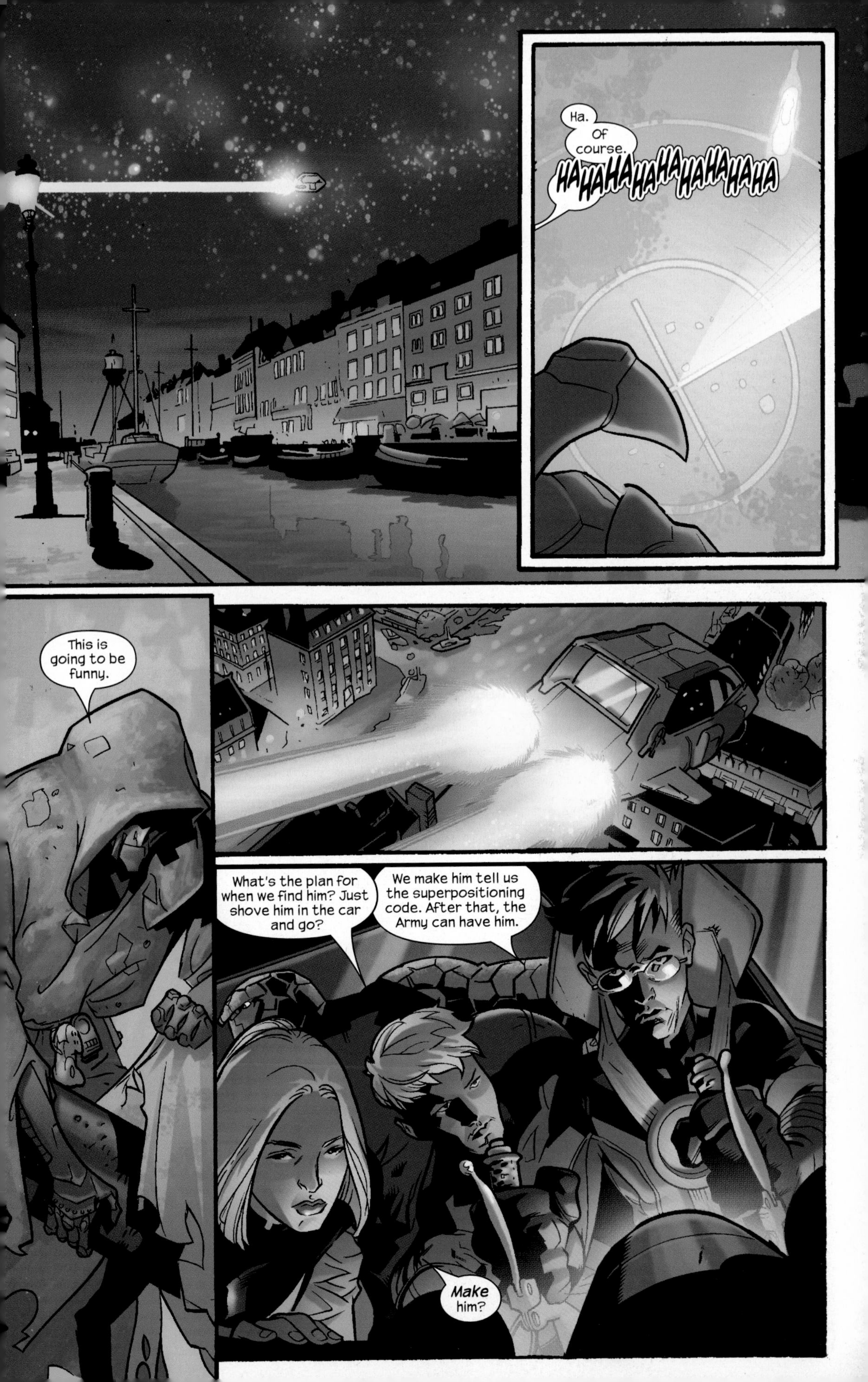
Ha.
Of course.
HAHAHAHAHAHAHAHAHAHA
This is going to be funny.
What's the plan for when we find him? Just shove him in the car and go?
We make him tell us the superpositioning code. After that, the Army can have him.
Make him?

Yeah, I know what that sounds like.

And I don't care.

We *make* him tell us the code. I'm not jerking around with this.

Yes.

Who else but you, Richards, would travel across the Atlantic in a flying toy car?

I'm not saying you're wrong, Reed, I'm just saying--

Yeah, okay. There it is. That's the launch point.

Looks like someone's built a shantytown on it...

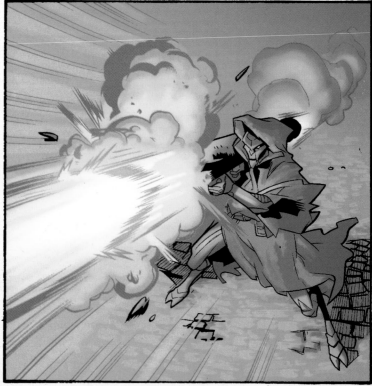

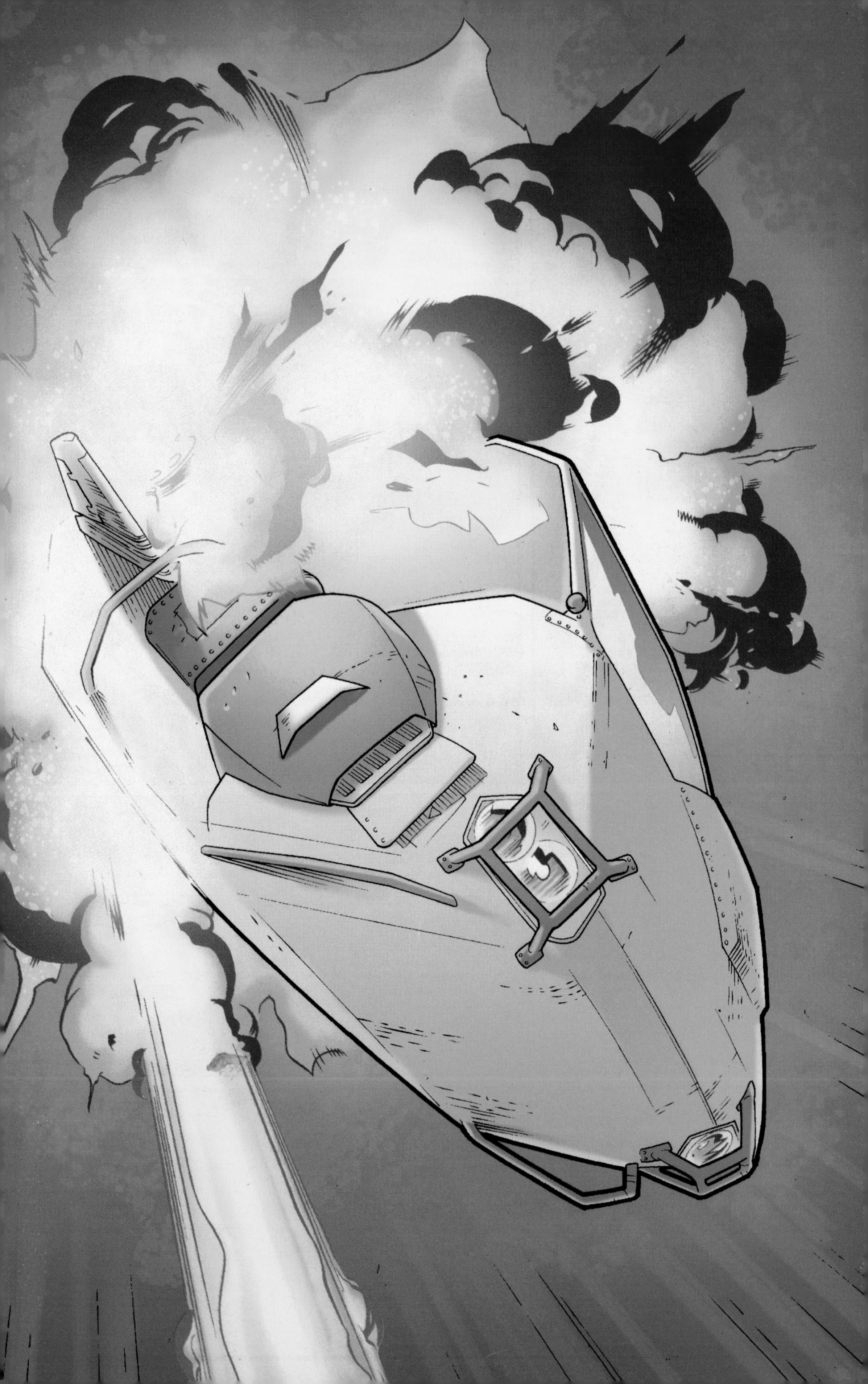

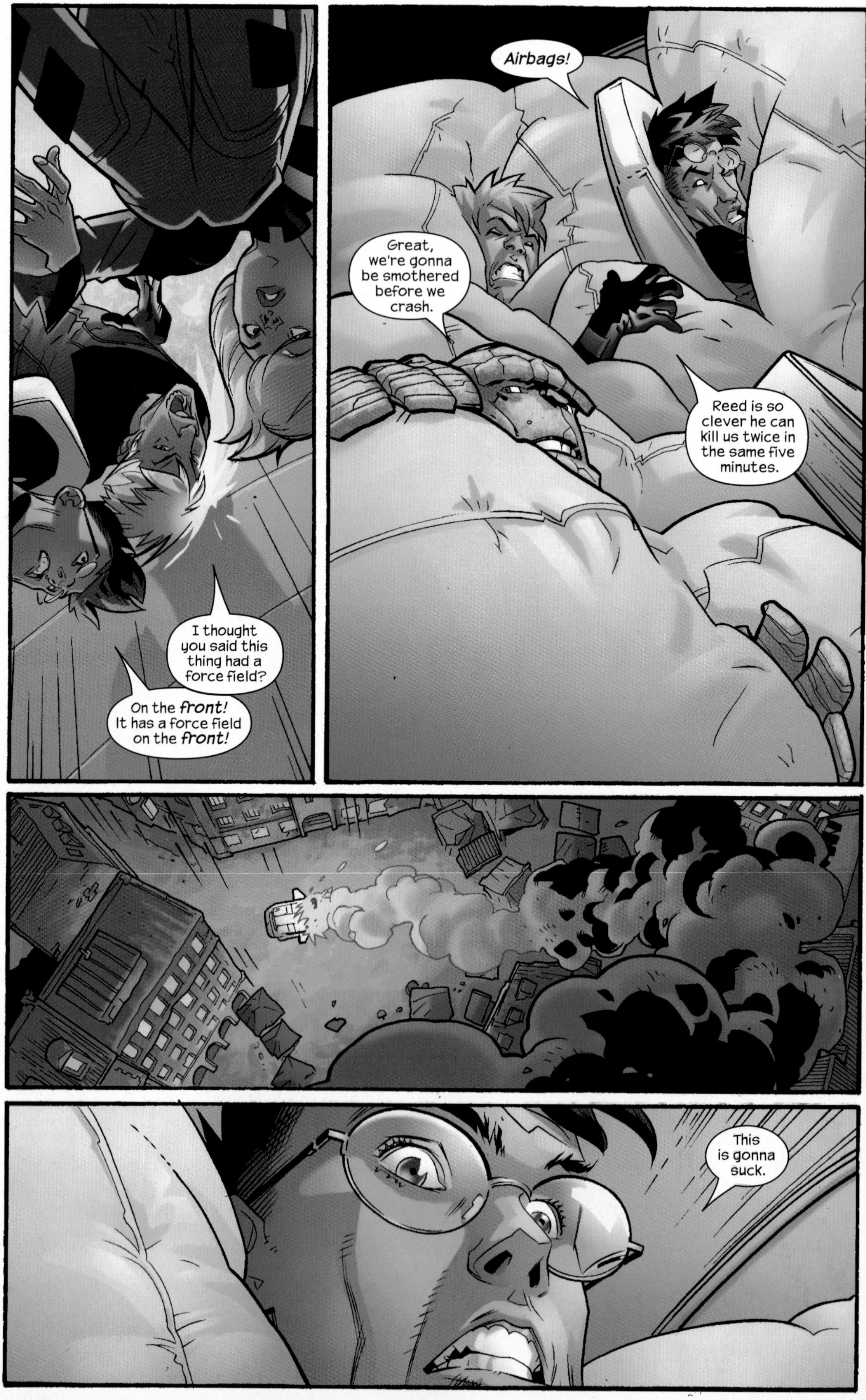
I thought you said this thing had a force field?
On the *front!* It has a force field on the *front!*
Airbags!
Great, we're gonna be smothered before we crash.
Reed is so clever he can kill us twice in the same five minutes.
This is gonna suck.

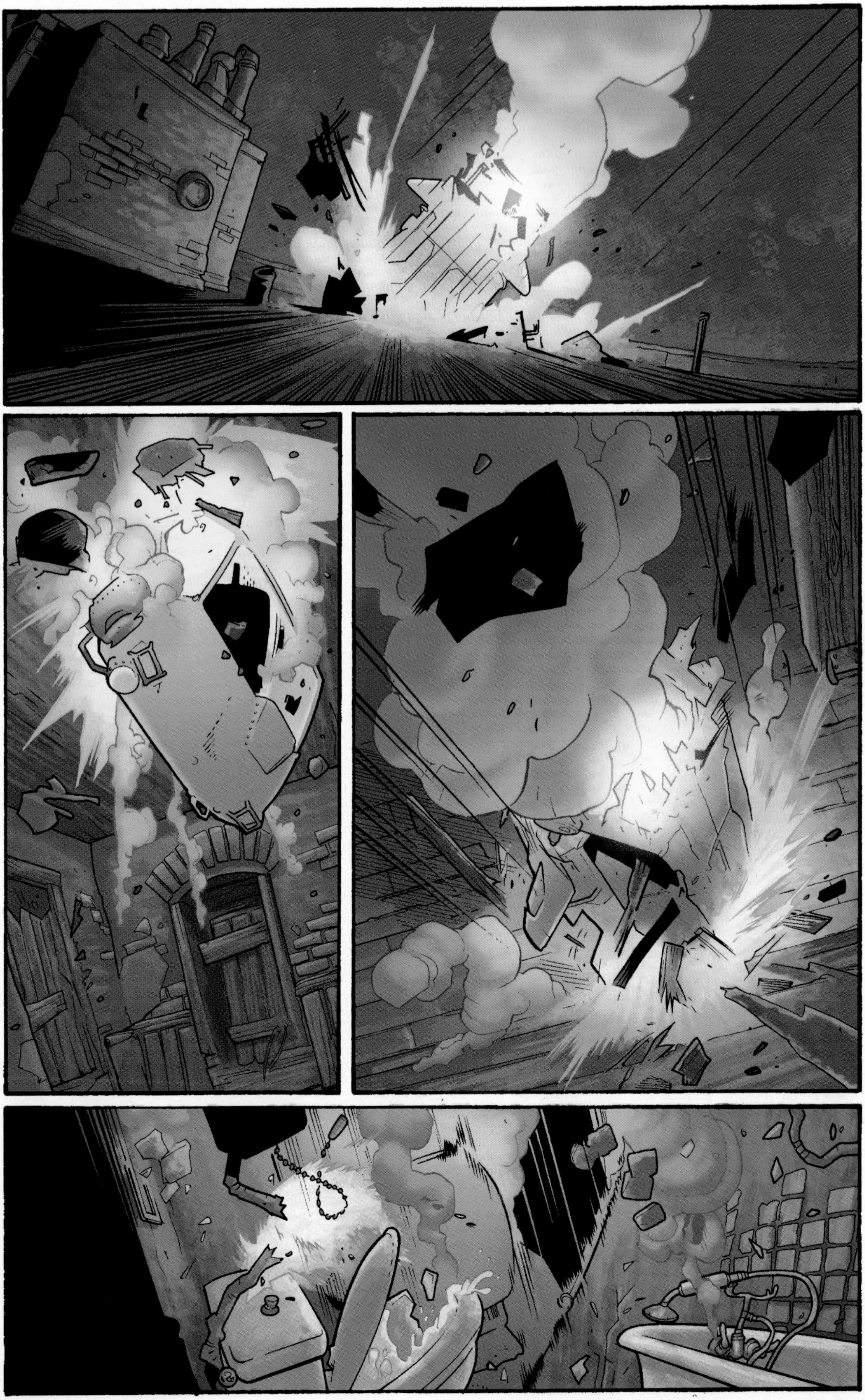

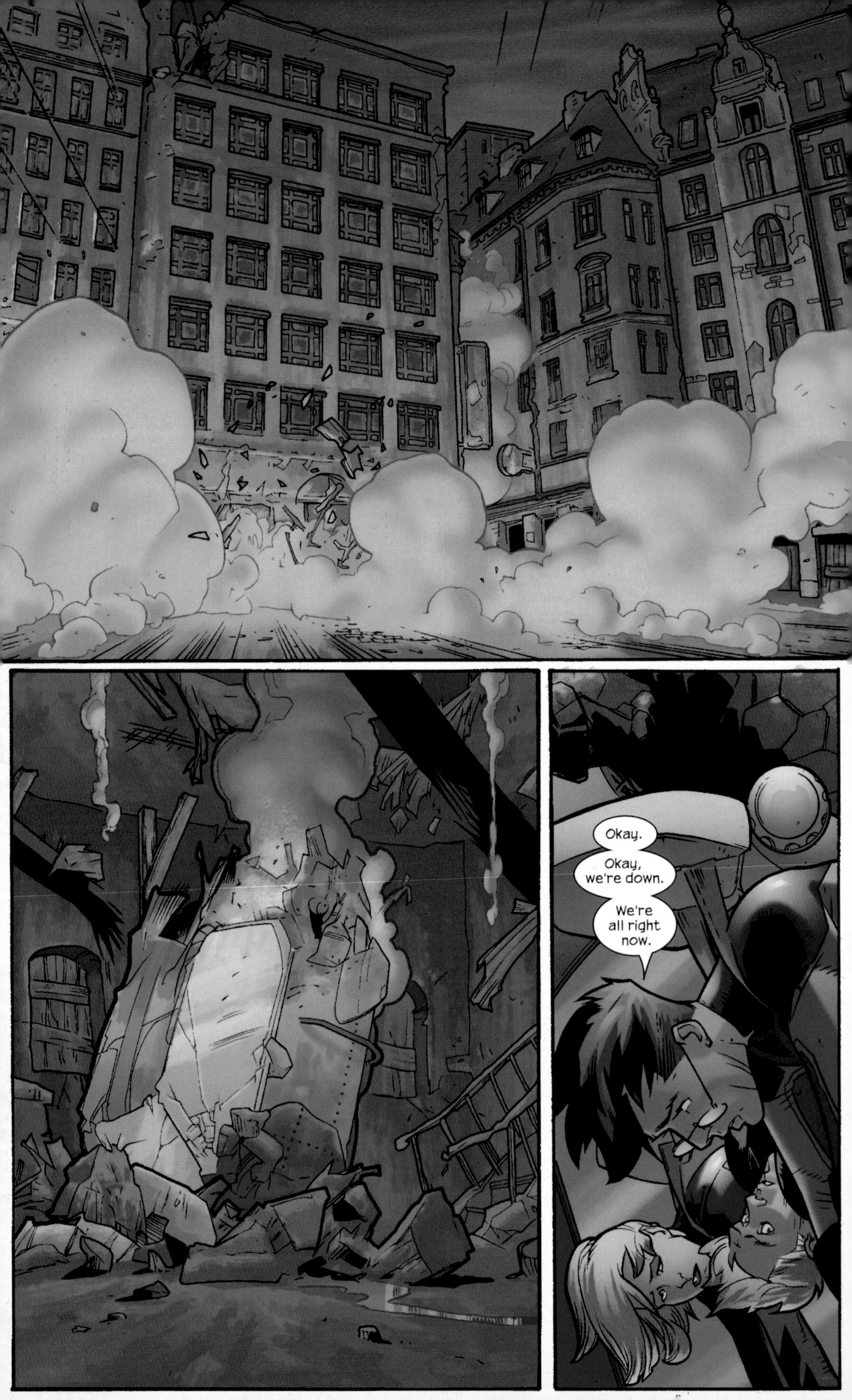
Okay.
Okay, we're down.
We're all right now.

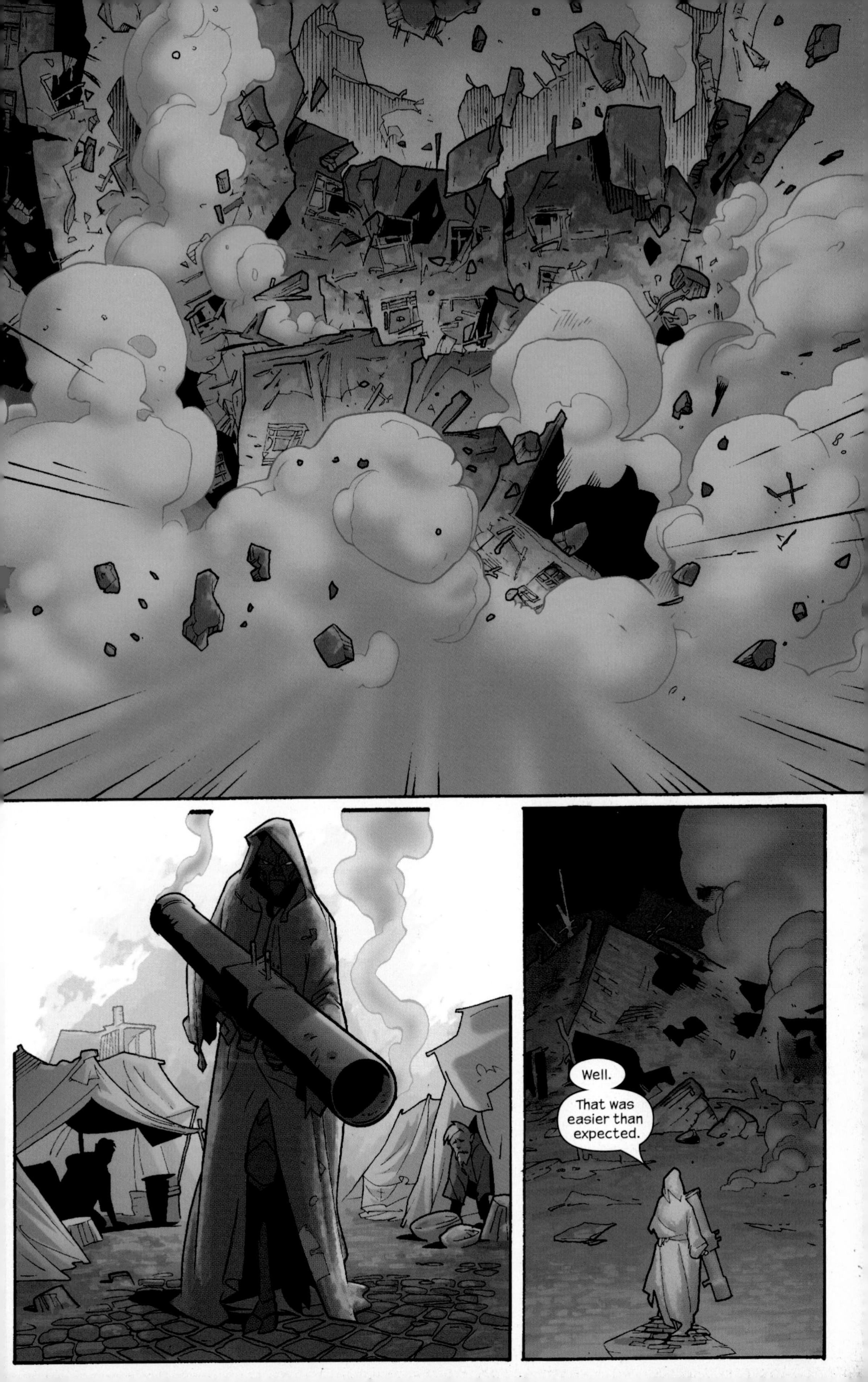
Well.
That was easier than expected.

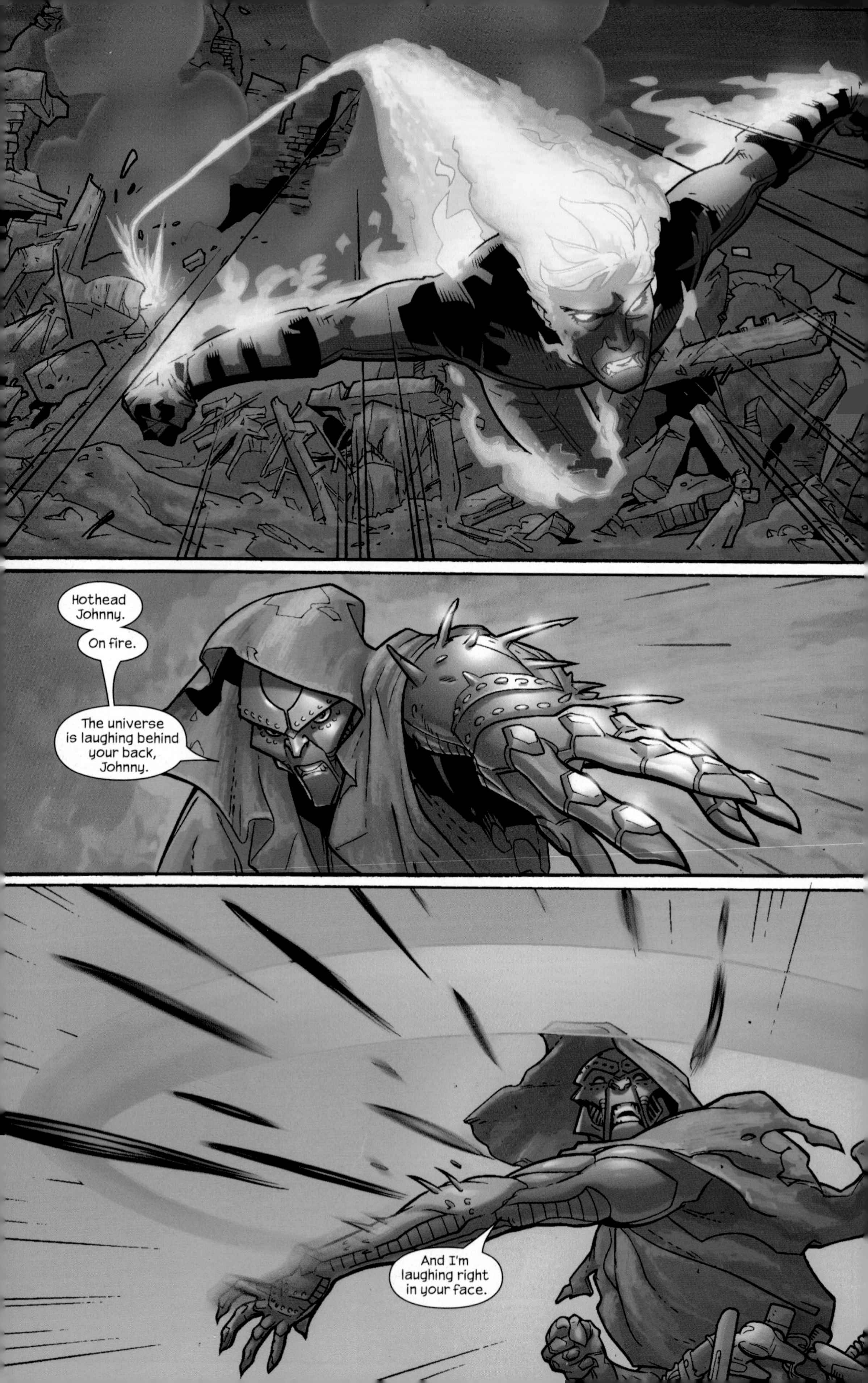
Hothead Johnny.
On fire.
The universe is laughing behind your back, Johnny.
And I'm laughing right in your face.

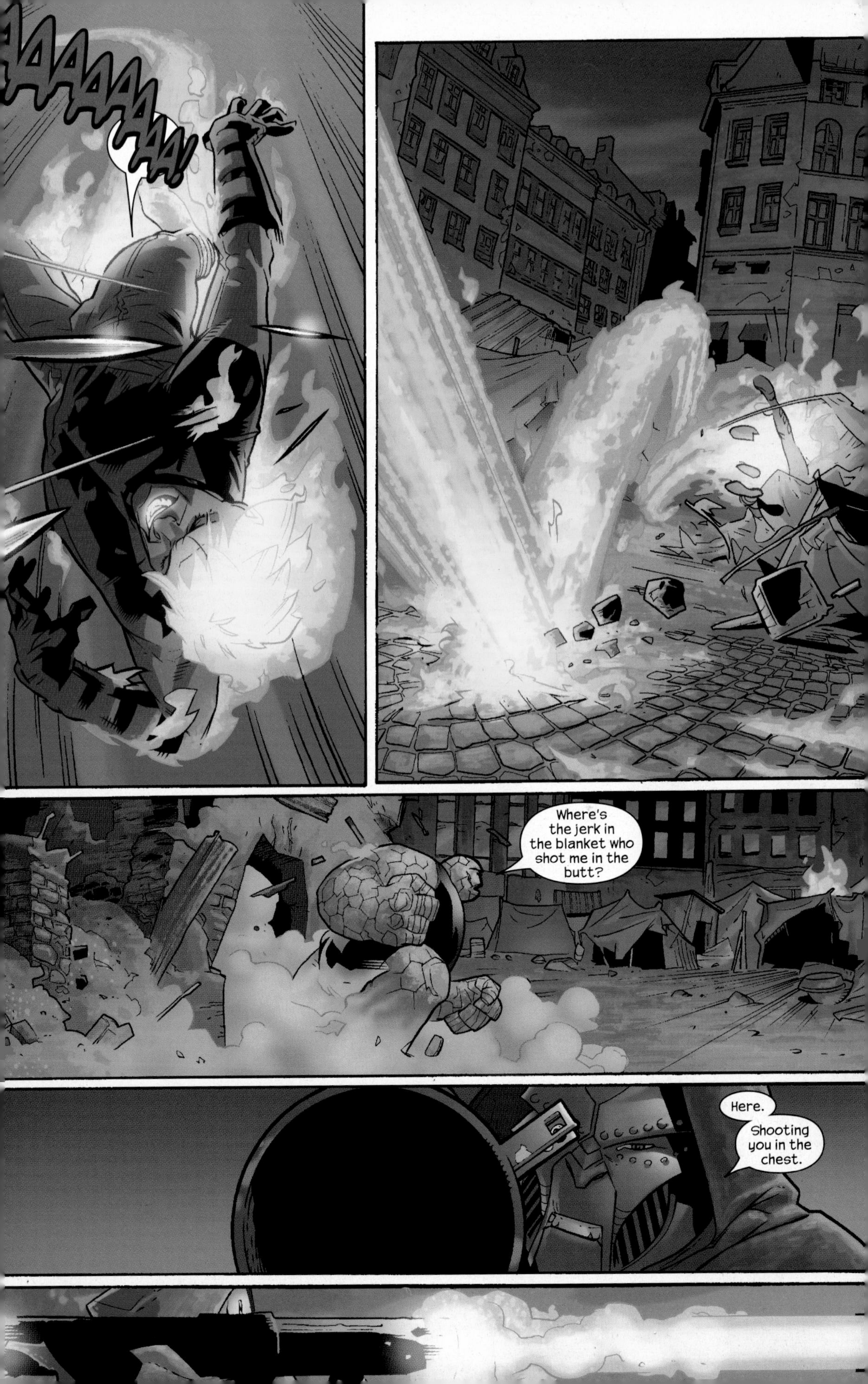
AAAAAAAAAA!
Where's the jerk in the blanket who shot me in the butt?
Here.
Shooting you in the chest.

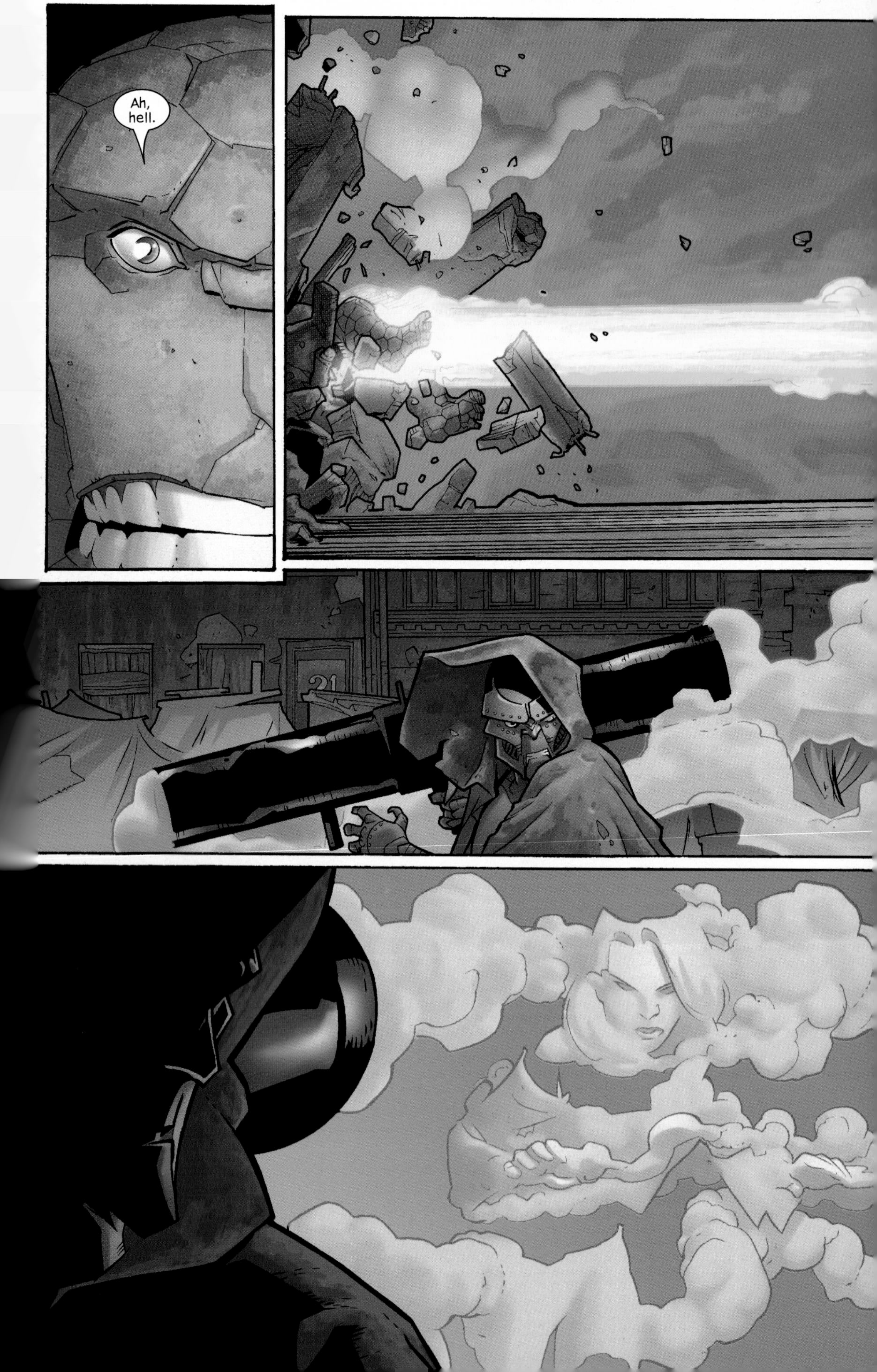
Ah, hell.

If that's you, Victor--

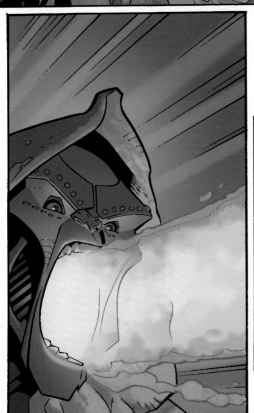

COUGH What the--

HHHKKGGHHH

I'm not sure myself.

I seem to be converting the remains of my internal organs into poison, Susan.

Could that be possible?

Perhaps if you took a deep breath, you could identify the poison for me.

You'll have to think fast. It works quite quickly.

And it is so painful that the victims break their own backs in the final convulsions.

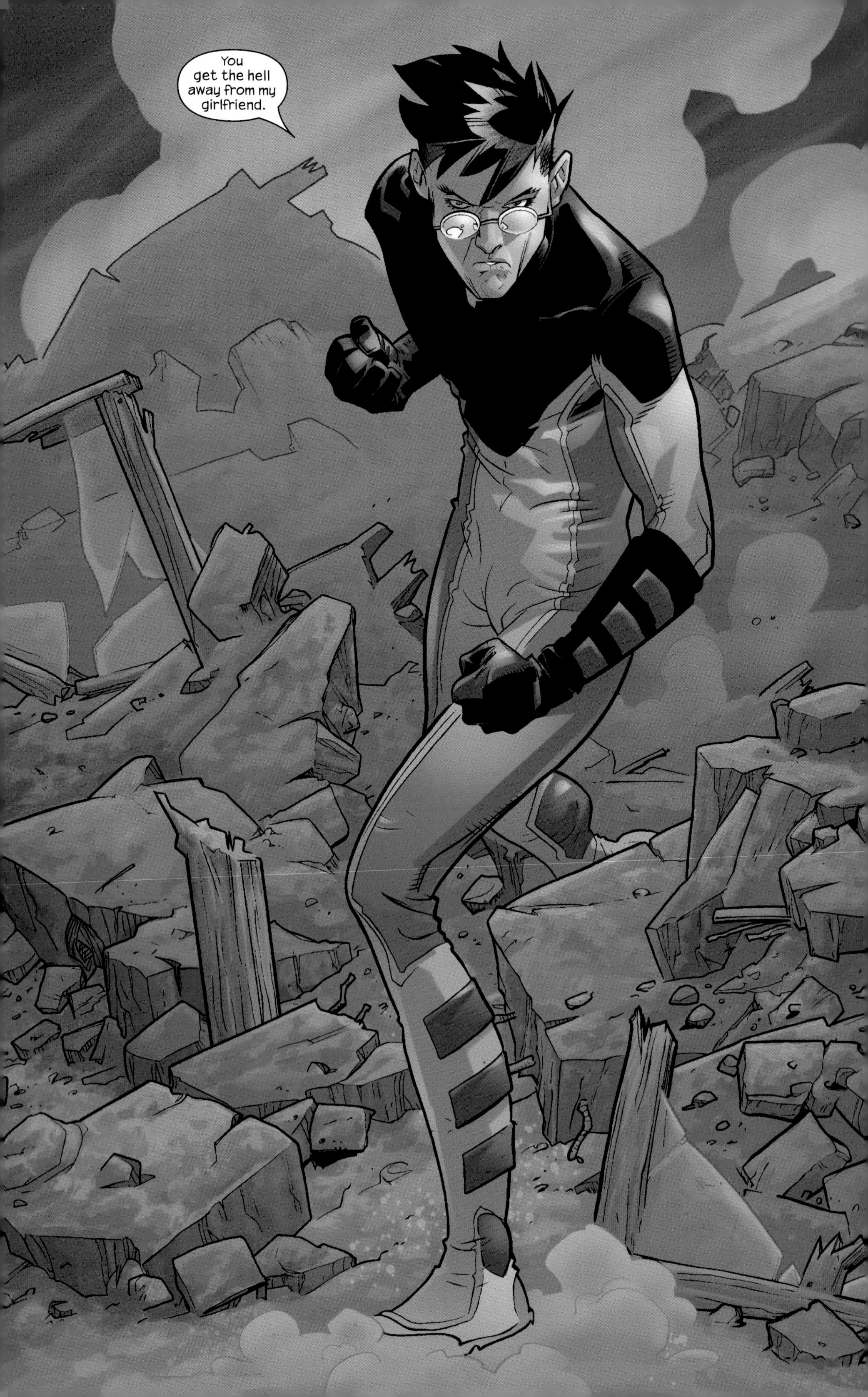
You get the hell away from my girlfriend.

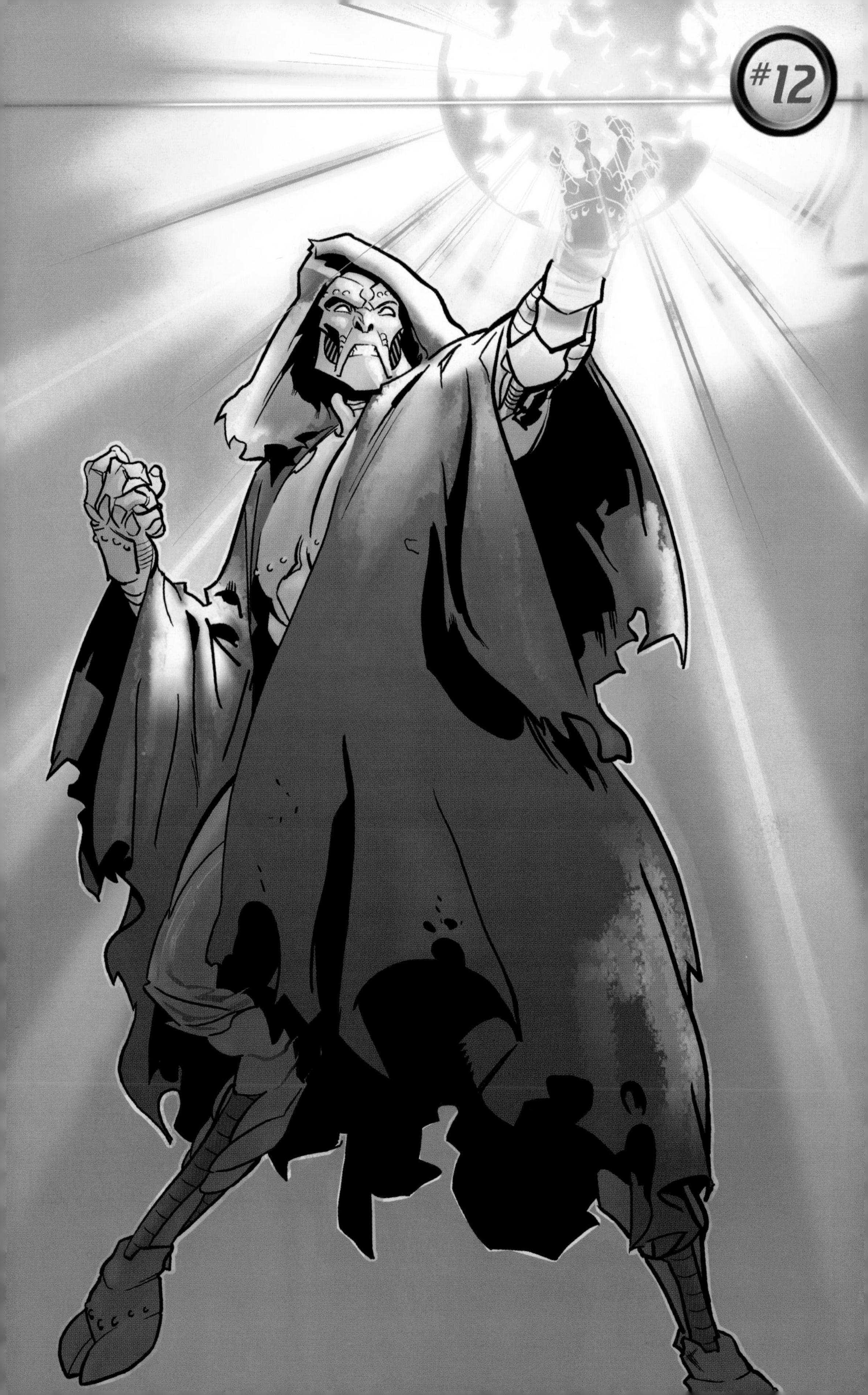
#12

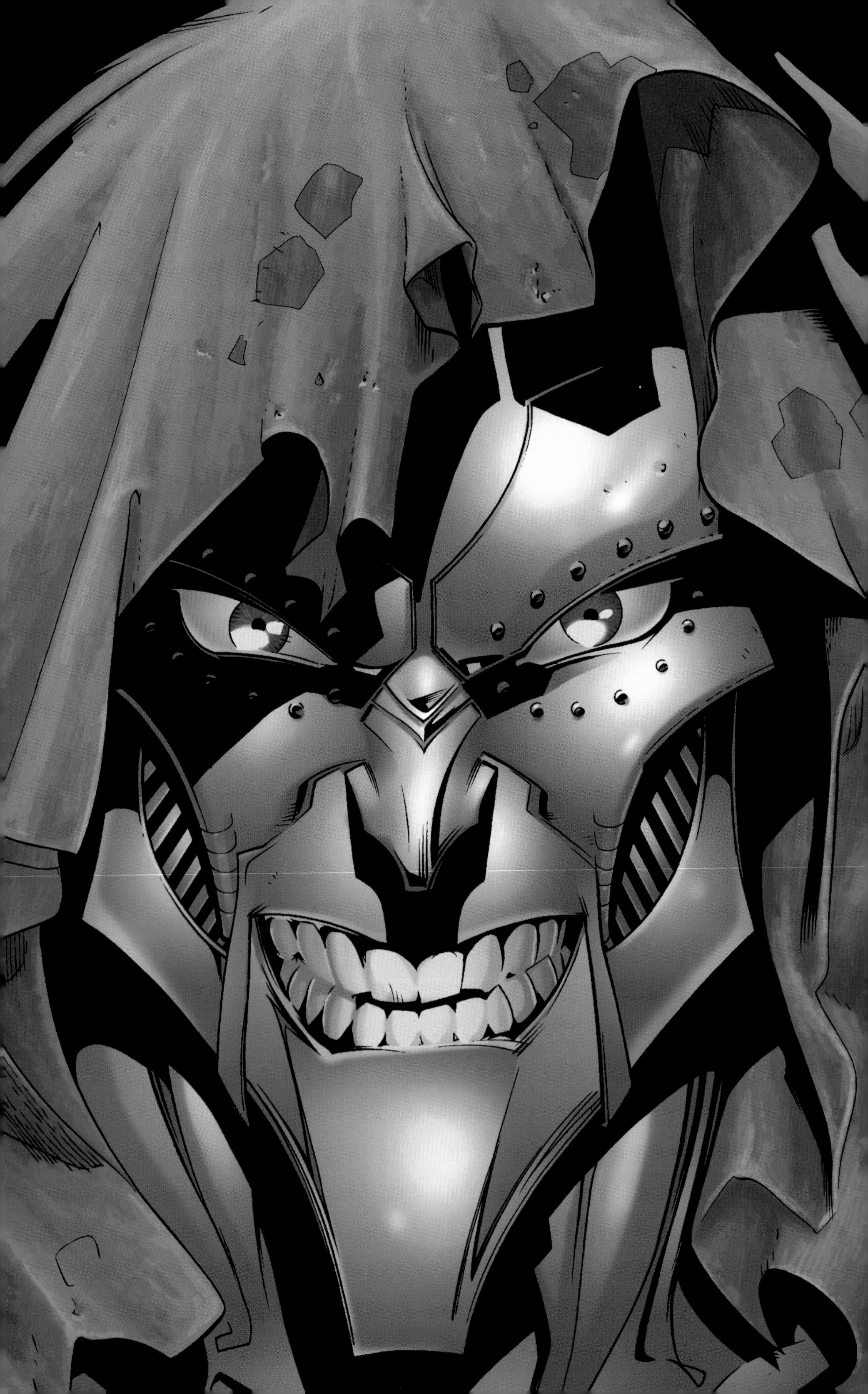

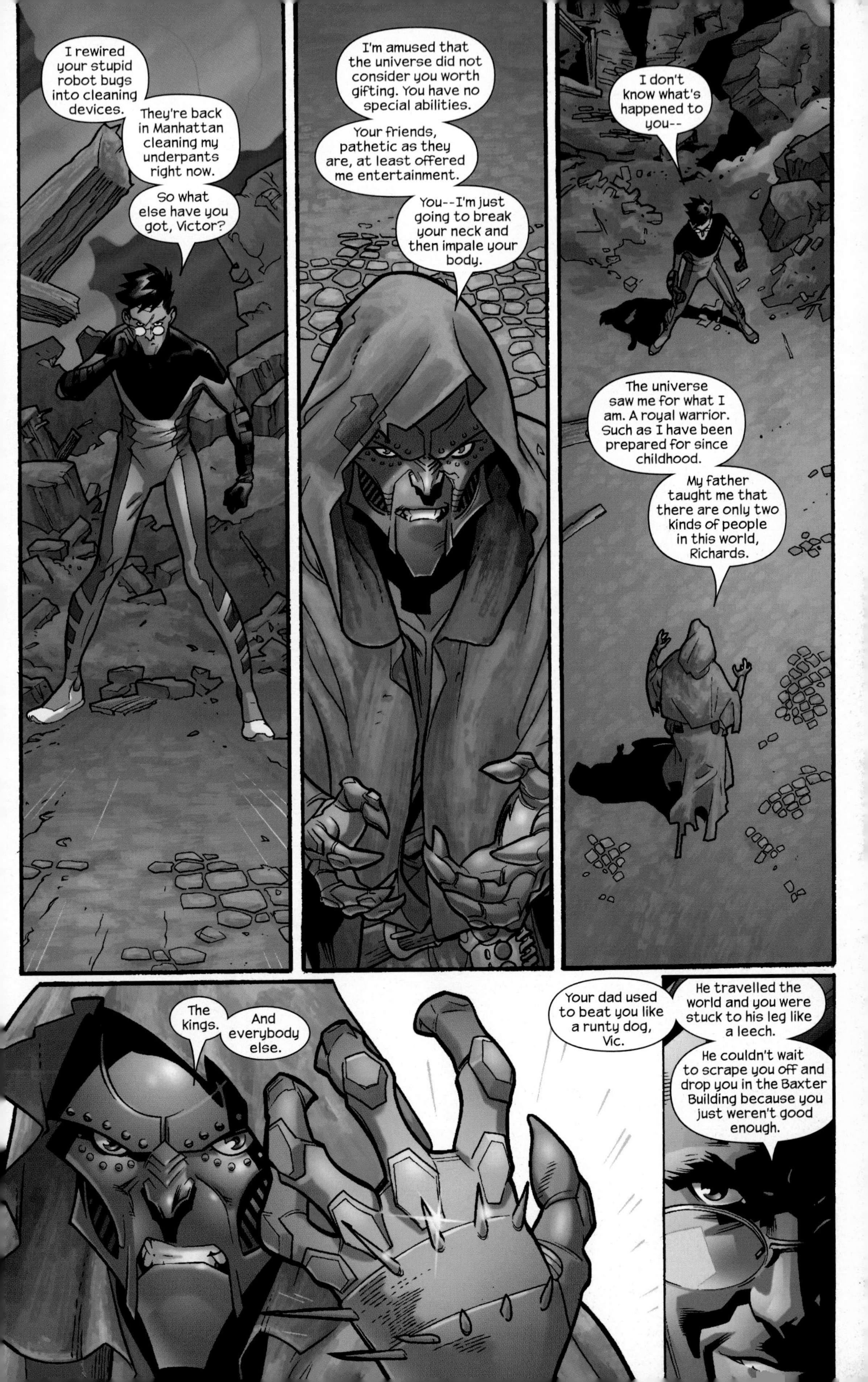

I rewired your stupid robot bugs into cleaning devices.
They're back in Manhattan cleaning my underpants right now.
So what else have you got, Victor?
I'm amused that the universe did not consider you worth gifting. You have no special abilities.
Your friends, pathetic as they are, at least offered me entertainment.
You--I'm just going to break your neck and then impale your body.
I don't know what's happened to you--
The universe saw me for what I am. A royal warrior. Such as I have been prepared for since childhood.
My father taught me that there are only two kinds of people in this world, Richards.
The kings.
And everybody else.
Your dad used to beat you like a runty dog, Vic.
He travelled the world and you were stuck to his leg like a leech.
He couldn't wait to scrape you off and drop you in the Baxter Building because you just weren't good enough.

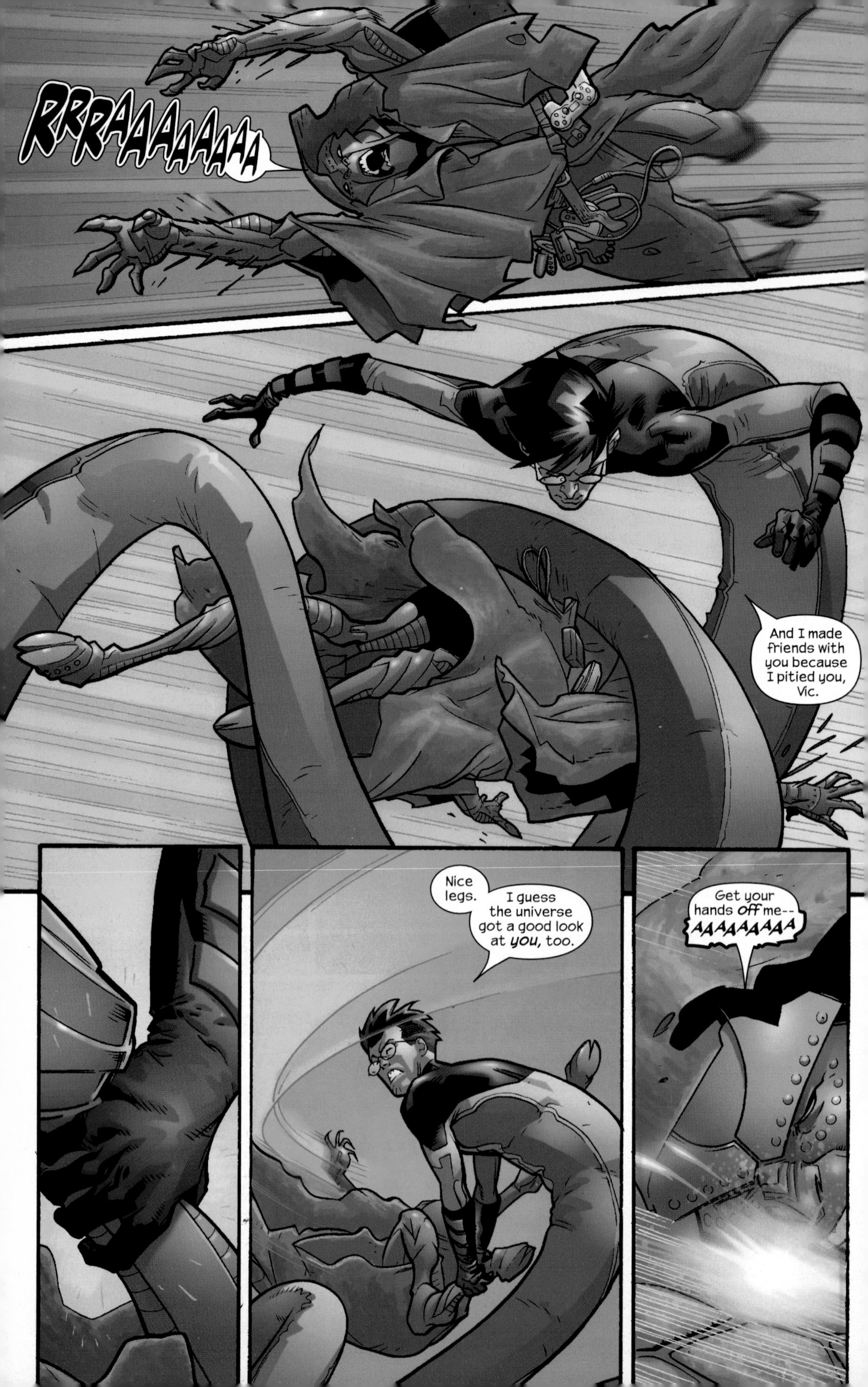
RRRAAAAAAAAA
And I made friends with you because I pitied you, Vic.
Nice legs.
I guess the universe got a good look at *you*, too.
Get your hands *off* me--AAAAAAAAA

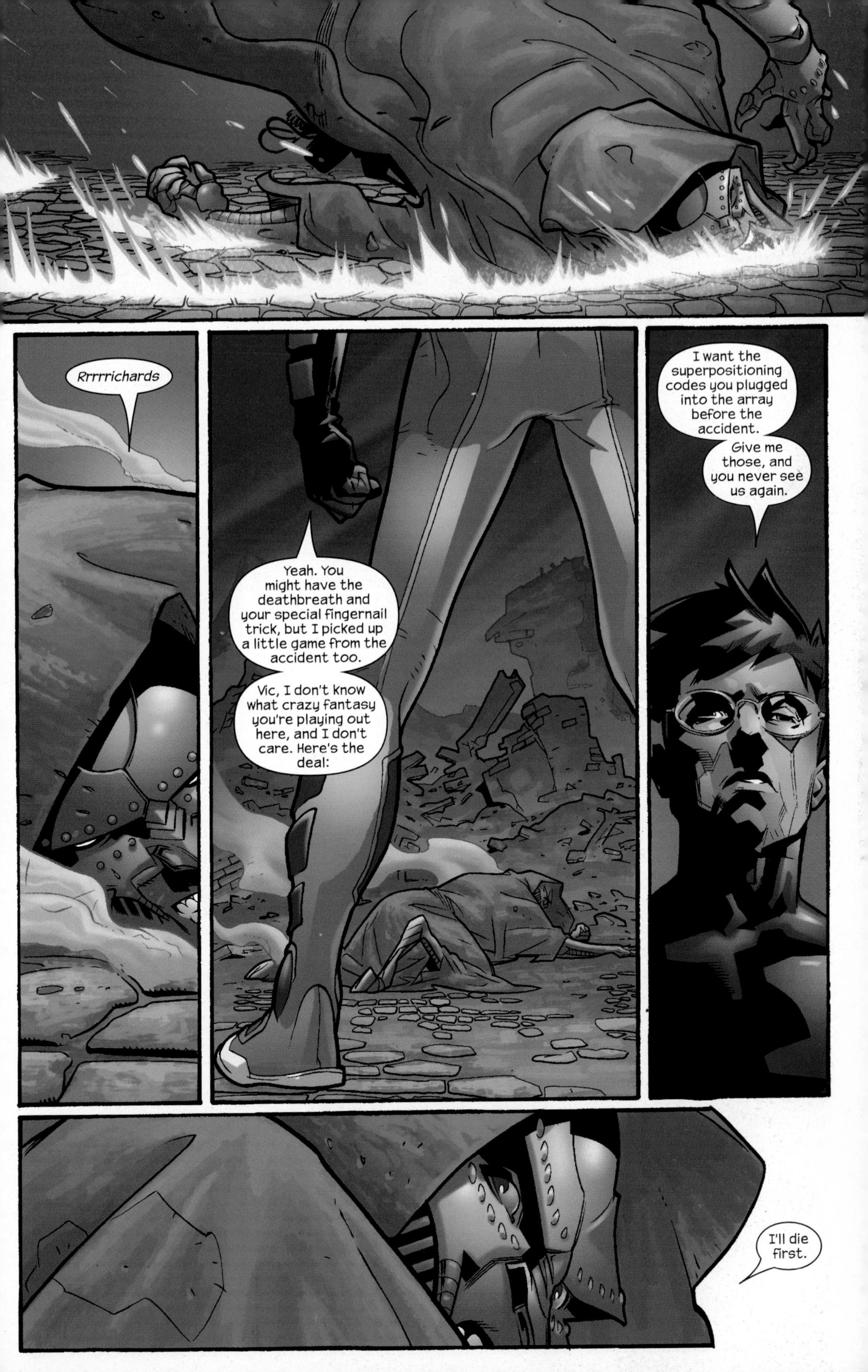
Rrrrrichards
Yeah. You might have the deathbreath and your special fingernail trick, but I picked up a little game from the accident too.
Vic, I don't know what crazy fantasy you're playing out here, and I don't care. Here's the deal:
I want the superpositioning codes you plugged into the array before the accident.
Give me those, and you never see us again.
I'll die first.

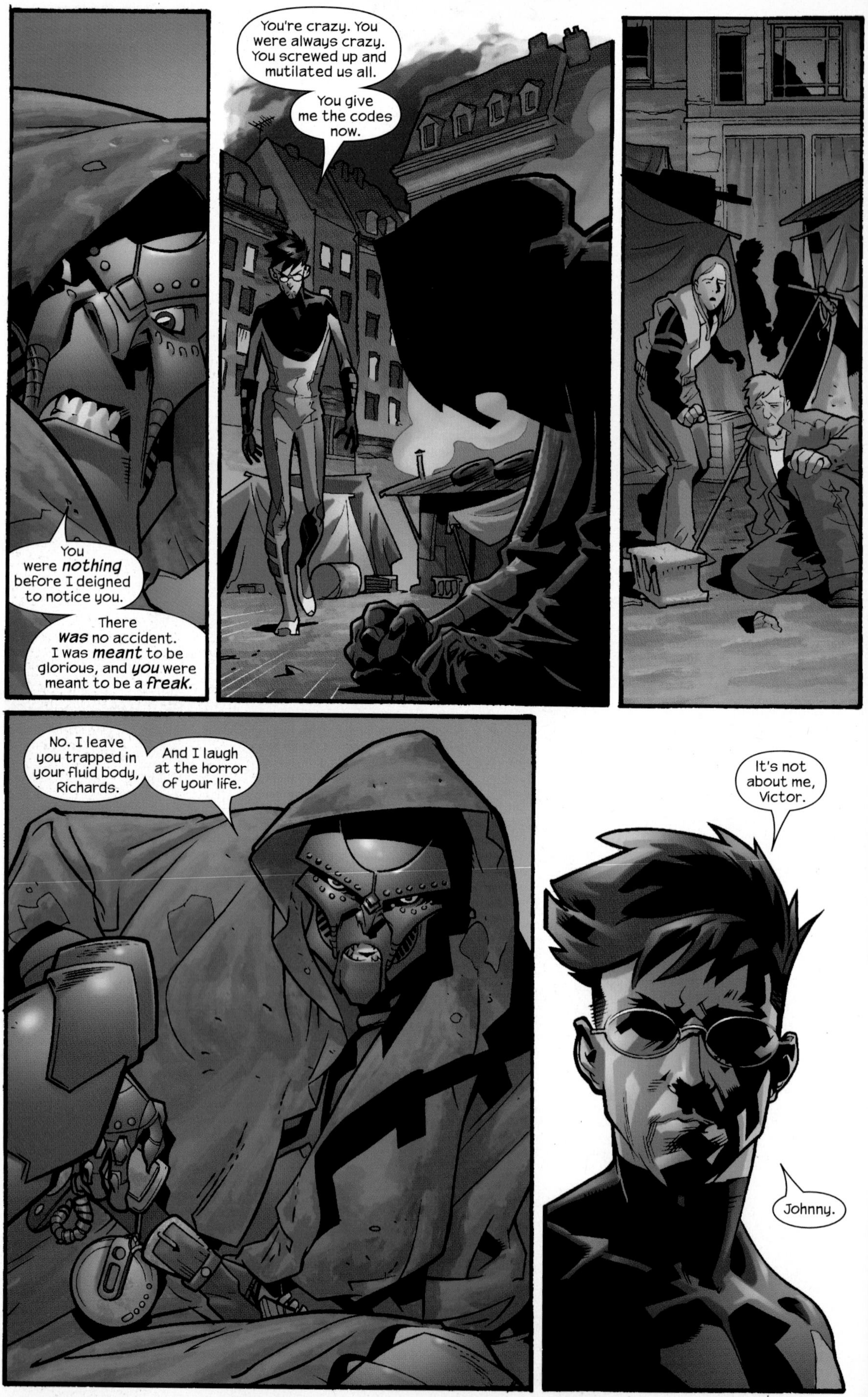
You were *nothing* before I deigned to notice you.
There *was* no accident. I was *meant* to be glorious, and *you* were meant to be a *freak.*
You're crazy. You were always crazy. You screwed up and mutilated us all.
You give me the codes now.
No. I leave you trapped in your fluid body, Richards.
And I laugh at the horror of your life.
It's not about me, Victor.
Johnny.

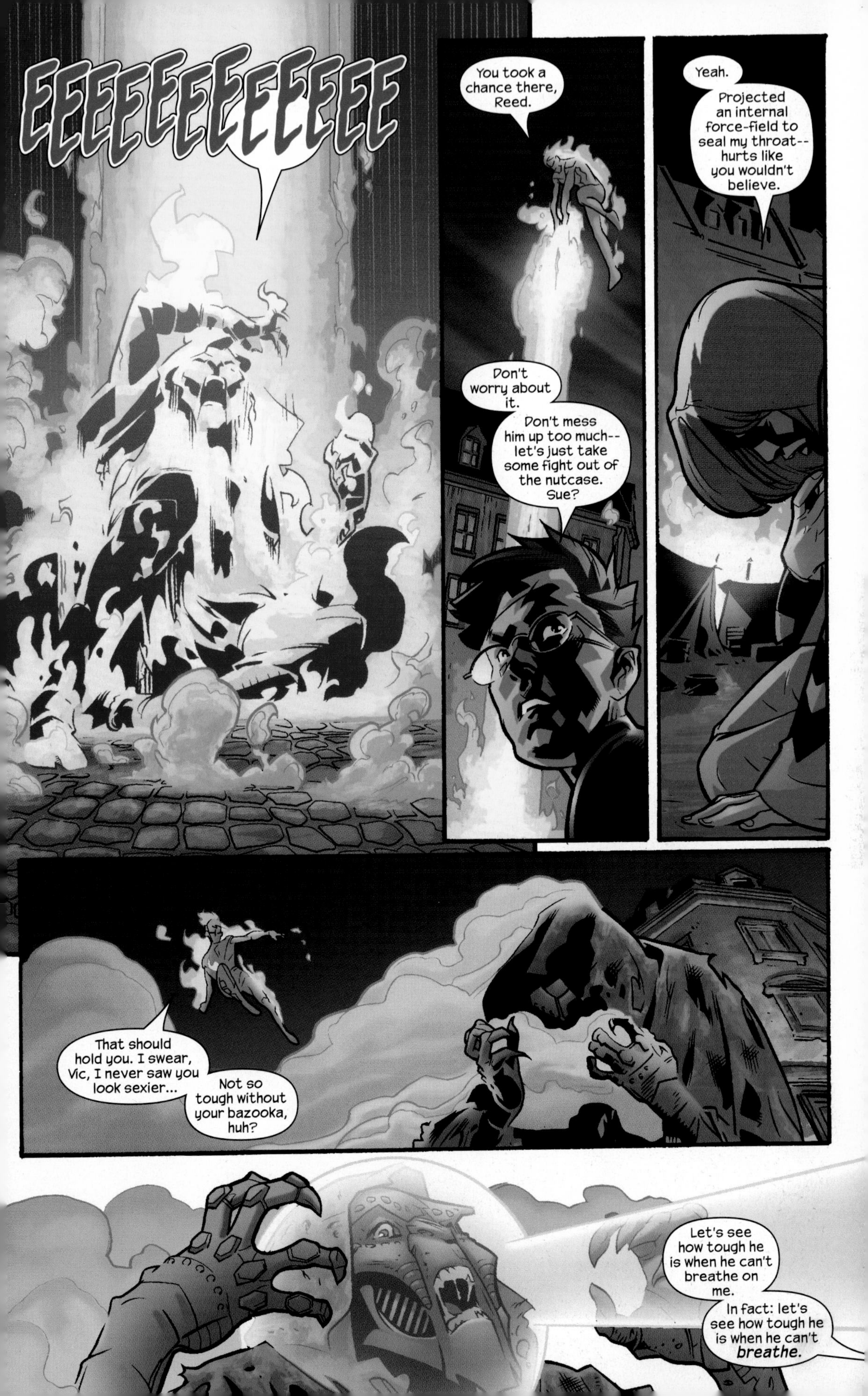
EEEEEEEEEEEEE
You took a chance there, Reed.
Yeah.
Projected an internal force-field to seal my throat--hurts like you wouldn't believe.
Don't worry about it.
Don't mess him up too much--let's just take some fight out of the nutcase. Sue?
That should hold you. I swear, Vic, I never saw you look sexier...
Not so tough without your bazooka, huh?
Let's see how tough he is when he can't breathe on me.
In fact: let's see how tough he is when he can't *breathe.*

I've got him, but he's clawing at the field and I can *feel* it--

How hard *is* that stuff he's in? *Ben!*

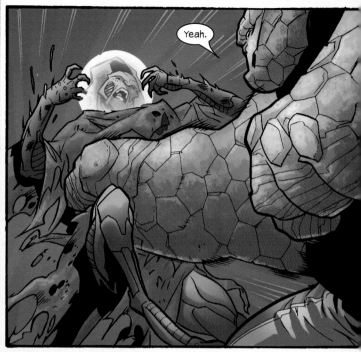

Yeah.

I only met you like twice.

And I hate you already.

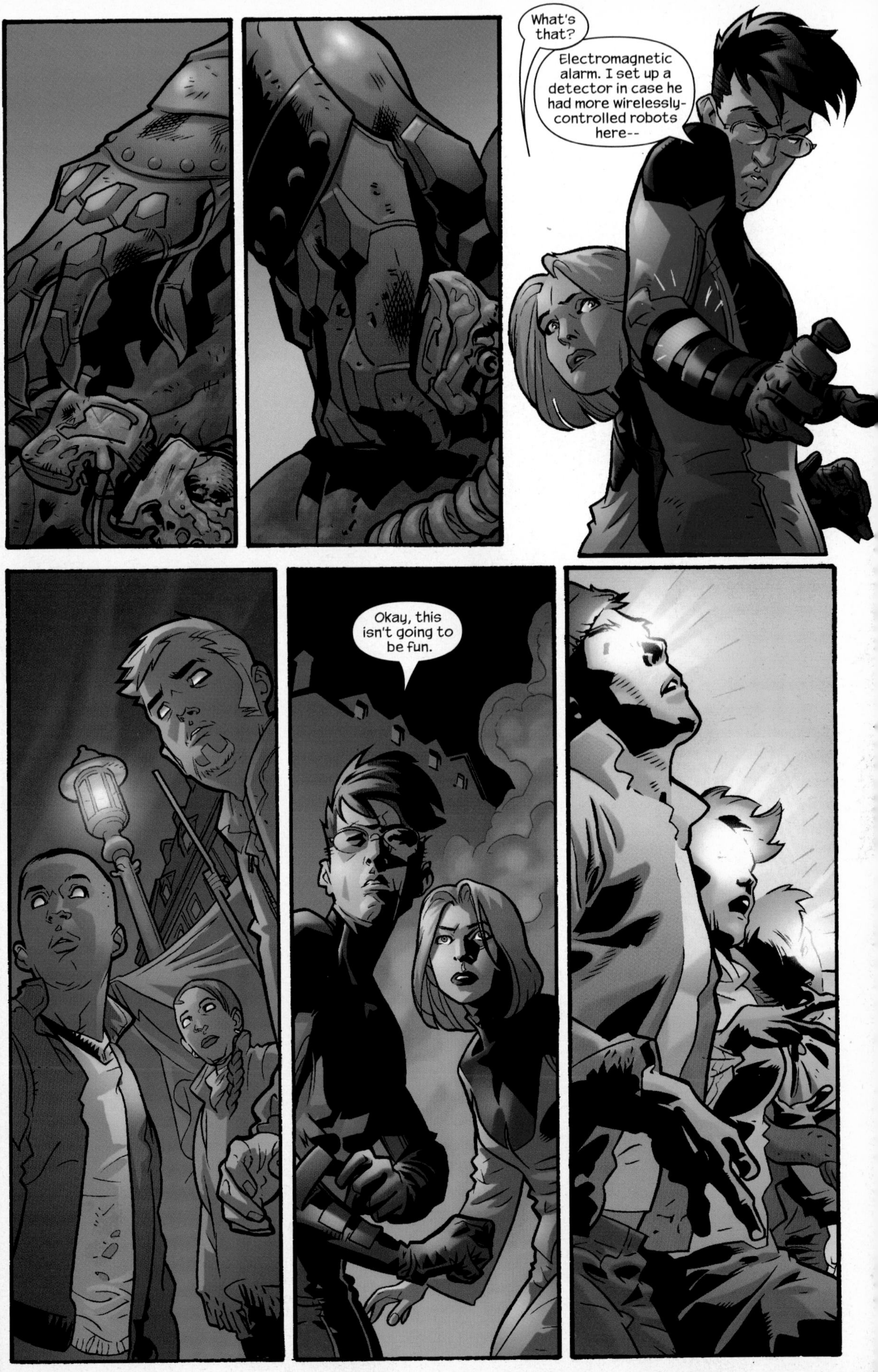
What's that?
Electromagnetic alarm. I set up a detector in case he had more wirelessly-controlled robots here--
Okay, this isn't going to be fun.

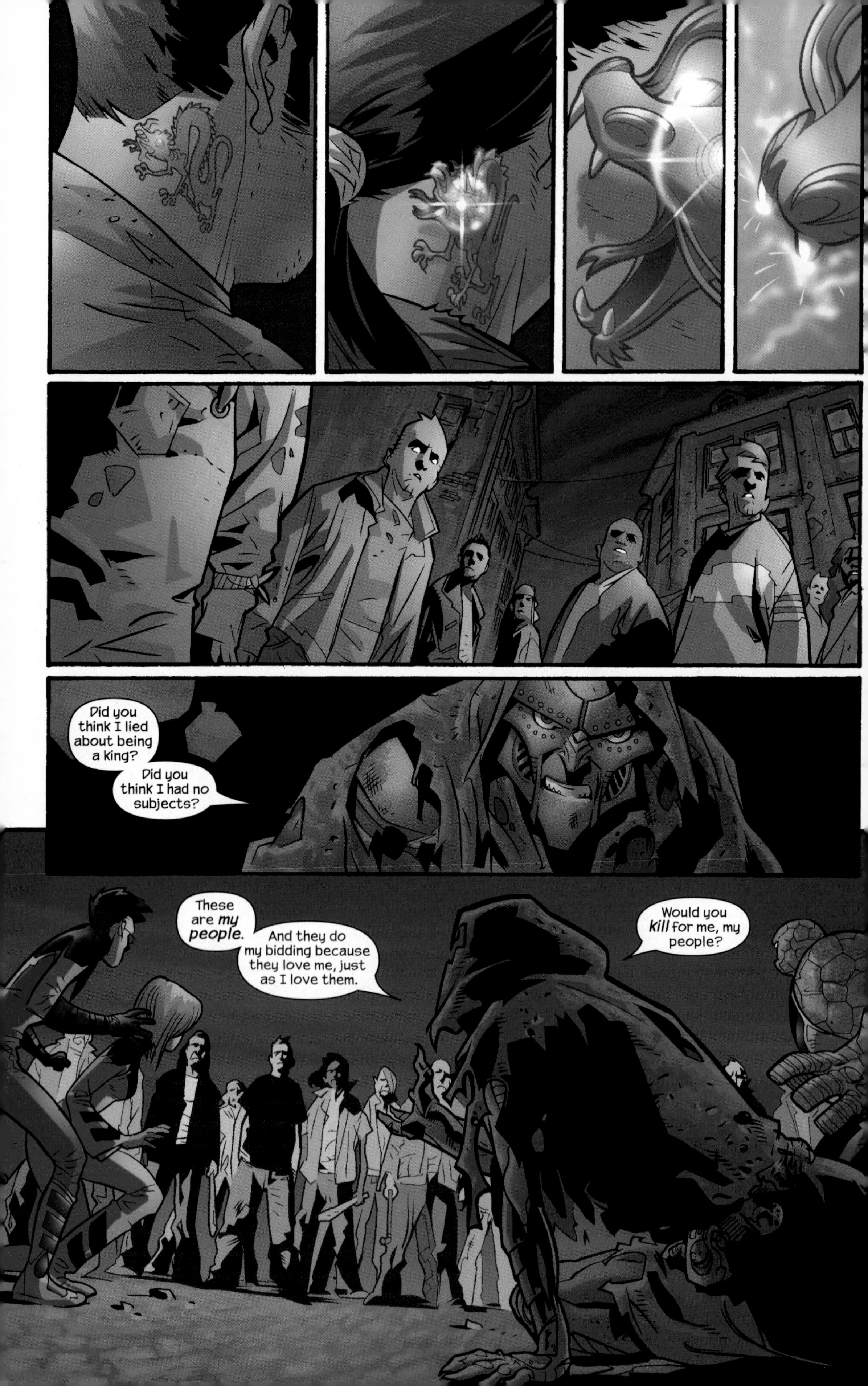
Did you think I lied about being a king?
Did you think I had no subjects?
These are *my people*.
And they do my bidding because they love me, just as I love them.
Would you *kill* for me, my people?

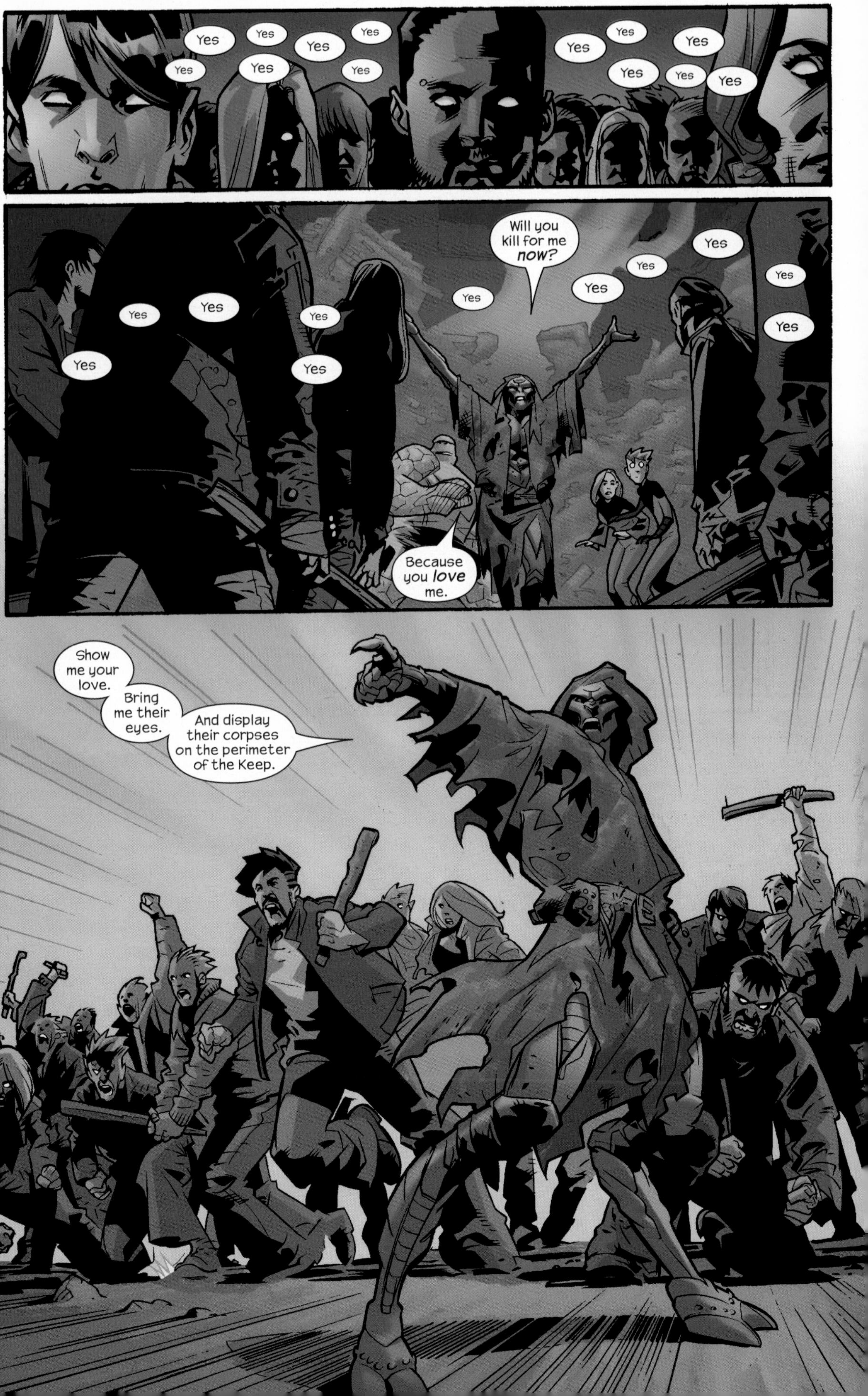
Yes
Yes
Yes
Yes
Yes
Yes
Yes
Yes
Yes
Yes
Yes
Yes
Yes
Will you kill for me *now?*
Yes
Yes
Yes
Yes
Yes
Yes
Yes
Yes
Yes
Yes
Yes
Because you *love* me.
Show me your love.
Bring me their eyes.
And display their corpses on the perimeter of the Keep.

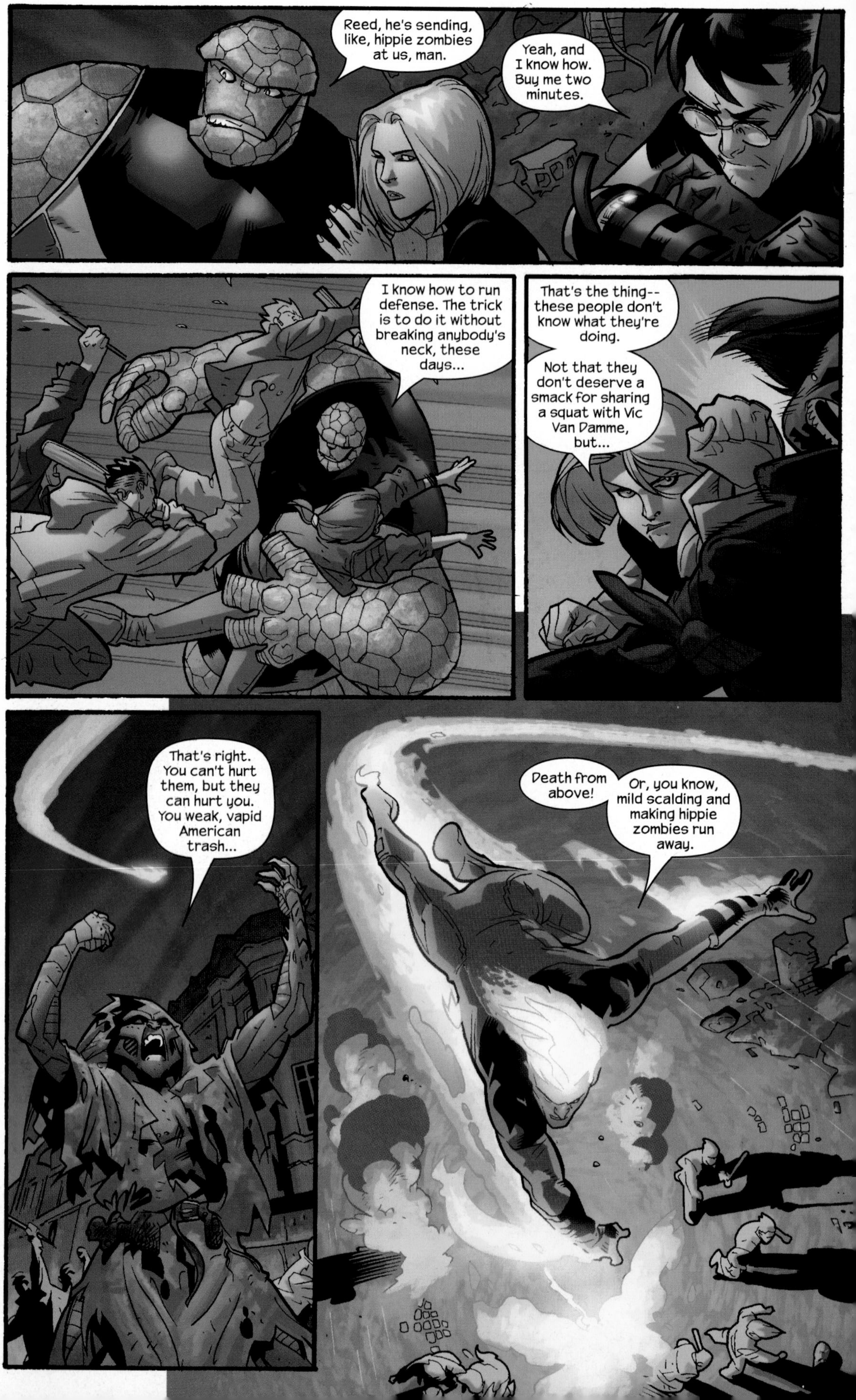
Reed, he's sending, like, hippie zombies at us, man.
Yeah, and I know how. Buy me two minutes.
I know how to run defense. The trick is to do it without breaking anybody's neck, these days...
That's the thing-- these people don't know what they're doing.
Not that they don't deserve a smack for sharing a squat with Vic Van Damme, but...
That's right. You can't hurt them, but they can hurt you. You weak, vapid American trash...
Death from above!
Or, you know, mild scalding and making hippie zombies run away.

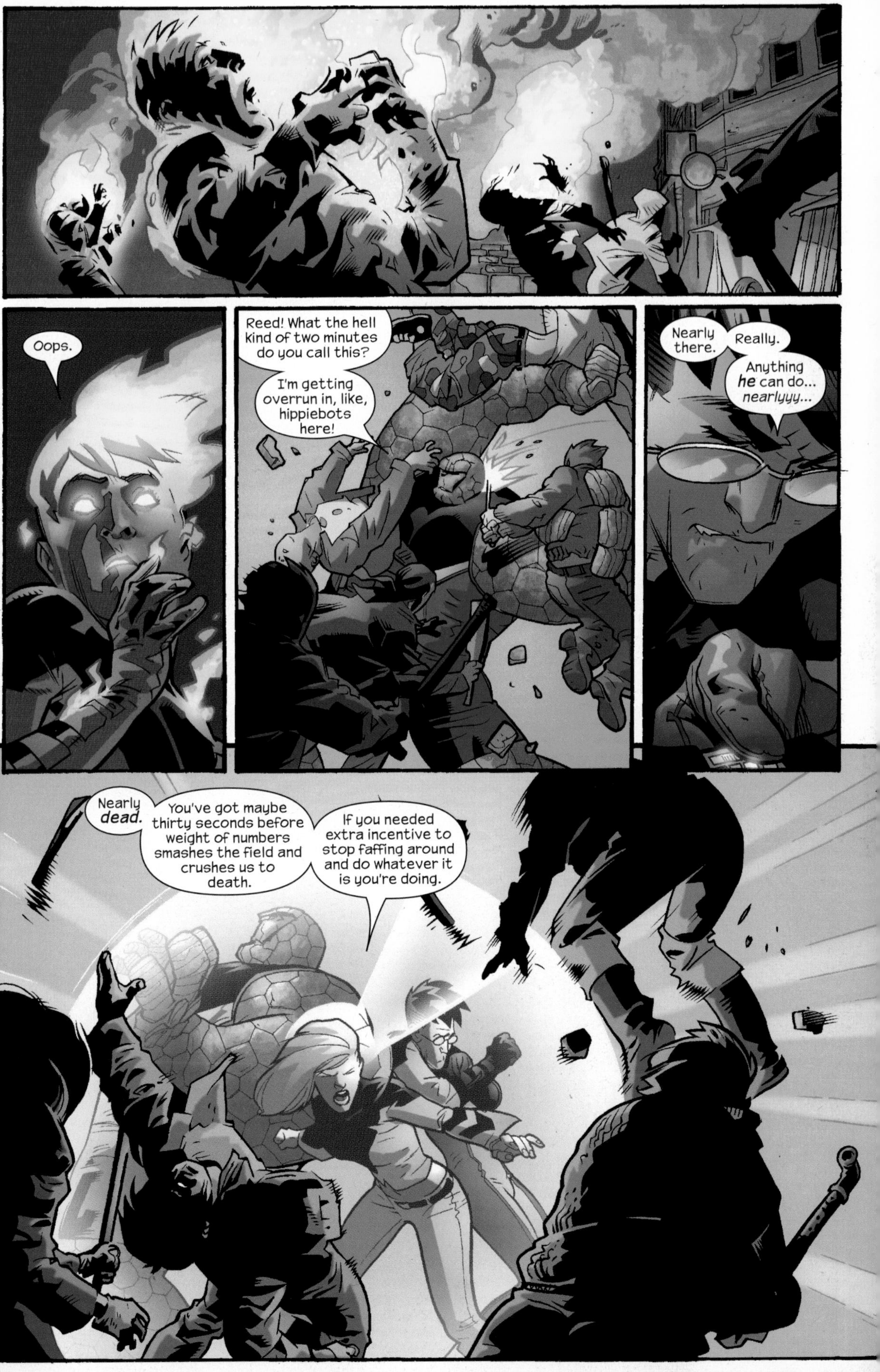
Oops.
Reed! What the hell kind of two minutes do you call this?
I'm getting overrun in, like, hippiebots here!
Nearly there.
Really.
Anything *he* can do... *nearlyyy...*
Nearly *dead.*
You've got maybe thirty seconds before weight of numbers smashes the field and crushes us to death.
If you needed extra incentive to stop faffing around and do whatever it is you're doing.

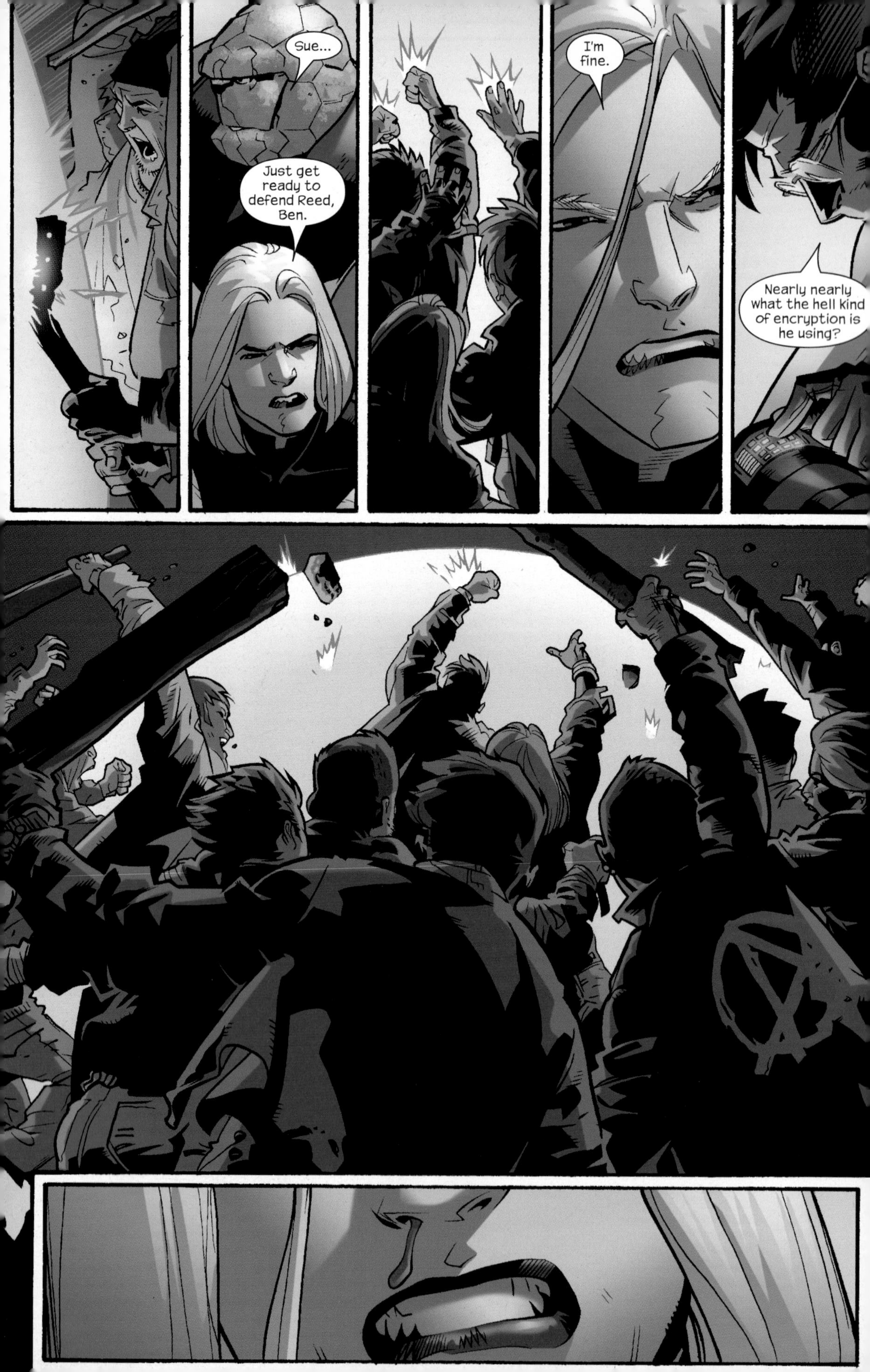
Sue...
Just get ready to defend Reed, Ben.
I'm fine.
Nearly nearly what the hell kind of encryption is he using?

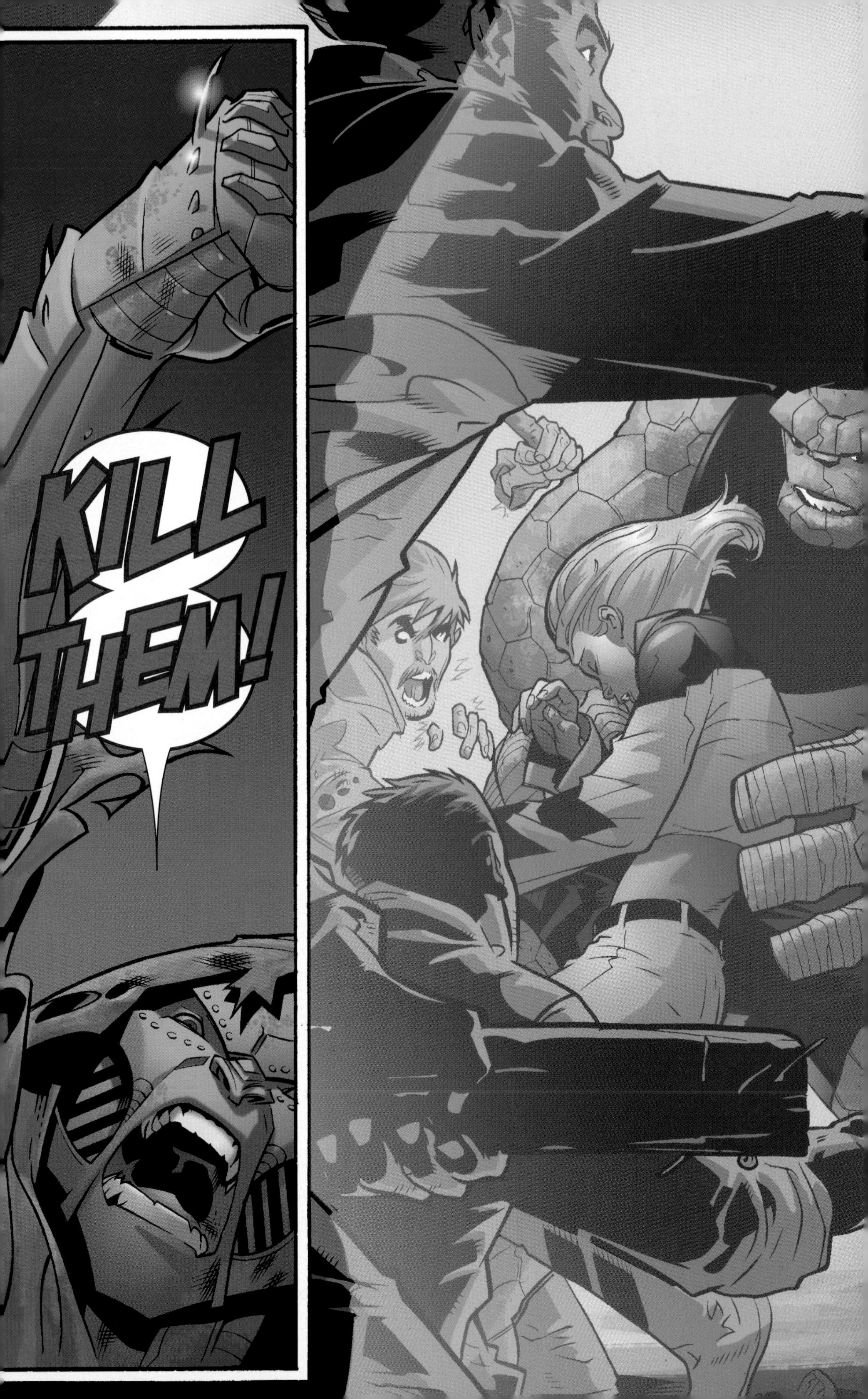
KILL THEM!

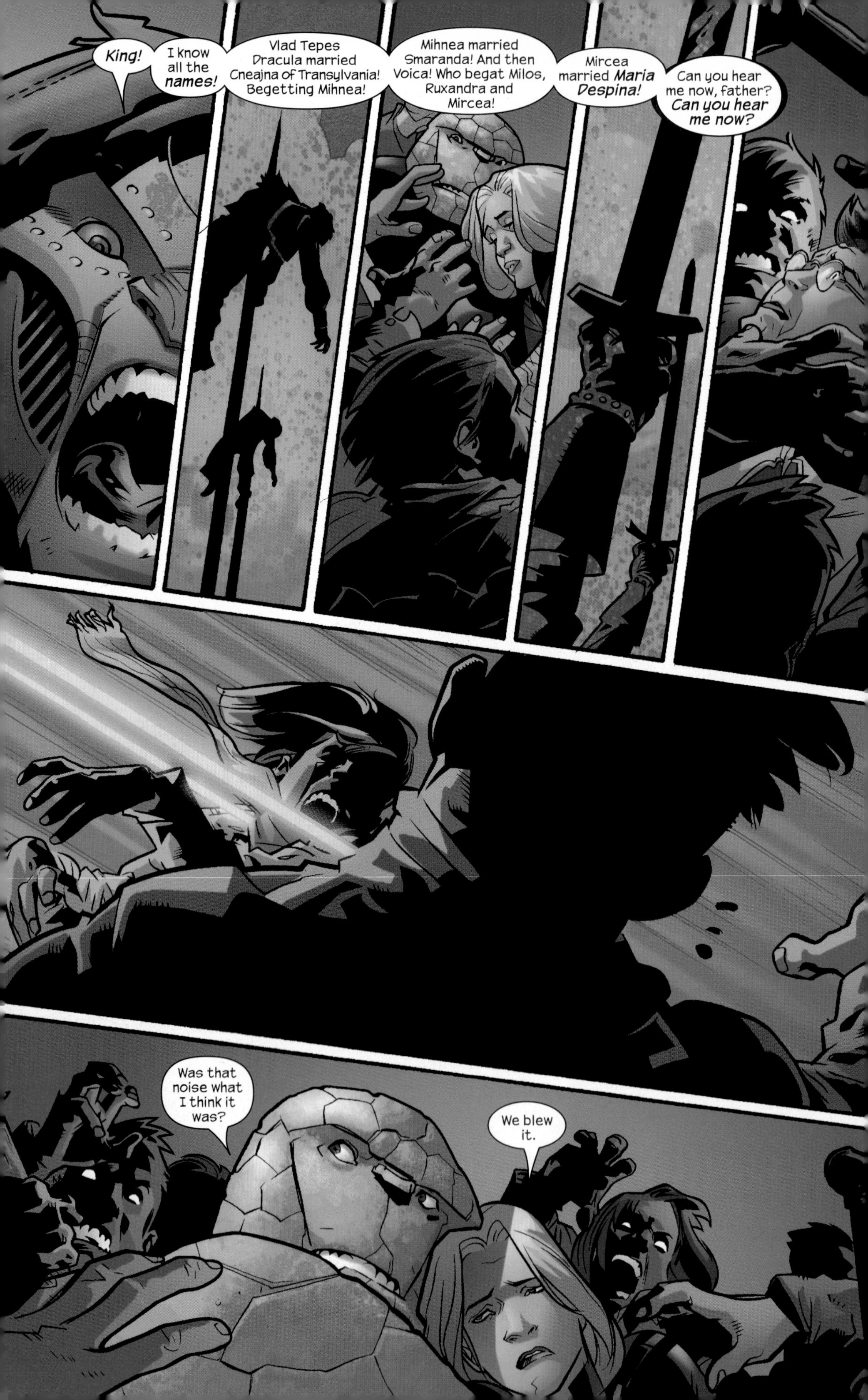
King!
I know all the names!
Vlad Tepes Dracula married Cneajna of Transylvania! Begetting Mihnea!
Mihnea married Smaranda! And then Voica! Who begat Milos, Ruxandra and Mircea!
Mircea married Maria Despina!
Can you hear me now, father? Can you hear me now?
Was that noise what I think it was?
We blew it.

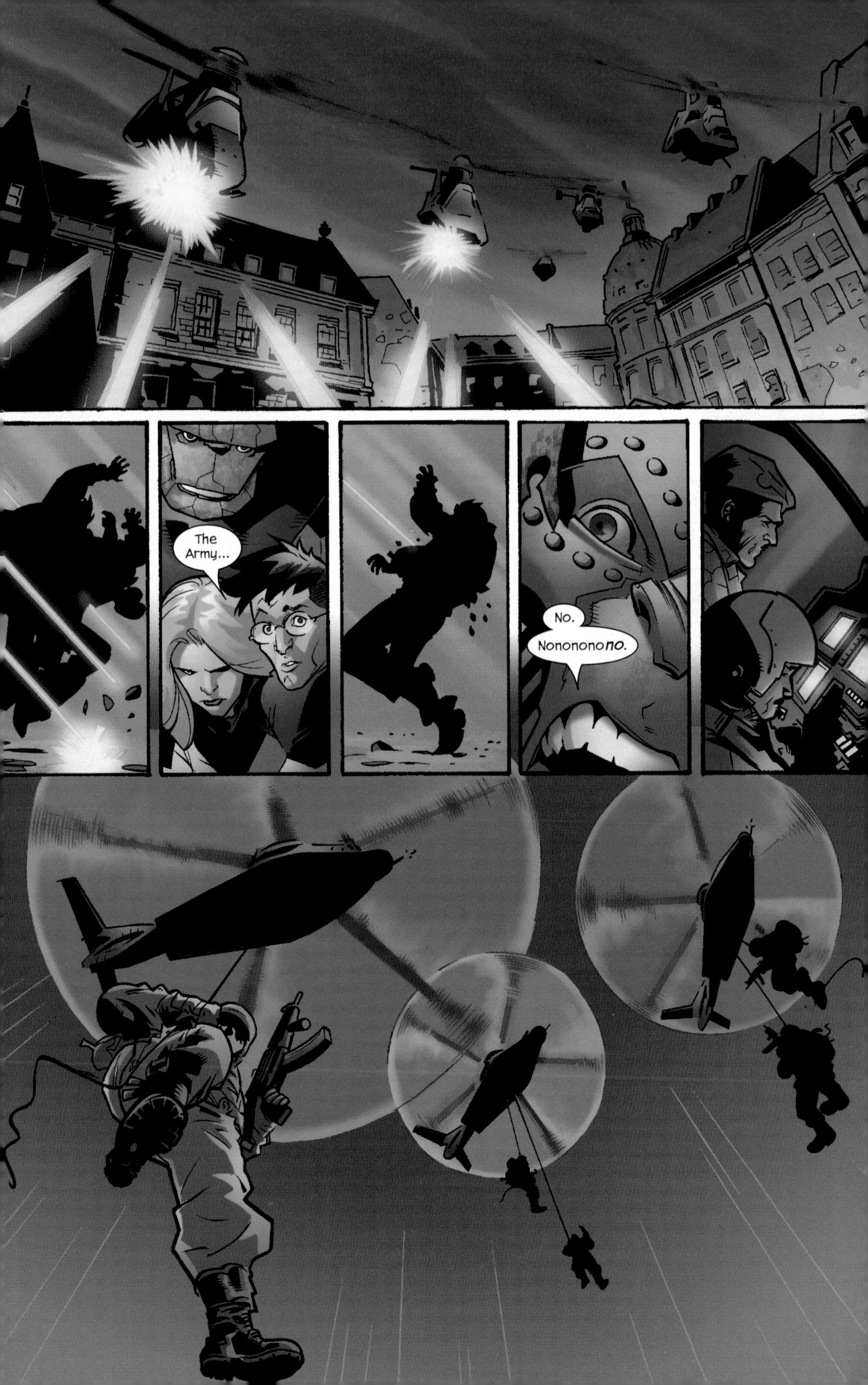
The Army...
No. Nonononono*no*.

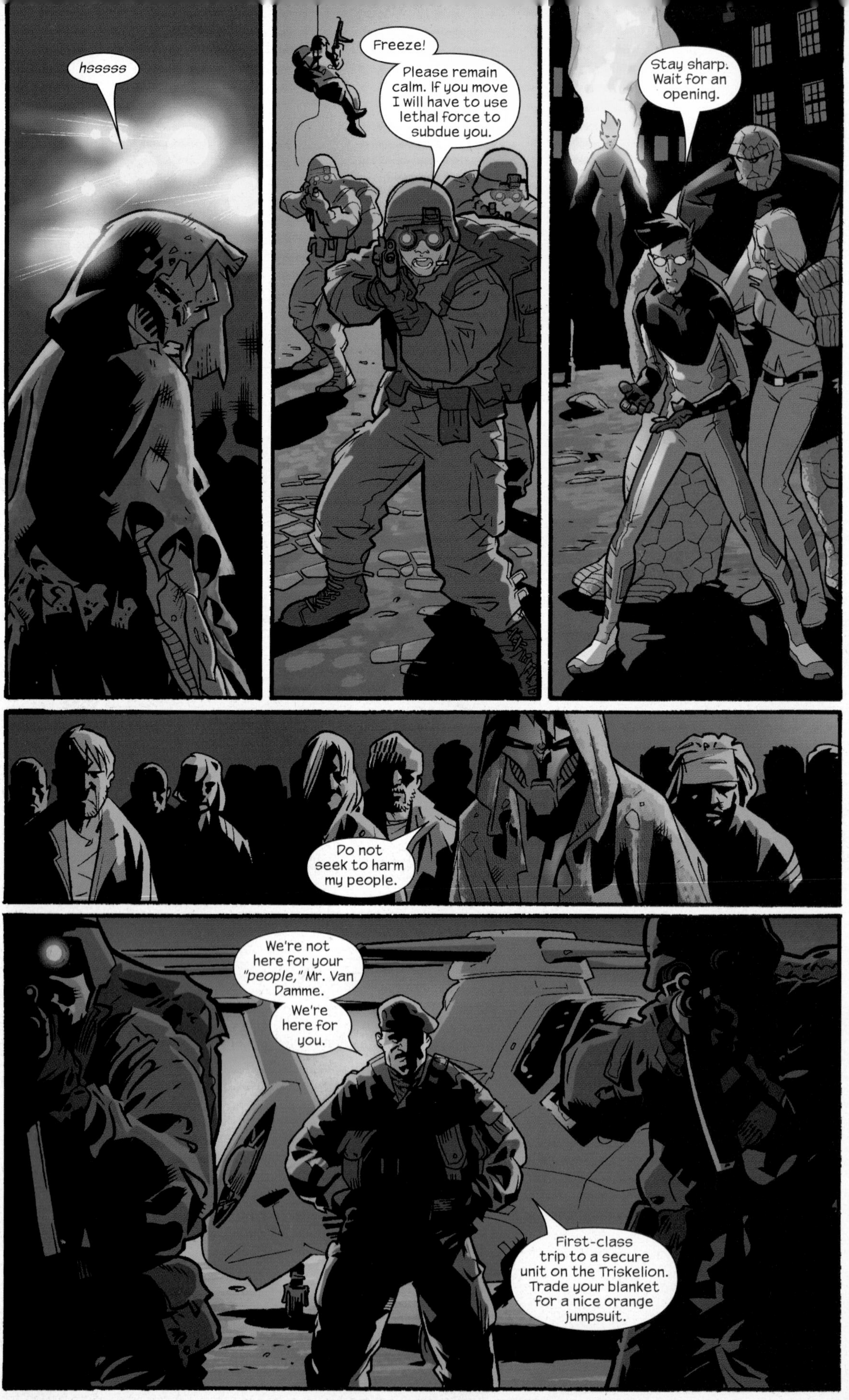
hsssss
Freeze!
Please remain calm. If you move I will have to use lethal force to subdue you.
Stay sharp. Wait for an opening.
Do not seek to harm my people.
We're not here for your "people," Mr. Van Damme.
We're here for you.
First-class trip to a secure unit on the Triskelion. Trade your blanket for a nice orange jumpsuit.

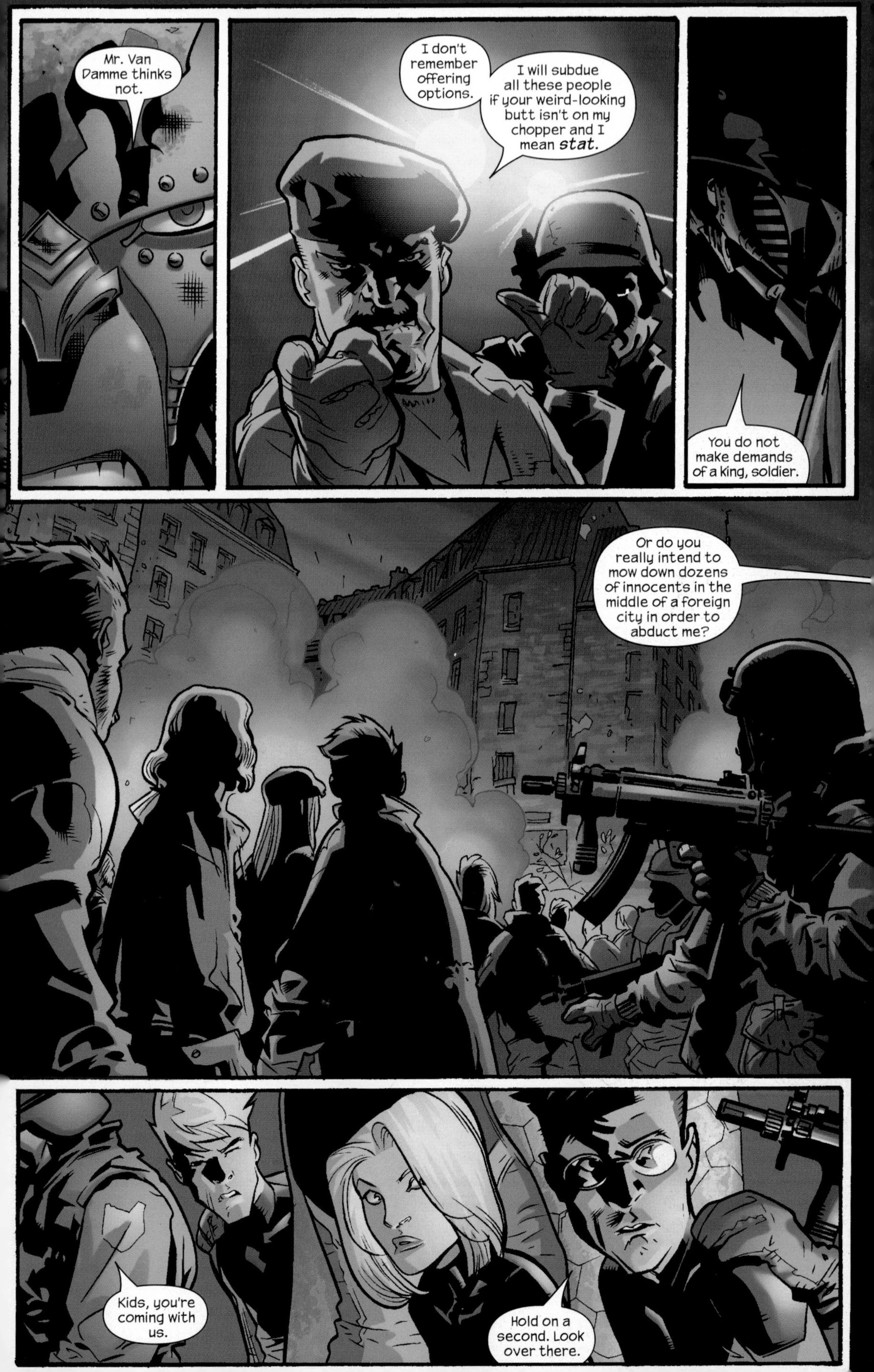
Mr. Van Damme thinks not.
I don't remember offering options.
I will subdue all these people if your weird-looking butt isn't on my chopper and I mean stat.
You do not make demands of a king, soldier.
Or do you really intend to mow down dozens of innocents in the middle of a foreign city in order to abduct me?
Kids, you're coming with us.
Hold on a second. Look over there.

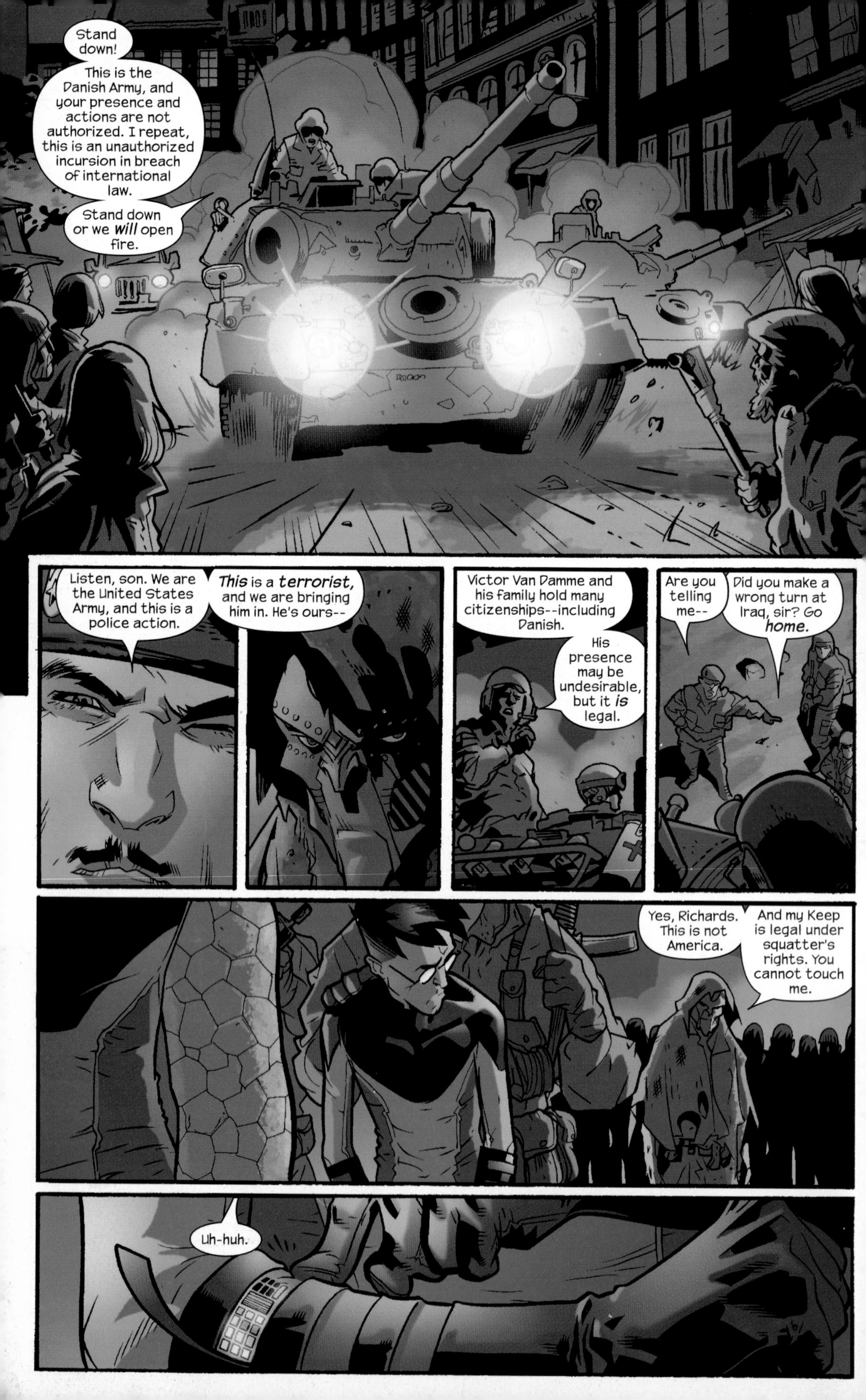
Stand down!
This is the Danish Army, and your presence and actions are not authorized. I repeat, this is an unauthorized incursion in breach of international law.
Stand down or we *will* open fire.
Listen, son. We are the United States Army, and this is a police action.
This is a *terrorist,* and we are bringing him in. He's ours--
Victor Van Damme and his family hold many citizenships--including Danish.
His presence may be undesirable, but it *is* legal.
Are you telling me--
Did you make a wrong turn at Iraq, sir? Go *home.*
Yes, Richards. This is not America.
And my Keep is legal under squatter's rights. You cannot touch me.
Uh-huh.

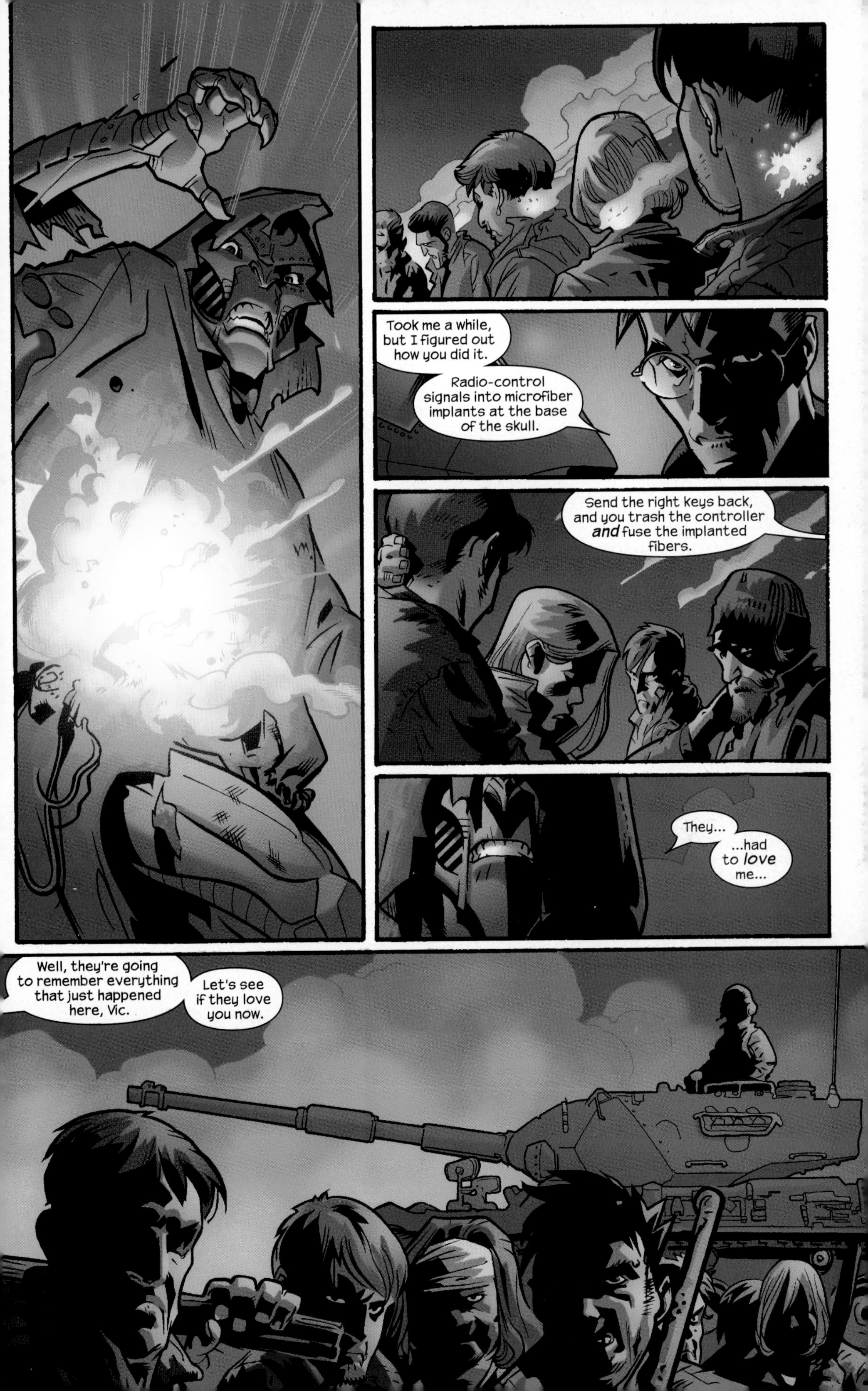
Took me a while, but I figured out how you did it.
Radio-control signals into microfiber implants at the base of the skull.
Send the right keys back, and you trash the controller **and** fuse the implanted fibers.
They...
...had to *love* me...
Well, they're going to remember everything that just happened here, Vic.
Let's see if they love you now.

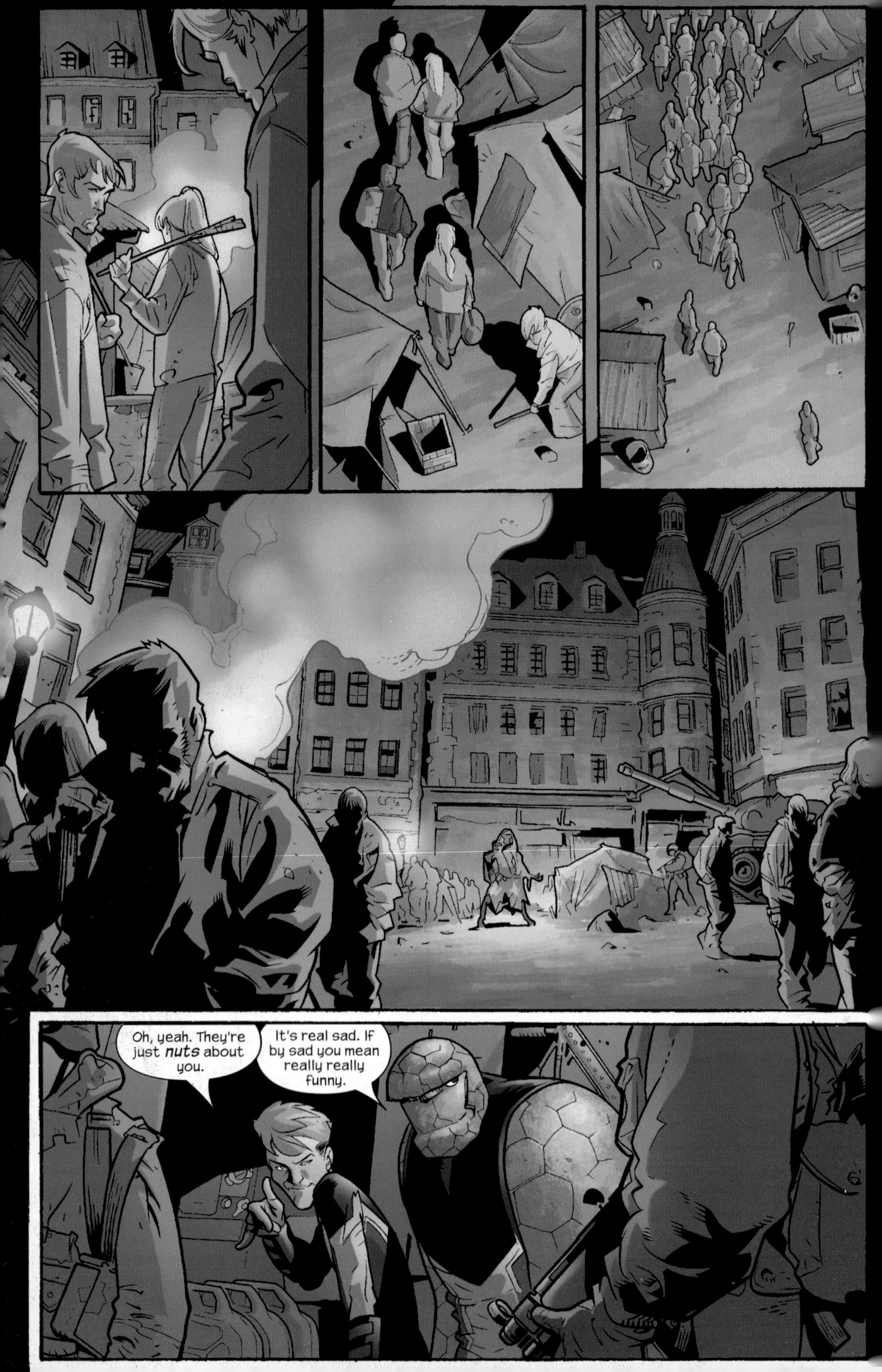
Oh, yeah. They're just *nuts* about you.
It's real sad. If by sad you mean really really funny.

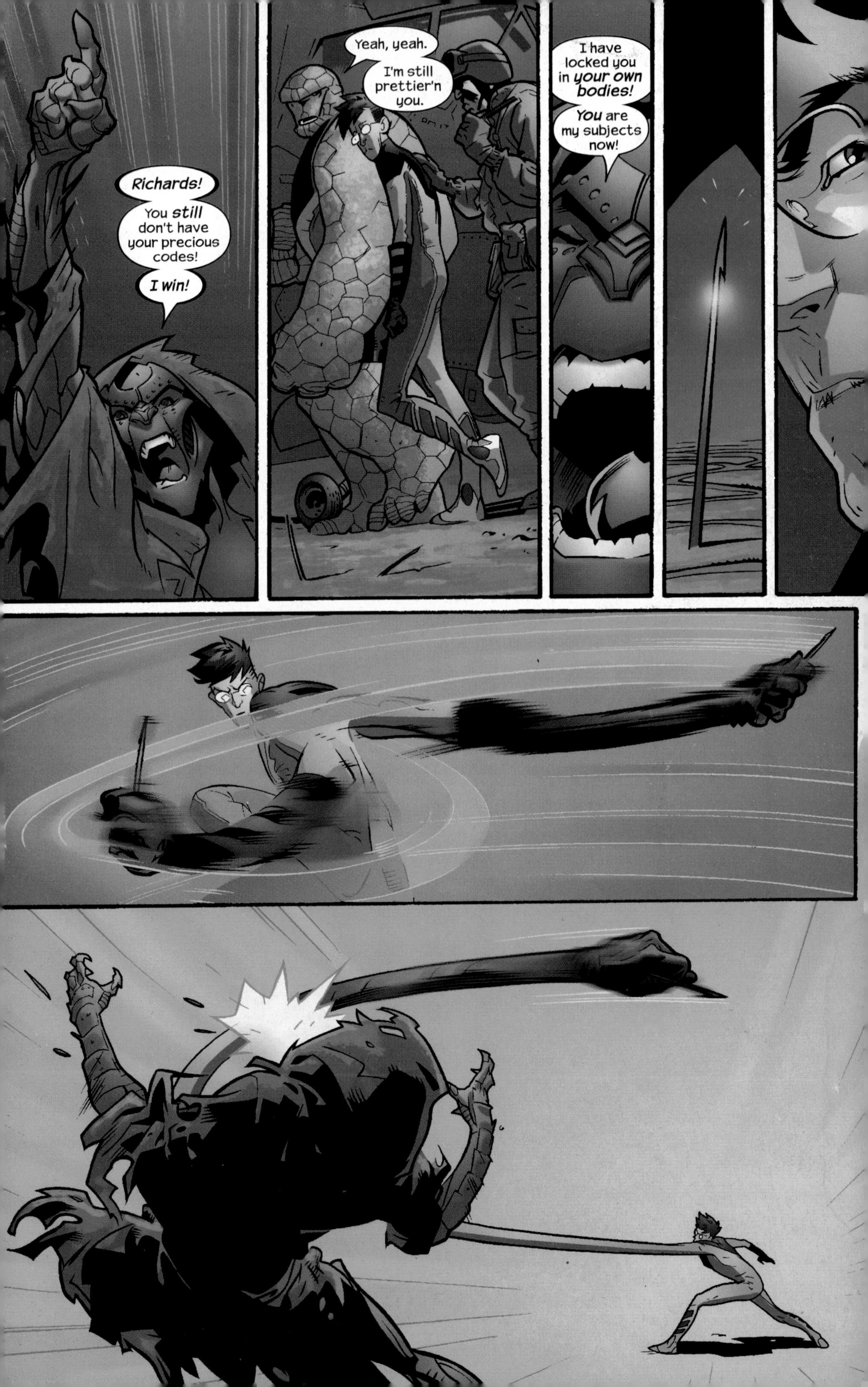
Richards!
You still don't have your precious codes!
I win!
Yeah, yeah.
I'm still prettier'n you.
I have locked you in your own bodies!
You are my subjects now!

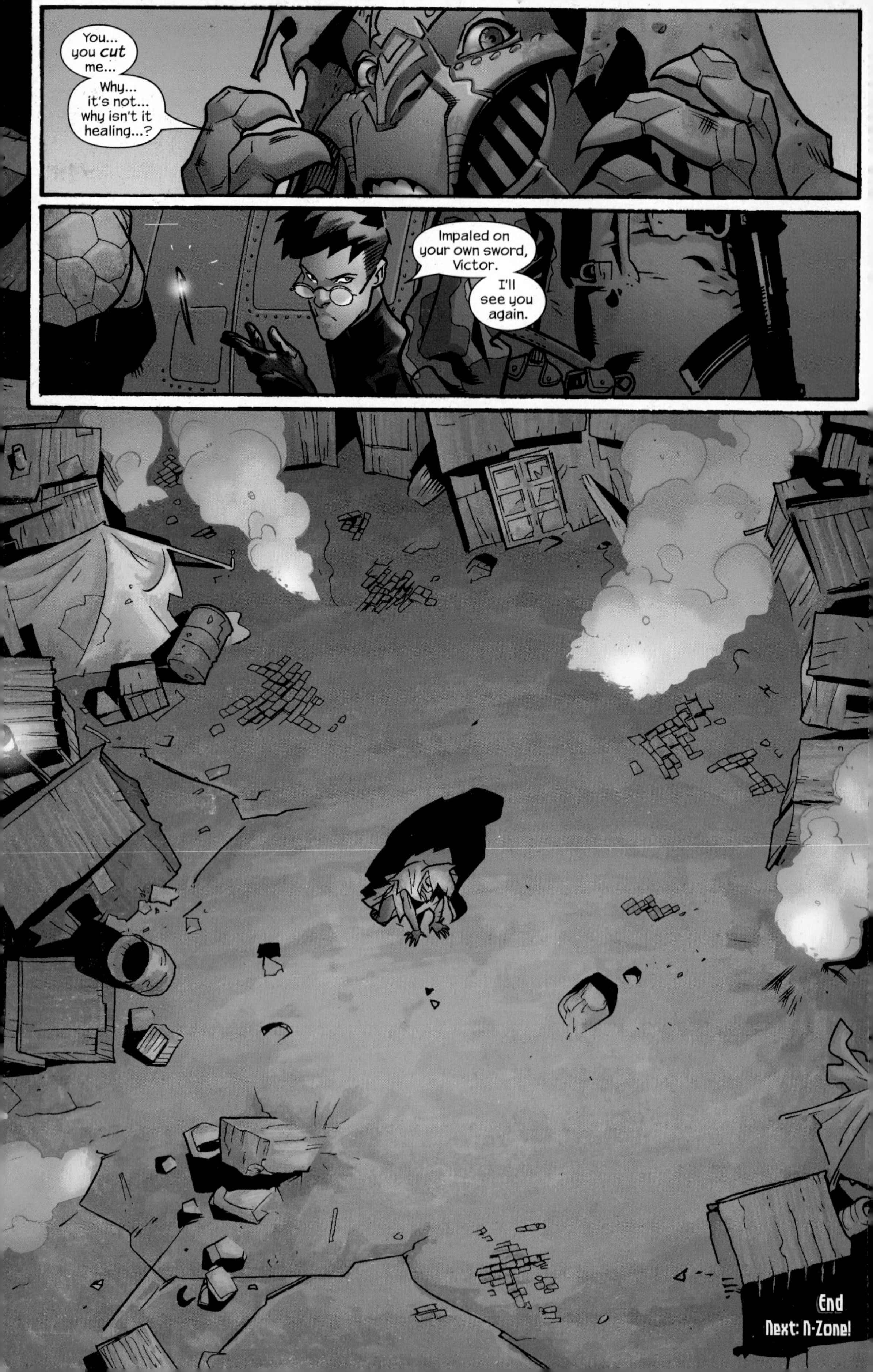
You... you cut me...
Why... it's not... why isn't it healing...?
Impaled on your own sword, Victor.
I'll see you again.
End
Next: N-Zone!